THE

NEW CHILDREN
AND
NEAR-DEATH
EXPERIENCES

THE
NEW CHILDREN
AND
NEAR-DEATH
EXPERIENCES

@

P.M.H. ATWATER, LH.D.

FOREWORD BY
JOSEPH CHILTON PEARCE

Bear & Company
Rochester, Vermont

Bear & Company
One Park Street
Rochester, Vermont 05767
www.InnerTraditions.com

Bear & Company is a division of Inner Traditions International

Library of Congress Cataloging-in-Publication Data
Atwater, P. M. H.
  [Children of the new millennium]
  The new children and near-death experiences / P.M.H. Atwater ;
foreword by Joseph Chilton Pearce.
      p. cm.
Originally published: Children of the new millennium. New York : Three Rivers Press, 1999.
Includes bibliographical references and index.
ISBN 1–59143–020–8
  1. Near-death experiences in children. 2. Human
evolution—Miscellanea. I. Title.
  BF1045.N42A88 2003
  133.9—dc22
                            2003018534

Printed and bound in the United States at Lake Book Manufacturing, Inc.

10 9 8 7 6 5 4 3 2

Text design by Rachel Goldenberg and layout by Priscilla Baker

This book was typeset in Sabon

GRATEFUL ACKNOWLEDGMENT IS MADE TO THE FOLLOWING FOR PERMISSION TO REPRINT FROM THEIR MATERIALS

*Janet Blessing: "Fly" by Janet Blessing. Reprinted by permission of the author.

*Doubleday, a division of Random House, Inc.: excerpt from *The Famished Road* by Ben Okri. Copyright (c) 1993 by Anchor Books. Reprinted by permission of Doubleday, a division of Random House, Inc.

*Joseph Benedict Geraci: excerpt from published work for his Ph.D. dissertation, "Students' Post Near-Death Experience Attitude and Behavior Toward Education and Learning," on file at the University of Connecticut at Storrs. Reprinted by permission of the author.

*Guadalupe Press: excerpt from *It's All Cod* by Walter Starcke. Copyright (c) 1998 by Guadalupe Press. Reprinted by permission of the author.

*Hampton Roads Publishing Company, Inc.: excerpt from *Solstice Shift: Magical Blend's Synergistic Guide to the Coming Age*, edited by John Nelson. Copyright (c) 1999 by Hampton Roads Publishing Company, Inc. Reprinted by permission of Hampton Roads Publishing Company, Inc.

*Dr. Valerie Hunt: excerpt from *Infinite Mind: Science of the Human Vibrations of Consciousness* by Dr. Valerie Hunt (Malibu Publishing Company). Copyright (c) 1996 by Malibu Publishing Company. Reprinted by permission of the author.

*Mata Amritanandamayi Center: excerpt from *Mata Amritanandamayi: A Biography*. Copyright (c) 1988 by Mata Amritanandamayi Center. Reprinted by permission of M.A. Center.

*The Matrix Institute: excerpt from *Notes from the Cosmos: A Futurist's Insights into the World of Dream and Prophecy and Intuition—Includes Global Prediction for 1998–2012* by Gordon-Michael Scallion. Copyright (c) 1997 by Matrix Institute. Reprinted by permission of the Matrix Institute.

*Todd Murphy: excerpt from "The Structure and Function of Near-Death Experiences: An Algorithmic Reincarnation Hypothesis." *Journal of Near-Death Studies*, Vol. 20, No. 2, Winter 2001. Reprinted by permission of the author and *Journal* publisher, Kluwer Academic/Human Sciences Press.

*Rainbows Unlimited: excerpt from *The Millennium Children: Tales of the Shift* by Caryl Dennis. Copyright (c) 1997 by Rainbows Unlimited. Reprinted by permission of Rainbows Unlimited.

*Linda Redford: the Honor Pledge and Honor Code from The Adawee Teachings. Reprinted by permission of the author.

Woodrew Update Newsletter: excerpt from *Woodrew Update*, vol. 17, no. 3. Reprinted by permission of Greta Woodrew, LL.D.

It is with the deepest love and affection that I dedicate this book to Kenneth L. Johnston, my father, a man considered by most who know him to be one of the finest police officers ever to have worn a badge. I grew up immersed in police work thanks to him; the police station in Twin Falls, Idaho, was my second home. Life extremes were daily fare then, and my father's insistence that I learn the techniques of investigative fieldwork later evolved into the research protocol I came to use in my explorations of the near-death phenomenon. I call myself the "gumshoe of near-death" because of this, and I am forever grateful to my father for his teachings and his love.

Contents

FLY

To think that i could
  FLY, like you,
above this complicated place
  to know that it is
    i, untrue,
is something i can't seem to face
  at all. To feel that
    sun, like you,
upon my cotton candy back . . .
  aware that i am
    one who flew
so long ago, i cry and rack
  my brain for one faint
    memory
of freedom high above the earth,
  of FLYING . . . but i
    cannot see.
'Twas way before my second birth.

—Janet Blessing, Pittsfield, Massachusetts.
Her near-death experience occurred at nine
months of age during a bout of pneumonia.
She wrote this poem when she was nineteen.

Foreword

IT MAY BE that the greatest value of a book is its ability to disturb, unless one wants only to be entertained. In either case, *The New Children and Near-Death Experiences* is quite a cup of tea. This heady adventure into the inner world just may be P.M.H. Atwater's magnum opus, though it can become threatening and disturbing to our commonly held assumptions. (At least it was to mine.)

Read with an unprejudiced eye, or mind (which, again, was not easy for me), it surely should rank with William James's classic *The Varieties of Religious Experience,* if nothing else. Like James's work, it raises a rich substrate of unanswered questions concerning the nature of the human mind and its incomparable, awesome creativity. Thus this is a seminal work, demanding further and deep philosophical inquiry and objective pursuit, while at the same time a work of astonishing thoroughness, brilliance, insight, and prodigious admirable research.

Atwater has simply covered her subject with impeccable thoroughness, even as her rigorously disciplined approach opens her subject to a wider question that might be beyond the scope of any single book. And she wisely knows when to leave a question hanging (always risky academically), rather than trying to make the definitive statement about *everything,* as some of us are wont to do. Every time I think she has boxed herself into an untenable position, she offers counterexperiences that prove to be outside that box and that show her objectivity toward any part of the remarkably rich material she has gathered. And much of this material is academically suspect—politically incorrect, so to speak—even as it is undeniably a rich segment of actual human experience, material that resonates with my own history as it will with that of many readers (whereas the academically/politically correct tends to leave *me* as a lived experience rather out of the picture).

Surely there are unresolved issues in this book, as there would have to be in a work of this scope. Time and again I wanted to stop and insist on battling out some issue, though it might take years. Memory itself is a gaping black hole of mystery, in spite of all the research into this area. False memory has been the subject of much study. Shared, archetypal memory is almost surely a real phenomenon. Nobelist Gerald Edelman claims that memory is quite organic, shifting, growing, changing, the brain-mind continually updating and reshuffling its memory. Contrary to current academic opinion, David Chamberlain denies that memory is "in the brain" at all, and gives serious evidence to back his point. I just received a disturbing paper concerning our "biomythological memory" that remakes itself continually on behalf of rationalization, self-aggrandizement, apology, and what Caroline Myss calls "woundology." Atwater's contribution to this perplexing and open-ended issue should prove rich and ongoing. I trust this book will be read and accepted by a wide population.

—JOSEPH CHILTON PEARCE,
AUTHOR OF *THE BIOLOGY OF TRANSCENDENCE:
A BLUEPRINT OF THE HUMAN SPIRIT*

Preface

Only those who have dared to let go can dare to reenter.
—MEISTER ECKHART

TWENTY SOME YEARS AGO I DIED, not once but three times within a span of three months. The year was 1977. A miscarriage and extreme hemorrhaging started it all, followed by a major thrombosis in the right-thigh vein that dislodged and the worst case of phlebitis the specialist had ever heard of, let alone seen. These events happened on January 2 and January 4, respectively. Three months later I suffered a physical, mental, and emotional collapse. Doctors were seen after the fact, so no one was in actual attendance when I died, yet it is the opinion of a gynecologist that I did indeed die, and that is my opinion also.

Regaining full use of my body and my faculties proved to be a daunting task, made more difficult by three relapses in September and October, one of which was adrenal failure. My blood pressure reading at that time was sixty over sixty. For me, coming back from death meant relearning how to crawl, stand, walk, run, climb stairs, tell the difference between left and right, and see and hear properly. It also meant redefining and rebuilding my belief systems.

The specter of insanity became the greater challenge, though, as dealing with three different near-death episodes demanded more from me than dying ever had. I was absolutely overwhelmed by the experience *and* its aftereffects. My previous background in the paranormal and altered states of consciousness was of little help. Dreams and visions offered no solace. For a while, I was lost between worlds, belonging to none of them.

What I dealt with in reidentifying myself and my place in the human family is described in chapter 2 of my first book, *Coming Back to Life: The Aftereffects of the Near-Death Experience*[1] and chapters 11, 13, and 15 in *Future Memory: How Those Who "See the Future" Shed New Light on the Workings of the Human Mind*.[2] Although bits and pieces of my personal story have been inserted into every book I have ever written, my primary work, first and foremost, is *research*. Why? Because it's my job.

Let me explain.

During my third near-death experience, I reached what I believe to be the centerpoint of existence. Many revelations about creation and consciousness and the journey of the soul were given to me while there. Afterward, a voice spoke. I came to regard it as the Voice Like None Other, for it was all-powerful, all-knowing, omnipresent, and of God. The Voice said: "Test revelation. You are to do the research. One book for each death." Books two and three were named, but not book one. I was shown what each book was to contain, but not how to proceed or what such a project might entail. I accepted the assignment.

My research of the near-death phenomenon began in earnest once I was back in my body and had sufficiently recovered from the trauma of my deaths, and had left my home state of Idaho and zigzagged across the continent to the Old Dominion of Virginia. It was mid-November 1978, and I had work to do. Immediately, I set about doing it.

For a quarter of a century, with only what monies I could scrape together, I have quietly moved among a special populace, those who had, like me, survived their deaths—asking questions and observing ever so intently the *behavior* of those who answered, as well as that of their families, friends, and caregivers. I learned through hard experience how to speak in "sound bites" once the media discovered I existed, but, fortunately, any fame I tasted was fleeting enough to allow me the time I needed to investigate the field of near-death states and consciousness transformations from 360 degrees . . . what was really there, whether or not it was what I wanted or expected to see. I was able to look through the eyes of over three thousand near-death survivors—a figure that doubles in number if you count the people I worked with and interviewed back in the sixties and early seventies when I was actively involved in exploring "otherworld journeys." (My work in the sixties led me to initiate Idaho's first nonprofit metaphysical corporation dedicated to an objective examination of mysticism and spiritual awakenings. Headquartered in Boise, Inner Forum existed for six years under my tutelage and one year under the direction of a board of directors, before it was replaced by the Creative Living Institute.)

Like other experiencers in the annals of near-death studies, I was shown my mission. Researching the near-death phenomenon and what it implies is why I returned from death. In my books, I pass along to others clear and tested material that provides a context for further inquiry and lends perspective to intriguing but elusive mysteries—about the mind, and about life and death.

I also do what I do because it's my passion, because, as the great paleontologist and Jesuit scholar Pierre Teilhard de Chardin once said, "Research is the highest form of adoration."

I came to know God in death . . . and I haven't stopped celebrating since.

The book you are now reading is actually a rewrite of *Children of the New Millennium*. Yet it is no ordinary rewrite. Thanks to the encouragement of Jon Graham at Inner Traditions, I was able to restore much of the material removed by the previous publisher, including two of the Appendices. I was told at the time that the deletions were for budgetary reasons. This book, therefore, is a bigger, more dynamic version than the original. It includes new research and new case studies spread throughout, as well as corrections and changes to the original text.

Child experiencers of near-death states have *a real voice* in this edition . . . much to the benefit of us all.

Acknowledgments

MY SINCEREST GRATITUDE goes to the 277 people who participated in this study of child experiencers of near-death states. Although many were youngsters when I interviewed them, the rest had reached their teen years or were in varying stages of adulthood. All of them bared their souls and shared their secrets about what it is really like to experience the near-death phenomenon as a child. I am awestruck by their courage in being so open, and humbled at their willingness to trust me with their joy and their pain.

Those who provided extra support are listed below. As is true of any endeavor of this magnitude, it is impossible to name everyone. So, to each and all, I give my deepest thanks!

Terry Young Atwater

Stephany Evans

William G. Reimer

Melvin Morse

Diane K. Corcoran

Theresa A. Csanady

Todd Murphy

Leslie Dixon

Joseph Benedict Geraci

Pat Kennedy

Donald Riggs

Andrew Swyschuk

L. Suzanne Gordon

Alejandra Warden

Sarah Hinze

Mellen-Thomas Benedict

Kelly John Huffman

Natalie DeGennaro

Paulie Litke

Dennis Swartz

My whole life is an aftereffect.

—JOHN RAYMOND LIONA, BROOKLYN, NEW YORK.
HIS NEAR-DEATH EXPERIENCE OCCURRED DURING BIRTH TRAUMA.

ONE

Evolution's Nod

The test of a first-rate intelligence is the ability to hold two opposed ideas in the mind at the same time, and still retain the ability to function.

—F. SCOTT FITZGERALD

TODAY'S CHILDREN really are different from those of previous generations. They are unusually smart, even gifted; identify with "alien" existences whether past-life oriented, extraterrestrial, or multidimensional; and they are natural creative intuitives.

William Strauss and Neil Howe, authors of *Generations: The History of America's Future, 1584 to 2069,*[1] label the children born between 1982 and about 2003 as our nation's fourteenth, or "millennial," generation. These youngsters are arriving at a time in our history when countless measures for the protection of the young are being swept into law. They are turning out to be the most wanted, the most nurtured, the most educated, the most dedicated to public service, ever.

And this is true globally.

Millennial children are not confined to the boundaries of any one country, as this observation from Ibarra Chavez, a Mexican pediatrician, proves: "The new crop of infants are coming in more *aware* . . . eyes focused and alert, necks strong, lying in bassinets no bigger than chickens,

1

and with a *knowingness* I cannot describe [in Spanish or in English]. They are very special babies, this new crop."

Sharon Begley, author of the *Newsweek* magazine article entitled "The IQ Puzzle,"[2] describes the situation this way: "IQ scores throughout the developed world have soared dramatically since the tests were introduced in the early years of this [twentieth] century. . . . The rise is so sharp that it implies that the average school child today is as bright as the near-geniuses of yesteryear."

The gene pool cannot change fast enough to account for this jump. So it has been supposed that better nutrition and more efficient schools are the cause. Yet neither factor explains the fascinating incongruity that appeared in IQ test scores: acquired intelligence, which comes from rote schooling, improved only slightly, while nonverbal intelligence, which is based on creative problem solving, soared!

Trying to make sense of this, experts have surmised that either kids are getting better at taking tests, or something in their environment accounts for this astonishing difference. Some top educators feel that the spread of image-intense technologies, like video games, for example, are probably at least partially responsible since they train a child to concentrate and respond—major components to learning (unlike regular television, which demands nothing of viewers). Other professionals suggest that it may be permissive or relaxed parenting, which results in the child leading the parent, that can promote the critical skill of vocabulary building.

Whatever the cause, the global jump in youngsters' intelligence amounts to about a 24- to 26-point rise over the IQ score used during the first half of the twentieth century as a marker for genius, at around 134. This directly challenges the entire academic understanding of what constitutes genius and how it is measured.

Surprisingly, the research of near-death states I began in 1978 shows that roughly half of those children who have experienced the near-death phenomenon fall within this same score range, upward to 150, 160, and even higher. But their jump in intelligence was sudden and could be traced to that moment when death seemed their only option—not playing with video games or trying to outwit parents. They were not born that way. And few of those I interviewed ever used image-intense technologies; the majority described parental bonding as "strained." Although the end result of their experience matches the changes currently being observed with millennial kids, how they got that way differs radically.

The incongruity in test scores, though, concerns nonverbal intelligence or creative problem solving. Nearly all of the child experiencers in my twenty-six-plus years of researching near-death states came to exhibit this trait (genius or not), followed by a noticeable decrease for most of them in the ability to express themselves and socialize.

Commonalities between the millennial generation and child experiencers of near-death episodes are so numerous (nonverbal intelligence being just one) that to understand what might be happening with the new crop of young people worldwide, we would be wise to take a closer look at the near-death experience *and* its aftereffects—at how children are really affected by the phenomenon of experiencing life *after* death.

Near-death studies in the past have focused on adults. The classical model that emerged was an adult model—of adults, for adults. What is lacking has been an in-depth study of near-death states as seen through the eyes of the child experiencer, beyond the initial work done by Melvin Morse, M.D., and chronicled in his book *Closer to the Light: Learning from the Near-Death Experiences of Children.*[3] Because of this, the fuller story of what happens to kids has been bypassed. In seeking to remedy the situation, I made a most amazing discovery: child experiencers of near-death states have all the markers to indicate that they are the precursors, the advance wave, who not only set the stage for the millennial generation but also offer persuasive evidence to indicate that a new race is aborning— evolution in our lifetime.

A poll taken by *U.S. News & World Report* in early 1997 estimates that there are 15 million near-death experiencers in the United States,[4] or about one-third of those who "died" but later revived. That already high figure does not take into account child experiencers. The best estimate we have for kids comes from the work of Morse. He reported the occurrence rate for youngsters at around 70 percent, more than double that of adults in the same situation: brushing death, nearly dying, or being resuscitated or reviving from clinical death.

In other words, *the vast majority of children who face death experience a near-death scenario. And these children contend with the same aftereffects, both psychological and physiological, as do adults . . . but in a different manner. Good and evil jumble together for them, and the line separating one reality from another disappears.*

Modern technology and ever-improving resuscitation techniques are returning more people from the brink of death, especially children, than even ten years ago. We've already explored adult versions of encountering the Other Side; now it's time to focus on kids. Except that, when we talk about little ones, we must also address evolutionary factors. Actually, any reference to near-death states, whether concerning adults or kids, can no longer be limited to an analysis of "the experience" as a single, anomalous event— because it isn't.

Near-death states comprise a complex and many-faceted phenomenon that is part of a much larger genre, *transformations of consciousness*. As such, they model broader issues that impinge upon the human family as a whole. Label them evolution's nod, God's will, or the adaptation of the species; whatever they're called, the experience and its aftereffects are reflective of a powerful force for change that is undeniable in its impact.

Recent attacks on Charles Darwin's theory of evolution put what I have just said into perspective. Bear with me as I show you why.

Darwin based his theory on the doctrine of uniformitarianism, which states that all geological phenomena may be explained as the result of existing forces operating uniformly from the origin of life on earth to the present, and that biological advancement from species to species is equally gradual and caused by similar forces.

How then, ask Michael Cremo and Richard Thompson, authors of *Forbidden Archaeology: The Hidden History of the Human Race*[5] do you explain the existence of an ornate vase inlaid with silver embedded in rock over 500 million years old? And how, asks Richard Milton, author of *Shattering the Myths of Darwinism,*[6] can you account for the many examples of rapidly forming fossils (e.g., that of a fish formed as it was swallowed by another fish, or of an ancient amphibian in the process of giving birth), and rocks off Britain's coast that took shape in a matter of hours rather than millions of years?

Thanks to computer modeling, satellite photography, and a new breed of scientist willing to ask the unthinkable, a new theory of evolution is developing—one based on evidence from the fossil record in rock strata— that posits that the Earth has suffered severe convulsions, volcanic upheavals, and worldwide flooding at various stages in its prehistory. These catastrophes, and the sudden changes that resulted, are proving to have been a greater influence on the path evolution took than graduated pressure over time.

The brilliant paleontologist Stephen Jay Gould applied the catastrophe theory to species adaptation by detailing how a species can go for millions of years without change and then, within a brief span, perhaps a hundred years or much less, make a *quantum leap* in evolution and accomplish the impossible.

Sudden changes. Quantum leaps. Evolution can alter its direction in a heartbeat—transforming geological formations, continents, plants, animals, human beings, even us moderns—irrespective of the natural order.

None of the present theories on evolution addresses biochemical molecules. Found at the core of the tiniest life-forms, biochemical molecules, the "living machinery of consciousness," know and are uniquely sensitive to light. According to Michael J. Behe, associate professor of biochemistry at Lehigh University in Pennsylvania and author of *Darwin's Black Box: The Biochemical Challenge to Evolution,*[7] "Light sensitivity could not have evolved, but must have been designed by some form of prior intelligence."

Intelligent design, responsible for the encoding of light sensitivity and a knowingness of light in all life-forms, accommodates evolution's nod as if responding to a greater plan, one that is replete with growth contingencies.

Take entropy, for instance. Contrary to its definition as the law of diminishing order and the decreased availability of energy, entropy *always* leads to new forms and a higher order—as illustrated by chaos mathematics. This theory tells us that in any system where unpredictability suddenly increases to the point that order disintegrates into chaos, that very chaos gives birth to new order. Life utilizes random unpredictability to guarantee continuous change and advancement.

Evolution operates the same way in the human family.

Always, sudden changes, quantum leaps in physiology and consciousness, have catapulted the growth and development of humankind beyond that which can be explained. As "missing links" are still standard fare in trying to understand the evolution of our bodies, so, too, are there missing connectors in any attempt to rationalize the evolution of consciousness.

Until now.

My work in the sixties and early seventies researching altered and transformed states of consciousness, and since 1978 studying near-death states, has enabled me to recognize that these experiences have less to do with anything paranormal, religious, mystical, or offering proof of an afterlife, than they do with how evolution might really work.

I have come to realize that what is involved in a transformation of consciousness, whether precipitated by the cataclysm of a near-death experience or a shamanic vision quest or a kundalini breakthrough or a baptism of the Holy Spirit, has all the markings of a structural, chemical, and functional change in the brain. This sudden change, sometimes akin to a quantum leap, flings the experiencer from one mode of existence to another—as if on cue. Social justice and moral integrity take on the vigor of "new light" when this occurs.

I call the phenomenon a *brain shift/spirit shift,* and I suspect that, because of the gravity of its aftereffects, such a shift is the engine that drives evolution—that which transforms, transmutes, and advances our species while triggering the development of the higher brain. This suspicion of mine is based on the interviews and observations I have conducted since 1978 with over 3,000 adult near-death experiencers (not counting the significant others I also spoke with), as well as research with nearly the same number of people during the middle sixties to the middle seventies who had undergone transformations of consciousness through other means. This research base was expanded by work with 277 child experiencers (about half still youngsters when we met, the rest having reached their teen or adult years).

Since near-death states model consciousness transformations in a neutral fashion, as they happen to anyone, at any age, under any condition, anywhere, I will use my research in this field to explore the broader subject of brain shift/spirit shift and what that implies.

Before I do, it would be helpful if I commented on why and how I do research. I was "told" during my third near-death experience that it would be my job, when I returned to life, to bring clarity and perspective to what I had just survived while testing the validity of its revelation. Thus, it has never been my intent or interest to verify or challenge anyone else's findings. As fate would have it, however, my research has indeed become a challenge to the generally accepted classical model.

The protocol I use is that of a police investigator, a skill I learned from my police-officer father (that's why some people call me the gumshoe of near-death). I specialize in interviews and observations, cross-checking everything I notice a minimum of five times with different people in different sections of the country, as a way to ensure that any bias I may have as a near-death experiencer will not cloud my perception and that my work is not completely dependent on anecdote. Questionnaires for me are auxiliary, used only to further examine certain aspects of near-death states. All of my work is original, and most of it has since been verified by other researchers. Near-death studies has been a full-time profession for me since 1978, in addition to employment that pays for the groceries.

My interview style is straightforward. I ask open-ended questions, such as "What happened to you?" If I want to know more, I signal that intent with forward body movement, a tilt of my head, a smile, and the incredibly magical word "and . . ." Language used is determined by the experiencer as he or she responds to questions. To obtain a greater depth of material, I learned early on to avoid telling anyone I was a researcher, and to rely more on facial expressions and body posturing than on words. I watch as well as listen, ever mindful of feelings and sensations, for the dance we humans engage in as we relate to one another is quite revealing.

I altered my style somewhat with children, in this manner: no parents were allowed when I was with them; the same eye-level contact was maintained throughout the interviews; I replaced note-taking with gentleness; I encouraged them to share feelings as well as memories; and I opened myself to sense the wave of consciousness they rode.

Parents were interviewed too, as I wanted to know their point of view and whether they might have applied any pressure on their child by making a big deal out of it. This is important, as children are capable of slanting their stories to fit the emotional expectations of their parents and/or teachers. If I suspected such a compromise had been made, I would retire the account to the dustbin. I rejected about 15 percent of the interview opportunities I had with children for this reason. Fascination with "out of the mouths of babes" reports can mislead more readily than enlighten.

These claims, though, are most often right on target, as a report from Richmond, Virginia, demonstrates. In February 1996, a mother with two small daughters aboard lost control of her car and flipped it over into a ditch. The oldest nearly lost a leg, and three-year-old Victoria died. Refusing the grim verdict, a police officer began CPR (cardiopulmonary resuscitation) on the lifeless body. Five minutes later the little girl breathed. Her first words were: "I saw Jesus. But he told me it wasn't my time and I need to go back and be with my daddy." The child's grandfather, a man who drank heavily and "messed around," was so overcome by Victoria's message that he quit drinking and started to read the Bible. (This report is from Pat Kennedy, a friend of Victoria's family.)

Why are we so awestruck with what children have to say? Because we've forgotten what it is like to be one.

In 1994, I devised a lengthy questionnaire to probe the memories of those who had had a near-death episode as a child. My goal was not only to test recall, but to track the aftereffects throughout various life stages. Of the fifty-two people who participated, forty-four had experienced the near-death phenomenon by their fifteenth birthday. The youngest to fill out the questionnaire was twelve, the oldest a seventy-two-year-old who had been pronounced clinically dead at four and a half. (The other eight had significant experiences that were near-death-like, and were helpful in cross-comparisons.)

Because questionnaire findings so closely mirror what I have observed throughout the bulk of my work, I will reference them often and provide direct quotes. Each time a quote appears, the experiencer's name (a few requested anonymity), location, age of occurrence, and cause will be noted. For starters:

Francis Piekarski, New Martinsville, West Virginia. NDE at age five from drowning; at twelve from high fever and bone infection. "I got a bone infection and my temperature shot up to 105 degrees. I was very sick and my body began to shake. My mother was scared. So as not to scare her more, I stiffened up my muscles to stop the shaking. All of a sudden my body shook violently. My mother ran from the room yelling, 'He's dying.' At that moment, I was out of my body and looking up from the foot of my bed. I saw two men in their mid-twenties. One was looking to the left and the other to the right. They were about ten feet tall. It made me feel better that they were there. I felt they were angels and were guarding me."

Carl Allen Pierson, Hinton, West Virginia. NDE at age eight or nine, hit by lightning. "During a thunderstorm, with a metal washtub over my head, I went to untie a cow from the tree for my uncle. When I got approximately fifteen feet from the tree, lightning hit it and bounced to the tub. I was barefoot, standing on wet grass. Lightning took all the galvanizing off the tub, and knocked me and the tub away from the tree. The tub traveled about 250 feet and it knocked me 25 feet away. Burned me everywhere that I had contact with the tub. Turned the tub black. I was hovering above as my family encircled my body, which was lying on the grass. It was communicated that I was dead. I was trying to tell them I was not dead, but I made no sounds. Soft light. Warm, glowing feeling. Something or someone told me that everything would be okay, then there was blackness. Next I was lying in a dark house on a couch but could not hear or see, yet I was aware of what was going on. I could not move anything, like my body muscles were locked up. Great pain. Blackness. Then I was in a hospital or doctor's office on a gurney. I had a vision and saw myself hovering over my body again, but this time no one was present. My body was larger (adult size). I remember hearing the news on the radio, something about a boy who had been killed by lightning. There was mention of it in the local paper, too. Both turned out to be false reports, as you can readily see."

Barbara True Bradley, Des Moines, Iowa. NDE at age four and a half, pneumonia, complications from surgery. "I was in the hospital with lobar pneumonia and a pus pocket in the lung, along with an extremely high fever. In 1926 there was no sulfa or penicillin. The doctors told my mother I was critically ill. I had two operations. Two of my ribs were removed in order to open my lung and keep it open for the pus to be siphoned out several times a day. It was painful and frightening for a little kid! Sometime during this illness, my mother was told that that particular night would be the turning point. She and the Episcopal pastor prayed over me all night. I was better the next day. My 'dream' happened that night, although I'm not sure. This 'dream' was in black and white frames except one picture of me all dressed up in skirt, sweater, hose, and heels, and wearing a yellow carnation, going to a football game. (At the time, my family lived in Nebraska—Big Red Country. Later, when I married, my husband and I moved to Iowa—Yellow and Black Country.) In other scenes I saw myself walking toward the rear of an airplane that had two seats on each side of one aisle. I rode on a train that had a glass-domed top with pine and birch trees flashing by outside. (According to my encyclopedia, the first glass-domed train ran in 1945.) I watched myself being married to a dark-haired man in front of an altar that had a cross in the back. I had long, dark hair and wore a white dress with a white veil and a long train. Everything subsequently happened as shown to me."

John Raymond Liona, Brooklyn, New York. Complications at birth. "I was strangled by my umbilical cord during birth. Once born, I was given a tracheostomy to get me breathing—black eyes, swollen face, cuts from forceps. My mother didn't see me until the third day. I relive the event in my dreams from time to time, vividly. I remember being bent over or kneeling down, fighting with these knots. I was very upset and angry. Just when I was thinking I was getting in control of these things, I got hit in the face (the doc with the forceps). I started struggling even more. All of a sudden I became very peaceful. Everything I was feeling before just poured out of me and I was so calm. I remember looking at my hands, but the details are not clear. I think I was floating, because I was trying to move forward but could not. I was trying to reach this woman in the distance. The material of her gown was glowing with little specks of light trailing off.

John Raymond Liona, complications at birth.

There was a buzzing or humming sound. She floated away toward the left.
I was calling to her, yelling, but the light, it was all around. It was coming
from the right, and was so bright. She could not hear me. I was so upset,
as I wanted to go with her."

***Tonecia Maxine McMillan, Oxon Hill, Maryland. NDE at age eleven,
drowning.*** "I was on an inner tube in the water off a beach in Delaware.
I had ventured out too far. My grandmother (who raised me, as I never
lived with my siblings) motioned for me to come back to shore. I mis-
judged the depth. I stepped out of the inner tube and began to drown. I
left my body. I could see myself in the water. I saw my grandmother trying to come and get me, and I saw my brother cut his left foot. Then I was
in a very beautiful, peaceful, picturesque place like a meadow. I felt very
loved. The colors were brilliant; they were nothing like I have ever seen
before. There is simply no comparison—the yellows, greens—so very
beautiful, so peaceful. At the time of my drowning, I was on a 'black
beach,' so to speak. Delaware still was practicing segregation. I was told
that two white men were on the beach at the time. These two men saved
my life by pulling me to shore, then *they simply disappeared.* On the way
to the hospital, when I asked my brother how his cut foot was doing, I was
met with stony silence. He couldn't deal with the fact that I saw his accident while I was out of my body."

Anell Q. Tubbs, Boise, Idaho. NDE at age seven or eight, blow to head.
"I was playing on a hassock in the living room. It rolled and I fell off

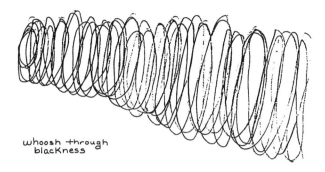

whoosh through
blackness

Anell Q. Tubbs, NDE at age seven or eight.

backward, striking the base of my head on the sharp corner of the coffee table—right in the little area where the neck and skull attach. Everything went black and there was this *whoosh,* and I felt like I was traveling at an extremely high rate of speed through the blackness. Then, in a split second, I relived my entire life, every bit of it, and it was in color just like it was happening all over again—emotions and all—but it only took a split second. The next thing I remember is sitting up and thinking, 'So that is what it is like to die.' I don't remember telling anyone. But it has always been fresh and right in the front of my mind."

Laura, San Francisco, California. NDE at age three and a half, child abuse, surgery. "My father, in a blind drunken rage, raped and sodomized and beat me to death in the middle of the night. At the most extreme outpost of pain, I cried out to God and in that moment I was torn from life. As I died I felt myself raised up by angels in robes of many colors. I did not know where they were taking me as they flew, carrying me up higher and higher in the sky. Finally, we reached a place where emptiness gave way to form, and form took the shape of huge cloudlike masses on which other angels seemed to be walking, although they too floated through the air. The angels carrying me lay me at the feet of a beautiful female angel whose radiating love was more powerful than any of those around her. She said to me in a voice whose sweetness and tone are unknown here on earth, 'Tell me your story.' I said to her, not in spoken words but in thoughts, 'I will, but now I need to rest.' My spirit had no energy, even to answer this loving lady. God in the manifestation of infinite light appeared off to my left, and I was engulfed in a form of all-powerful, all-nourishing love. That divine being appeared as a massive column of golden light, with the suggestion of a human shape inside. I both saw and felt his light, feeling as if I were in a warm bath that completely healed and protected me. I never wanted to leave. No conversation passed between us, but in those infinite moments I acquired the knowledge that allowed me to go back to earth to complete my life. After this infinite moment had passed, there began a battle for my life between the angels in heaven and the doctors on earth. Every time the doctors pounded on my chest, my spirit was sucked into my body for a split second, only to be pulled back again by the angels. They held me by my feet, struggling to keep me from coming back. Finally, the doctors pounded one last time. I heard an angel say, 'They're stronger than we are,' and I was sucked back into my body, sat up, screamed, and passed out. To this day, I always have the feeling that I need to go back, that there was something more I was meant to do there before returning. That feeling of incompleteness keeps me half in the other world all the time."

Regina Patrick, Toledo, Ohio. NDE at age four, pneumonia. "From infancy until I was ten years old, I was chronically in and out of the hospital. At age four, it was because of pneumonia. It was night and I lay on my stomach, having just awakened from what I took for a dream. A group of five to ten ethereal people had just given me a lot of instructions. The instructions were important and I needed to remember them. I was trying, but there were so many that I couldn't. I even tried repeating them to myself again and again, but to no avail. I was getting them jumbled and confused. I sensed that these instructions would be important to me someday, even if I didn't understand them. I was starting to get frustrated. Just at that moment, we separated. Because there was no sense of movement, I can't say whether I moved away from them or they from me, or if we separated from each other simultaneously. I awoke with a strange thing, something I had never had before, a great sense of peace, which confused me. What was the purpose of this peace? Normally, when I awoke in the hospital like this, I worried about my family back home: What were they doing? Were they worried about me? Were they okay? The peace obliterated my worry. I tried again to remember what they had told me but found I could remember even less now that I was awake. I was concerned that 'they' (the ethereal people) would be mad at me for forgetting their message."

TWO

@

Brain Shift/Spirit Shift

There is a soul force in the universe, which if we permit it
will flow through us and produce miraculous results.

—MAHATMA GANDHI

THE "ENGINE" OF EVOLUTION, that force that drives the adaptation and refinement of species, is normally so gradual that centuries must pass before we can even glimpse the changes it fosters. Brain shifts/spirit shifts jump-start that process in the human family. They are in essence evolution's quantum leap. The way experiencers are impacted by the spread of physiological and psychological aftereffects has all the appearances of a structural, chemical, and functionary change in the brain, and alterations in the nervous and digestive systems—not to mention a sudden "awakening" to things sacred and spiritual.

These two shifts are the invisible weights that tip perceptual scales toward spiritual realities instead of physical actualities. Whereas brain shifts can be examined, verified, and explained, at least to some degree, spirit shifts can be identified only by interpreting responses; that is, by recognizing the type of behavioral changes exhibited by the experiencer.

Among adult experiencers, I regard a brain shift/spirit shift as a growth event—a sudden, unexpected twist in life that operates like a "washing machine" in how it motivates us to clean up our habits, flush

13

out our minds, and overhaul our lifestyles. Some examples of growth events are: losing when we were certain we would win, or winning when we were certain we would lose; being forced to slow down in life when we wanted to go faster, or being speeded up when we wanted to go slow; suffering when we wanted to prosper, or prospering when we were unprepared or even unwilling. Growth events, if we are open to the messages they would impart, not only give us the opportunity to turn our lives around but allow us to make course corrections in favor of that which is spiritual. Growth events engendered by the near-death phenomenon are unusually powerful and far-reaching in their impact.

Among child experiencers, I regard a brain shift/spirit shift as an evolutionary event—for, regardless of how others are affected by a child's near-death scenario, the second birth the child seems to undergo reorders or "seeds" the youngster in ways that are exceptional to regular behavior development. Also, the brain is affected to a greater degree in children than in adults, propelling them into abstractions and learning enhancements as creative expression soars. This marks them as different from their agemates and at variance with family and social structures. Once grown, they attempt to enter the traditional workforce with a nontraditional mindset, ever pushing for change and new, even exotic, options and alternatives. The "second-born" challenge every aspect of society on every level, continuously. They inspire the kind of cultural growth that fuels social revolution.

To advance the idea that at the core of near-death episodes and other similar states is a brain shift/spirit shift, we need to explore the subject from various angles (as does the report *Phase II—Brain Shift/Spirit Shift: A Theoretical Model Using Research on Near-Death States to Explore the Transformation of Consciousness*).[1]

BRAIN SHIFT

Any manner of occurrence can trigger a brain shift. I would include here those of a more turbulent nature, such as: religious conversions, near-death episodes, kundalini breakthroughs, shamanistic vision quests, sudden spiritual transformations, certain types of head trauma, or having been hit by lightning. I would also count those more tranquil in how they are experienced—like the slow, steady application of spiritual disciplines, mindfulness techniques, meditation, sacred rituals, or a prayerful state of mind in which an individual simply desires to become a better person.

With turbulent experiences, I have noticed that the brain organ (structure, chemistry, function) seems to shift before the mind, or the degree of consciousness present. With tranquil experiences, the mind, or consciousness level, tends to shift before the brain.

Which shifts first makes a difference with the aftereffects: consequences from tranquil episodes are gradual and usually happen in increments, giving a person time mentally to think and prepare; turbulent ones are so immediate and so powerful that the brain organ itself can be overwhelmed, compounding the challenges of whatever might be encountered. Certain major characteristics tend to be displayed by people who have gone through a brain shift, as described in the following two lists.

These characteristics can be positive or negative, depending on how they are applied. Based on my previous investigations of spiritual awakenings and enlightenment done in the 1960s and 1970s, these characteristics match across the board with the universal experience of a transforming and evolving consciousness—in other words, a brain shift.

Physiological Aftereffects

Changes in thought processing (switch from sequential/selective thinking to clustered thinking and an acceptance of ambiguity)

Insatiable curiosity

Heightened intelligence

Able to abstract easily

More creativity and inventiveness

Unusual sensitivity to light and sound

Substantially more or less energy (even energy surges, often more sexual)

Reversal of body clock

Lower blood pressure

Accelerated metabolic and substance absorption rates (decreased tolerance of pharmaceuticals and chemically treated products)

Electrical sensitivity

Heightened sensations of taste, touch, texture, and smell

Synesthesia (multiple sensing)

Increased allergies and sensitivities

A preference for more vegetables and grains (less meat) with adults, just the opposite with children

Physically younger appearance with adults, more mature with children (before and after photos can differ)

Psychological Aftereffects

Loss of the fear of death
More spiritual/less religious
Philosophical
Possible bouts of depression
Disregard for time
More generous and charitable
Capable of forming expansive concepts of love while at the same time
    challenged in initiating and maintaining satisfying relationships
Exaggerated "inner child" issues
Less competitive
Convinced of a life purpose
Rejection of previous limitations and norms
Increased psychic ability, awareness of future, and future memory episodes
Charismatic
Childlike sense of wonder and joy (adults); a more mature wisdom (kids)
Less stressed
More detached and objective (dissociation)
"Merge" easily (absorption)
Hunger for knowledge and learning

These lists above highlight the aftereffects that are normal and typical to a brain shift. Because of the intensity of impact, it takes at least seven years for the average adult experiencer to fully integrate them.[2] With kids, it depends—some adjust quickly, but most not until they reach adulthood.

Almost every single one of the aftereffects can be traced to enhanced, accelerated limbic system involvement as a point of origination in the brain. For this reason, it would behoove us to learn something about this little-known area.

THE LIMBIC SYSTEM AND EMOTIONS

The limbic system, a conglomerate of various small but important brain structures located in a semicircle in the middle of the brain, caps off the topmost extension of the brain stem. It wraps around our primitive reptilian brain, translating our basic instincts for sex, hunger, sleep, fear, and survival into more flexible and social forms of behavior. Often referred to as the emotional or feeling center (the "gut brain"), the limbic system is also the seat of the immune system and the body's ability to heal itself.

Few people realize that it is the limbic system that operates as the "executive office" in deciding what information is stored in memory, what is forgotten, and what will be further elaborated upon and refined in the two main hemispheres and throughout the brain/mind assembly. And it has a direct neural connection to the heart.

Although this small but extremely efficient system has been part of us for hundreds of thousands of years of brain evolution, only recently has it been recognized as the most complicated structure on the earth. Many brain researchers now believe that if the limbic system doesn't actually originate "mind," then it certainly is the gateway within the brain to higher realms of mind and more powerfully diverse and collective types of consciousness. Thus, the staging arena where the organ called the brain accesses and filters what is referred to as the mind is the limbic system.

The brain, incidentally, has been discovered to be more emotional than cognitive. Nicholas Humphrey, a senior research fellow at Cambridge University, has explained, "A person can be conscious without thinking anything. But a person simply cannot be conscious without feeling."[3] Combine this with the scientific finding that feedback between the limbic system and the heart is *instantaneous,* and it becomes clear why in most near-death scenarios experiencers are "flooded with love."

THE LIMBIC SYSTEM AND CHANGES IN THE BRAIN

When the limbic is stimulated, it leaves "prints." With a little bit of stimulation, we get excited, perk up, emotions flow, and receptivity is enhanced (music, rituals, and celebrations promote such a response). Passion/compassion turns on with more stimulation, along with displays of psychic/ intuitive abilities and the inspiration to take action (hearing charismatic speakers and reading shocking news headlines often accomplish this; for instance, listening to the speeches of Martin Luther King Jr., or hearing of the tragic death of Princess Diana). Massive surges of love and light, faculty extensions, panoramic visions, and the emergence of wisdom and knowing can occur when the limbic system is deeply impacted by a sudden change or intense shift in its function.

When the limbic system is "spun around" or receives a good "blow," it's as if the temporal lobes, nervous system, and heart are signaled to do one of two things: shut down or accelerate response. Shutting down means damage or death. Accelerated function means healing or enhancement. What we refer to as "the aftereffects" in cases of near-death and near-death-like states may well be the spread, or cascade effect, or "imprinting," that various bodily systems come to exhibit in reaction to and in correspondence with the specifics of limbic enhancement/enlargement/ acceleration. The extent of the cascade effect seems to reveal the degree to which the limbic system was impacted.

The limbic system, far from being just a survival center, jump-starts:

Learning: "When emotions do not guide our awareness of the environment, thoughts, dreams, and images disappear. Our most subtle feelings have a physical basis within the limbic region, and the limbic should never be forgotten."[4]

Emoting: "The intensity of electrical current surrounding the heart's activity is about fifty times more powerful than that of the brain organ and precedes hemispheric action. There is 'heart intelligence' in how the heart gives intuitive input to the mind."[5]

And the limbic system, once accelerated in function, is the gateway of initiation for such conditions as:

Multiple Sensing (Synesthesia): Multisensory awareness, like hearing paintings, smelling sounds, tasting vision, seeing music. Neurologist Richard E. Cytowic believes sensing in multiple ways is not something new but has always existed and can be developed by anyone.[6]

Clustered Thinking: "Shaking together" or "clustering" information, instead of using linear logic, so data can be rearranged and tossed around in new ways; a sign of genius. Psychologist Howard Gardner speaks of Einstein seeing a light ray in his mind and knowing he was right, French composer Olivier Messiaen seeing color in tones, and Picasso experiencing numbers as patterns of contour.[7]

Parallel Processing/Simultaneous Brain Waves: Presence of all brainwave speeds (beta, alpha, theta, and delta) in simultaneous operation; the "awakened" mind. Anna Wise, a researcher of brain waves, and Max Cade, a psychobiologist and biophysicist, found that spiritual adepts can utilize the full range of brainwave levels simultaneously. Wise discovered that certain images, words, and timed pauses could actually shift anyone's brain into this state.[8]

Mind over Matter: Moving physical objects with brainwave emissions. Scientists at the New York State Department of Health, Albany, have discovered that people using thought alone can move a computer cursor around a display screen. Clinical trials are in progress to see if paralyzed individuals can be taught the same technique to help them communicate better and perform simple tasks.[9]

Any experience that overwhelms a person to the degree that thought processes are altered appreciably changes brain structure to some extent. We know this from clinical experiments using PET scans (positron-emission tomography). Near-death states and other transformative episodes of the same or similar magnitude affect an individual even more, engendering in most cases evidence to suggest permanent bodymind changes—accompanied by the awakening of higher levels of consciousness.

"Growth spurts" in the brain (intelligence and/or faculty enhancements) appear to be the result of brain cell branches suddenly increasing in number and spreading rapidly, which expands contact between cells. Scientists have long suspected that any rise in intelligence has more to do with these spurts than with the brain hemispheres (left and right) and neocortex (new or high brain). Growth spurts (or heightened brain cell branching) literally rewire and reconfigure the brain, making more complex, efficient neural pathways for transmitting information. Everything else proceeds from this factor—the brain and how it shifts structure and chemistry to suit the demands of new modes of usage.

THE TEMPORAL LOBES AND THINGS "FUTURE"

While studying cases of child experiencers, I came across clusters of reports at certain ages. Determining how significant these age clusters are requires larger studies than mine, but, for the present, my statistics suffice to support an intriguing observation: there appears to be a connection between the ages when most near-death episodes occur with kids and the more critical stages of childhood brain development.

Although these findings come from my work with near-death survivors, I use the term "brain shift" in the chart to reflect a broader range of inquiry, because large numbers of unusual and different incidents involving children cluster at the same ages as do the near-death reports in my research, especially with youngsters aged three to five.

I first began tracking anomalous events in the mid-sixties out of pure curiosity and noticed, much to my surprise, that three- to five-year-olds were much more apt than persons of any other age to experience past-life

AGE CLUSTERS FOUND IN REPORTED CASES OF A BRAIN SHIFT

Age Clusters	Correlations
Children and Young Adults	
Birth–15 months*	When the actual wiring of the brain is determined and synapse formation increases 20-fold; utilizes more than twice the energy of an adult brain. By about 18 months, excess neurons and synapses are pruned.
3–5 years*	Time of temporal lobe development; explore and experiment with possible roles, future patterns, action/reaction, environmental continuity. Brain usually reaches 90% of adult size by age 5.
7–9 years	Time of judgment/discrimination development; often when serious accidents and illnesses occur or problems with significant others. Dramatic growth spurts in brain region crucial to language and understanding of spatial relations.
11–15 years	Time of puberty; hormone fluctuations; sexuality and authority are questioned; identity crisis. Brain's gray matter thickens, especially in frontal lobes (the brain's region for planning, impulse control, reasoning).
Mature Adults	
27-32 years*	Crossover between adherence to values of friends, family, and the pressures of the workplace and the urge to establish self as an independent and mature ego; social crisis. Brain begins to shrink in volume; gray matter loss. Information processing slows.

NOTE: Among mature adults, smaller clusters are notable around the ages of 39, 49, and 59. Children's data is based on 1997 analysis; adults, on 1994 analysis. More research is needed for reliable confirmation of these groupings.

* With children, the first two age categories are where most of the reports cluster in my research base, as well as where I found the most compelling cases of genius. With adults, I found the largest cluster from ages 27 to 32.

recall, alien sightings, alien abductions, flying dreams, out-of-body episodes, spirit visitations, invisible friends, and other paranormal and psychic occurrences. This is the *same time frame* when long-term memory begins for most children and when storytelling has the greatest influence. It is also the period when kids are almost entirely future oriented and temporal lobe development predominates. (The temporal lobes are those sections of the brain located behind and upward from the ears to near the temples.) Traditionally, the temporal lobes are referred to as the "patterning center" or "library," that place where our original blueprints of shape and form are stored. For this reason, they are thought to be the seat of imagination.

Because youngsters who have near-death experiences come to have an extraordinary relationship with things future, I searched through studies done on childhood behavior development for anything that might explain why—and learned that kids between three and five have no natural sense of time or space. They gain this sense *by projecting into the future* and by intuitively engaging with futuristic ideas, images, feelings, and sensations. The future does not appear as "future" to children. To them it is simply another aspect of "now" (that which is immediate), and it remains so until they are able to establish the validity of continuous scenery and connected wholes. Once they accomplish this, they have the perspective and the sense of continuity they need to adapt to ever-changing environments and the meaningfulness of cause and effect (consequences). In other words, the imaginal adventures of childhood are necessary for the development of healthy minds.

Yet near-death states that happen during this same juncture in brain development appear to accelerate mental growth in child experiencers years ahead of what would be expected. Perhaps this critical timing is the reason. More than just imaginal worlds and magical imagery are involved in near-death states, though. The shift child experiencers undergo suggests the hand of evolution at work.

A fascinating fact is that adults as well as children who have undergone any type of brain shift regularly begin to "step" into the future. Many even begin to "live" the future ahead of time and remember having done so when the futuristic event actually occurs. Their feat mimics what happens to ordinary kids between the ages of three and five. I called this the "future memory" phenomenon and wrote a book about it,[10] defining the phenomenon as:

Future Memory: to live in advance (subjective/sensory rich). The ability to fully live a given event or sequence of events in subjective reality before living the same episode in objective reality. This is usually, but not always, forgotten by the individual after it occurs, only to be remembered later when some "signal" triggers memory. Sensory-rich future memory is so detailed as to include movements, thoughts, smells, tastes, decisions, sights, and sounds of regular physical living.

All this is actually lived and physically, emotionally, and sensorially experienced, *not* merely watched (which is clairvoyance), heard (clairaudience), predicted (prophecy), or known (precognition); and that living is so thorough, there is no way to distinguish it from everyday reality while the phenomenon is in progress.

Future memory is not to be confused with déjà vu, which is past oriented. What I refer to is a clear and cogent ability to somehow access the future and "live" it *before* physical manifestation. That sense of "living in advance" is acutely felt by experiencers. Some examples from interviews with adults:

A former military officer who now lives in Illinois pre-experiences conversations at meetings he attends. He claims this relaxes him and makes life more interesting.

A woman in Washington State is able to comfort troubled travelers because she prelives which bus and plane terminals to visit and who to look for and why.

A woman in Alabama meets fellow shoppers in advance and pre-experiences standing at cash registers, and seeing items rung up at other registers, including prices.

Distinguishing features of the future memory phenomenon are: *physical sensation at start and finish,* akin to a chill, rush, lift, tickle, or "high" (a signal of brain-chemical release); *pattern of occurrence,* universal regardless of experiencer; *mind state when it happens,* usually wide awake and alert, although some report having it during dream states; *content,* almost always mundane activity, but can cover significant events— feels as if it's a rehearsal of some kind; *awareness of power to change the future divided afterward,* with some claiming the pre-lived future can be changed, others saying it can't; *consequences,* handle stress better because of rehearsals, becoming more peaceful and confident—frequency of episodes tends to subside once experiencer feels more grounded.

The similarities between what happens naturally to children from ages three to five and what happens to experiencers of any age after a brain shift, once they begin having future memory episodes, is uncanny. Consider these striking comparisons.

CHILDHOOD BRAIN DEVELOPMENT AND THE BRAIN SHIFT EXPERIENCE

Typical Three- to Five-Year-Olds	Adult and Child Brain Shift Experiencers
Temporal Lobe Development	*Temporal Lobe Expansion*
Emerging Consciousness	Enlarging Consciousness
Prelive the future on a regular basis, spend more time in future than in present.	Prelive the future on a regular basis through dream states, visions, future memory episodes.
Play with futuristic possibilities as a way of "getting ready"; rehearse in advance demands soon to be made upon them.	Pre-experience life's challenges and opportunities before they occur as a way of preparing for demands they will soon face.
No natural understanding of time-space states; consider "future" an aspect of "now." Gain perspective and continuity by establishing the validity of action/reaction or "future" (continuous scenery and connected wholes).	No longer restricted by a sense of time-space states; an awareness of simultaneity and the importance of "now." Embrace broader dimensions of experience beyond that of "future" (unlimited perspectives held in tandem with the continuity of stable reference points).
Progress from mental imagery of universal archetypes to cultural stereotypes in a process of self-discovery.	Progress from mental imagery of cultural stereotypes to the individuation process in a journey of soul discovery.
The Birth of Imagination	*The Rebirth of Imagination*

This chart emphasizes how reliable the future memory phenomenon may be as a signal that a person's brain is in the process of shifting in structure, chemistry, and function—that it's undergoing a growth spurt. And that, as part of the shift, experiencers tend to *revert back to the brain-development stage of three- to five-year-olds,* and I believe for the same reason: *to reestablish continuity and order through futuristic rehearsals* so they can ready themselves for the greater challenge of higher mind states and spiritual maturity. I have observed that:

Being able to live the future in advance, and remember that one did, alleviates much of the stress and fear that worrying about unknown variables can cause. This advanced preparation enables the human psyche to negotiate the demands of sudden change more smoothly. The ability imparts an immense sense of confidence and peace in individuals, no matter what age, and often leads to frequent incidences of synchronicity (meaningful "coincidences") as if one's life were caught up in some type of "flow."[11]

THE TEMPORAL LOBES AND IMAGERY

Todd Murphy, himself a near-death survivor, researches near-death imagery cross-culturally. In his paper "The Structure and Function of Near-Death Experiences: An Algorithmic Reincarnation Hypothesis,"[12] he states:

> It is well established that, although there appears to be a universal *grammar* to NDEs, the specific vocabulary of any given case is determined by a variety of factors including age, culture, the specific circumstances in which the patient dies, psychological history, and possibly many other, still undiscovered factors. A dictionary containing this vocabulary might encompass the whole of human subjectivity including our symbolism, myths, and religions.

In discussions with Murphy, he reminded me that the left temporal lobe specializes in negative emotions and images (things fear based, like paranoia and sorrow), while the expertise of the right temporal lobe is with positive emotions and images (things love based, as joy and peace). Two excellent sources of scientific material on this subject are the article "Toward a Psychobiology of Transcendence: God in the Brain," by Arnold J. Mandell,[13] and the book *Neuropsychological Bases of God Beliefs,* by Michael A. Persinger.[14]

Persinger induced what appeared to be pleasant, heavenlike near-death experiences in subjects by stimulating the Sylvian fissure in the right temporal lobe. He used magnetic signals of the same strength as those produced by the earth's magnetic field to accomplish the feat. Because his work had results similar to that of Wilder Penfield, a medical doctor probing certain parts of the brain during surgery to target memory recall,[15] many researchers are now convinced that unpleasant/hellish near-death states are a product of exciting the left temporal lobe and pleasant/heavenly ones, the right.

Persinger's experiments and those of physicians like Penfield, however, failed to induce anything other than a *generalized pattern* of imagery, a basic template or "blueprint." This was also true with similar states caused by temporal lobe seizure, centrifuge pilot training, and excessive stress. The fact that classical near-death scenarios are easily created was undoubtedly a major impetus behind Raymond Moody's study of crystal or mirror gazing. Through resurrecting the centuries-old practice, he had hoped to see if volunteers really could contact the Other Side and experience a legitimate "visitation." His book *Reunions: Visionary Encounters with Departed Loved Ones,*[16] caused quite a stir, to say the least, and did result in a few claims of success.

Even so, no researcher or experiencer of any such created imagery/episode, including Moody, has ever induced or exhibited the full scope and impact of genuine near-death states, the incredible range of detail present in most of them (which only on rare occasions could have been known about in advance), or the spread of aftereffects (which in most cases increase with time and become permanent).

All anyone can accomplish when stimulating the temporal lobes (left or right), regardless of method or conditions, is to create *general pattern arrangements* of emotions and images. The reason for this is straightforward enough: the temporal lobes are storage receptacles or libraries of basic shapes, forms, feelings, and sounds. Implicit in this is the notion that together they may function as a resource center or data comparison device that children can tap into as they learn to discern differences. As we age, engaging in creative imagination and invention ensures that both lobes not only remain active but can take on more expansive and expressive projects.

But if mind states alter significantly, as during a brain shift, the temporal lobes seem to assume the role of mediator between worlds. This "mediator within" is strongly evident in near-death cases. Initial imagery, sometimes called "over-leafs," will always match what will accommodate the experiencer's most urgent need at the moment, and/or what will directly affect those around him or her. This phenomenon of accommodation occurs repeatedly, regardless of whether the imagery features God or religious figures or angels, animals, relatives, or friends.

This leads me to believe that the initial patterning of any otherworld journey is first and foremost to either relax the experiencer and put him or her at ease (through a pleasant episode), or tense the experiencer and alert him or her (through an unpleasant episode), so that whatever needs to be accomplished by the experience may be addressed. This primary directive of the temporal lobes can and often does alter once the scenario is fully under way (e.g., a child, once comforted by an angel, may then ask, "Is that what you really look like?" only to have the angel dissolve into a brilliant burst of light). Experiencers, when so alerted or relaxed, are more likely to go through intense scenarios that foster life-changing characteristics afterward.

Still, accommodations, personal history, what a person has been exposed to during the span of his or her life, even language constraints, do not fully explain all of the contents of near-death states. In *Beyond the Light: What Isn't Being Said about the Near-Death Experience*,[17] I described four levels of imagery found in otherworld journeys such as near-death. Briefly, these levels are:

Personal	Images from one's own life.
Mass mind	Images of a collective nature that reflect the human condition.
Memory fields	Primordial, archetypal images that are universal in nature.
Truth	That consistent, stable reality that undergirds and transcends creation and all created things (seldom any imagery per se; rather, a knowing).

(Many authors have written extensively about the imagery in otherworld journeys. I would call your attention to the works of Carl G. Jung, Joseph Campbell, Richard Heinberg, Manley P. Hall, and Ioan Couliano.)[18]

Scenarios can sometimes be better understood if one keeps in mind that subjective imagery has various interpretations. The initial "greeter" is not always who or what it seems to be. The fact remains, however, that the range of details present in the experience places near-death states front and center as a major challenge to anyone's belief that the life we have, and who we think we are, is all there is.

SPIRIT SHIFT

Spirit shifts bespeak a larger agenda, one that transcends personal and societal concerns and expectations, and seems determinant in why some individuals have a brain shift while others do not, even if conditions are similar.

I offer this observation without hesitation, for one cannot research near-death and other transformative states as long as I have without recognizing a greater power at work, as well as a subtle spirit or soul force that appears to be responsible for the outworking of that greater power.

Repeatedly, experiencers describe this subtle presence as a highly organized, intelligent luminosity that plays the role of emissary for the Divine, God, Source, or whatever title one prefers. Apparently, this intelligent luminosity can take on any form or color or substance or odor, yet is always available as a nonenergetic force, a Holy Spirit capable of moving in and through us once we are ready or once we surrender to it.[19] Experiencers claim that should we ignore its presence or remain locked in a particular lifestyle that denies our true purpose or "life mission," this subtle spirit can forcibly intervene, and if it does, a shift occurs.

How this plays out with child experiencers of near-death states is worth a closer look. The depth of maturity that emerges from these youngsters threatens as many people as it inspires. Since spirit shifts lack the physicality of brain shifts, I will rely more in this section on quotes from my case studies to convey the stirring of spirit.

Linda A. Jacquin, Missouri. NDE at age four and a half, drowning. "At a recent meeting I was talking about my childhood near-death experience. A few days later, I received a note from a fellow experiencer who was there. She said she received a message for me from a divine being. The message was: 'A good fisherman practices the catch-and-release philosophy. If the fish he catches is too small, it is simply returned to the water so it can grow some more.' She felt that my brush with death was reviewed and judged by the Divine and that the judgment was to return me to let me grow. I agree. Perhaps this is why children who have near-death experiences are sent back to earth. Like little fishes, they need time for their spirits to grow."

Anell Q. Tubbs, Boise, Idaho. NDE before age eight, blow to head. "I have come to the conclusion *I am normal.* Every person on this planet is here for the same reason—to grow and to learn—and everyone is at a different stage in their evolutionary process. Everyone has the same ability to heal and be psychic and know things. If they don't exhibit these abilities now, they will."

Emily, Seattle, Washington. NDE at age two from high fever; at five from complications during surgery. "I believe, in modern society, we mistakenly focus primarily upon physical and material needs and neglect our emotions and spirit. I am deeply committed to helping people achieve health in Mind, Soul, and Body through alternative medicine. I sense a change coming and I hope to be part of it in a positive way."

Regina Patrick, Toledo, Ohio. NDE at age four, pneumonia. "My ultimate mission is to have a home, a place where people can come to die, and to do spiritual work with the dying—to help them, strengthen them, and prepare them to go on. I've done hospice work, volunteered at nursing homes through my church. I have a ministry sharing The Journey, which is for people struggling with life-threatening illness."

Joe Ann Van Gelder, Newport, Vermont. Nine NDEs as a child, multiple illnesses and accidents. "My experiences have led me to believe that our human evolution involves the development of a different level of consciousness, which requires our physical bodies to adapt to higher vibratory frequencies. I was told by my guidance to move my geographic location to the forty-fifth parallel, halfway between the equator and the North Pole. When I did, everything improved for me."

Diana Schmidt, El Cerrito, California. NDE at age nine, undiagnosed seizure. "I have discovered the suppressed and forgotten feminine foundations of our culture, and think that the paradigm of the New Age is the Dark Goddess and Sophia—*Light comes from the Dark.* I celebrate and speak whenever I can on this paradigm change and teach a course called The Symbolic Life, which shows people how symbols are a source of renewal and healing. I do this through symbol systems such as tarot, I Ching, astrology, runes, etc."

Christina Moon, Eureka Springs, Arkansas. Two NDEs, complications at birth. "I describe my 'religion' thusly: take a computer card for each of the major religions of the world and stack them up. Mine would be where the holes match and go all the way through. In other words, I have a very eclectic philosophy and would describe myself as a Buddhist Pagan. I am guided by a concern and a compassion for all living beings no matter what shape, size, or species. I try to live in a way that will add to rather than detract from the world."

Laura, San Francisco, California. NDE at age three and a half, child abuse and during surgery. "I learned how to live with my murderer for another fifteen years by learning what I could from him and leaving the rest. I learned that the most important phenomena in the universe are love, truth, and the quest for knowledge. I received a clear sense of my purpose in life and how I must achieve it. I was given the gift of seeing things before they happen and the ability to visualize events, images, and forms, and then bring them into being. I learned that we are wounded, and heal, from deep wounds, not so that we may somehow be safe forever, but so that we may be wounded again in a new way. Most of all, I acquired a deep love of death and a longing to be in the presence of God again, a longing that is with me every moment of every day. It is only for the knowledge of his presence that I am able to live."

N.T.A., Omaha, Nebraska. NDE at age thirteen months, electrical shock. "I believe every person is a spiritual being and that we all have a special purpose that is spiritually oriented. I believe we are all light beings of love and that Christ came to teach us that we could be like him. I believe in the concept of unity of all things. I think that the history we have been taught for thousands of years is not the whole truth, and that these truths are coming out. Many earth changes are taking place and many ascended beings [Holy Ones] are helping and guiding us through this time of transition. It is time for us to be okay in questioning our beliefs and to take responsibility in healing ourselves and the planet—to hold more light. I believe 'bad' things, people, and experiences are opportunities for growth. As we awaken and remember, we will begin to create heaven on earth. My near-death experience has made me realize and know without a doubt that love and happiness, acceptance and joy, are possible for every person."

The majority of the child experiencers I interviewed had the gift of conversing directly with spirit afterward. And they spoke of divine intervention as an active force in their lives.

An example of divine intervention is what happened to Stephanie Lang of New York City. She nearly died at the age of three from a severe kidney infection complicated by measles, chicken pox, and a raging fever. Although she does not remember having had a near-death experience per se, she went on to exhibit most of the aftereffects. Along with a sharp mind and incredible artistic talent, she struggled with depression and a lack of motivation and felt somehow "off course." While lunching one day on the roof of a twenty-six-floor skyscraper, she walked to the railing with the intent of just looking around. She began to rock, absentmindedly lost her balance, and pitched forward toward the traffic below. Before she could react, she suddenly found herself ten feet back from the railing, sitting on her bottom with tears streaming. A clear voice in her head spoke: "Are you going or are you staying? If you are staying, you have to change." She credits this rescue to divine intervention. It totally changed her life; afterward, she became goal oriented and excited about taking advantage of every opportunity she could. Even though doubts still assail her from time to time, the deep depressions she once had are gone.

This closeness to spirit, a sense of the Divine, of God, propels experiencers into a search for more and better avenues of service, mission, and outreach. Says Tonecia Maxine McMillan of Oxon Hill, Maryland, who at age eleven drowned: "I was mean, self-centered, and egotistical before, but, when my episode was over, I was more peaceful and I really cared about people and wanted to help them." She became a nurse as a result, and has devoted her life to taking care of others' needs.

It is true that many are frustrated by a lack of any clear knowing or message telling them exactly what to do with their lives or how, but just as many are like McMillan—motivated and alive with the faith that where they're headed is the right path for them. Jungian analyst James Hillman addresses this in his book *The Soul's Code: Character, Calling and Fate.*[20] He states, "Psychotherapy has become an exaggerated self-searching to find out who we are but has neglected entirely the search for what the world wants from us—our *calling.*" David Spangler, author of *The Call,*[21] expands on Hillman's idea, saying: "You *are* your own unique self, and if you have the humility to break through the boundaries of ego you will hear the summons of your Call. Something you may not even know about yourself will emerge, and you will discover a service, a gift, a divine purpose behind your actions."

Prayer and meditation take on dynamic proportions immediately following a child's near-death experience, as does *visioning* (aligning in consciousness with the divine purpose within us to love and to express a greater degree of life and caring). Many of these youngsters actually saw prayers being said for them while they were out of body. They describe how the power of those prayers turned into beams of radiant, golden, or rainbow light that arced over from the one saying the prayer, no matter how many miles away, to where they themselves were "hovering." Once the prayer beam reached them, the feeling would be akin to a "splash" of love or an incredible warming. Because they have seen and felt the effectiveness of prayer, child experiencers consider it a valid and real way to talk with God while sharing God's healing love with others.

Larry Dossey, M.D., former chief of staff of Humana Medical City in Dallas, Texas, and current cochairman of the panel on mind/body interventions in the Office of Alternative Medicine at the National Institutes of Health, has a lot to say about the power of prayer, both in his books and personally.[22] "There is a quality that correlates with the effect of the prayer, and it's something that sounds very old-fashioned. It's love. And if the individual doing the praying does not have compassion and empathy and love and a deep sense of authentic and genuine caring for whoever they are praying for, these [medical] experiments [on the power of prayer] don't work very well. Love is the key to success."

Typically, children seem obsessed with worship and attending church after their episodes. Barbara True Bradley of Des Moines, Iowa (who "died" at four and a half from lobar pneumonia), said, "When I was well and returned home, I set up a table in my bedroom, covered it with a white cloth, and had a prayer book and cross on it. I remember kneeling there to pray."

Those who had been steeped in certain religious dogmas beforehand, though, oftentimes found the call to express the inner spirit running counter to their earlier indoctrination. To appreciate why child experiencers are more apt than adult experiencers to lose the pure spontaneity and utter joy of their new relationship with God, consider these incidents.

Judy, New York. NDE at age eleven, complications during a tonsillectomy. "I remember questioning everything the minister and Sunday School teacher said. I became belligerent in Sunday School. I stopped going to choir practice. I used science to prove religion (nothing can be created or destroyed, only changed) and applied it to body/soul."

Dorothy M. Bernstein, North Olmsted, Ohio. NDE as a toddler, twice stopped breathing. "I stood up in class and asked Father Marginen, "How is it you teach that if I stand by and say nothing when someone is doing wrong, I am as guilty as the person doing wrong? Yet you say it was the Jews who crucified Christ, when in truth it was the Romans who drove the nails into his hands and feet and pierced his side. Why are they not guilty?"

Robert C. Warth, Little Silver, New Jersey. NDE at age five, complications during a tonsillectomy. "I was brought up Methodist until I asked the "wrong" questions and was pulled out of church. My parents were

told by my Sunday School teacher that I was disrupting the class by asking [questions] about church dogma he could not or would not answer."

Child experiencers seldom remain alienated from God if they are ever
"turned off," but their feelings about religion and church attendance do
change. The split of those who stay in religious settings versus those who
choose a more eclectic spiritual path is about the same as with adult experiencers: one-third stay, two-thirds leave. But youngsters are *more* than
twice as likely as adults to cut ties permanently. (Adult experiencers usually rediscover the value of church with time, and return to a church setting, though rarely the one of their youth. They seem to prefer "new
thought" churches like Unity, Religious Science, or Baha'i.)

Kathleen Norris, a published poet and author, speaks to this schism
between the church of one's youth and the challenge to make peace with
what once seemed so divisive. Although she does not claim to be a near-
death experiencer, her behavior traits and memories suggest that she may
have had such an episode as an infant. She recalls:

"I didn't do living right, at first. When I was six months old, I nearly
died. All wrong, for an infant to be so caught up in the last things.
Naturally, the hospital was called Providence; in all likelihood, as I was in
danger of dying, a nun baptized me there. My official baptism came four
months later, in the arms of my grandfather Norris, a Methodist pastor.
Six months of age is too early to learn that one's mother and father are
helpless before death. But the struggle that took place in my infant body
and still-forming pre-verbal intelligence was between life and death, and I
am convinced that a sense of something vast, something yet to come, took
hold in my consciousness and remains there still."

In her journey to erase what she felt was religious bigotry, she turned
to the arts, revisiting her home church years later only to discover that she
liked being there and conversing with the ministers. She eventually joined
a monastery and immersed herself in Christianity. After becoming a lay
minister, she shared what she learned about religion and the spiritual quest
in two books, *The Cloister Walk* and *Amazing Grace*.[23]

While religion is a systematized approach to spiritual development
formed around set standards or dogmas, spirituality emerges from a personal, intimate experience of God. There are no standards or dogmas,
only precedents, as individual knowing or gnosis is honored. Needlessly at
odds with each other, both routes to a more positive, uplifting, and meaningful life are equally valid and worthy.

Ken Wilber, author of *A Brief History of Everything*,[24] puts this issue into perspective by describing it in evolutionary terms: "Consciousness evolution moves from pre-personal to personal to transpersonal; from subconscious to self-conscious to super-conscious; from pre-mental to mental to supra-mental; from instinct to ego to God."

An integral part of spirit shifts is the flowering of psychic abilities. This rankles more people and causes more misunderstandings than any other aspect of the phenomenon. Few can adequately address why this occurs. Cries of "It's the devil's work" are as commonplace as "This is God's gift." Here are some incidents of this nature as reported by child experiencers in my study:

Gracie L. Sprouse, Keene, Virginia. NDE at age eleven, drowning. "I believed myself to be psychic until I learned that psychic abilities may be from Satan. Yet constant, instant miracles have never ceased in my life; they have in fact increased. The more I recognize them, the more they happen. I now believe these to be Godly abilities."

P. Bradley Carey, Burlington, Washington. NDE at age thirteen, choked by boy at school. "I heard the radio playing when the dial indicated it wasn't. Then what sounded like a commercial started. In it, the company gave their telephone number, which I wrote down figuring to prove to myself that it was just my imagination. I dialed it. A ceramic store clerk answered (located in Spokane, on the other side of the state). After asking a few questions, I found out that their commercial was only being carried in their locality. There are so many miles and mountains between us that the signal can't get down here. It was totally impossible for me to hear this ad. I live in the middle of nowhere, no traffic, no neighbors, and there was no radio on. How did I hear the radio commercial?"

Cecil L. Hamilton, Palmyra, Virginia. NDE at age eleven, drowning. "How do you use the information you have? I see so many psychic fakes. I can tell where their experience ends and guesswork begins. I know the future, especially with little, ongoing things. I know when people are about to die. I try sometimes to turn it off—'cause you don't enjoy going out to dinner and seeing death on someone at the table."

Rhona Alterman-Newman, Cherry Hill, New Jersey. NDE at age six months, strangulated hernia. "Ten days after my mother died, she came back to her room and checked to see if we'd turned off the heating pad. The reason I think she did this is because, when we left for the hospital with her, we left the pad on and she was concerned about that. It scared me to see her that night. I was fully awake when she came."

Francis Piekarski, New Martinsville, West Virginia. NDE at age five, drowning, and at twelve, high fever, bone infection. "Perhaps the craziest thing that happened was when I was listening to JFK politicking in Charleston. I wanted to stand up with him onstage and tell him things that I knew about him. I could have changed his future, but I didn't. This has happened several times, like a time warp. The single greatest change my episodes gave me is an unwavering *knowing* that I had seen God and that I have two angels watching over me."

Lynn, Michigan. NDE at age thirteen, during open-heart surgery. "I know things about people. I have become very psychic. I find people react to this in different ways. Some want to be your 'friend' and then ask you questions all the time—about boyfriends, lottery numbers, interpersonal relationships. This type of 'friend' is a user. Some have accused me of being a witch. They confuse being psychic with witchcraft and devil worship. These are usually 'born again,' and they either want to 'save' me or kill me. Others hear about me and believe I can work miracles. It's amazing what this group thinks I can do. I have been credited with healing people, healing relationships, and uncrossing any situation a person might find themselves in. One woman went so far as to climb through my open bedroom window and sit on my bed one night, asking me to bring her husband back to her. I was only sixteen. I screamed when this woman touched my hand. My mother got her to leave."

Lauren Thibodean, Madison, Ohio. NDE at age six, electrocuted. "I became very psychic, although I'd already shown signs prior to my near-death experience. My childhood was lonely; I was nicknamed 'Jinx' and 'Witch Girl.' Some parents in the neighborhood would not let their children play with me or come to our house. I've had ongoing, very positive 'visits' from beings made of light, which I think of as the angels who rescued me when I was electrocuted, and past-life recall."

Carroll Gray, Atlanta, Georgia. One prebirth experience, five NDEs in childhood, mostly from child abuse injuries. "I have some precognition, like knowing who is on the phone before picking up, or knowing when Mother wants to be called. I see auras. There have also been several instances of telekinesis; I once tossed a child about fifteen feet backward from across the yard simply by 'thinking' it so. This surprised me, frightened my mother, and the child I tossed never came back to play with me again."

Clara Lane, Belmont, Ohio. NDE at age ten, complications during surgery for acute appendicitis. "Many times I have awakened in the middle of the night to see people standing in my bedroom and in the hallway. They turn to look at me, then vanish. I do not feel afraid. Several times we have lived in houses that were haunted. I could sense things. Seeing people in my bedroom at night still happens to me thirty-eight years later. I believe they are watching over me all the time, but only at night do they become visible."

Child experiencers often speak about the light they saw surrounding living things while they were out of their bodies. They claim this light was as beautiful as prayer beams and seemed to consist of a similar energy. Many, like Carroll Gray, continue to see this light or aura on an ongoing basis.

It can be a real challenge for youngsters to handle a phenomenon such as this, or, for that matter, any of the faculty extensions that typically occur. An excellent book for introducing kids to the psychic realities of near-death states is Kathleen J. Forti's *The Door to the Secret City*.[25] Forti had a near-death episode in her late teens, described in my book *Future Memory,* that accurately presaged events in her adult life, including being a storyteller for children.

The flowering of psychic abilities after a brain shift/spirit shift seems to be more of an enhancement of the limbic system than anything mysterious or paranormal. As such, it relates directly to perceptual enlargements of the electromagnetic range and to extensions of faculties normal to us. Although an issue for experiencers, the subject touches us all.

It is possible to extend and broaden our five faculties of sight, hearing, touch, taste, and smell to embrace *psychic dimensions* (those beyond reliance on physical forms), and *collective/spiritual realms* (the larger view, grander realities). Since the average person is only aware of 1 percent of what goes on around him or her, these extensions are advantageous and enriching, enabling us to circumvent whatever factors may seem to limit

the information we can access. Faculty extensions of this kind are not esoteric, but practical and easily learned by *anyone* with the will to try.

The following chart clarifies what I mean by faculty extensions.
Notice what happens to *intuition* and *perception* once our faculties extend
and broaden to reach the range of spiritual realities.

FACULTY EXTENSIONS

Physical Faculty	Psychic Extension	Collective and/or Spiritual Extension
See/Sight	See without use of eyes; research term: "clairvoyance"	Vision
Hear/Sound	Hear without presence of sound; research term: "clairaudience"	Music
Feel/Touch	Feel, or have an effect on an object, without touching; research term: "psychokinesis"	Art
Taste/Flavor	Taste without use of tastebuds; research term: "clairgustation"	Discrimination
Smell/Scent	Smell without use of nose; research term: "clairolfaction"	Integrity
Sense/Intuition	Sensing without or in advance of recognition; research term: "clairsentience"	Grace
Perceive/ Perception	Apprehending without or in advance of physical stimuli; research term: "precognition"	Knowing

The root of the word "psychic" means "of the soul." We might infer
from this that psychic abilities are really soul abilities, part of our inheri-
tance as children of God—our wellspring of wisdom from within. As with
everything else in life, *use determines value.*

Henry Reed, Ph.D., after years of innovative experimentation, found
that psychic abilities center around the traits of intimacy and closeness,
the bond we share in spirit. The workshops he now gives, called The
Intuitive Heart, and his paper titled "Intimacy and Psi: Explorations in
Psychic Closeness" are based on this fresh new approach.[26] He explains:
"Communicating heart to heart is another way of knowing; the way of

intuition, and intuition is the key to the twenty-first century. The consciousness revolution has discovered the psychic outside the brain, not within it. The intuitive heart is visionary, psychic, it has soul, and its essence is spiritual. Developing access to intuition is not a mental trick; it is a matter of caring."

The word "heaven" comes from the Greek language. In the original language of the Bible the word was often interchanged with the word "leaven." Jesus is quoted in Matt. 13:33 as saying, "The kingdom of heaven is like unto leaven." Leaven causes dough to rise. Leaven expands, yet the Greeks understood that heaven is *that which is already expanded*. With that clue from the Greek version of what heaven might be, allow me to conjecture. Brain shift/spirit shift may well function as does leaven, expanding the consciousness and faculties of the experiencer into the next phase of growth and learning. Individual consciousness, once expanded, could extend to and connect with other dimensions of reality and higher levels of consciousness—perhaps mass mind or even the One Mind. Having expanded in this manner, the person's consciousness could become *greater than before,* perhaps permanently . . . a true shift.

THREE

☉

A New View of
Near-Death States

*I believe there are two sides to the phenomenon known as
death, this side where we live, and the other side where we
shall continue to live. Eternity does not start with death.
We are in eternity now.*

—Norman Vincent Peale

ON AVERAGE, adult and child near-death experiencers are without pulse
or breath for about five to twenty minutes. It is not uncommon, at least in
my research, to hear of individuals being dead for an hour or more; some
"wake up" in the morgue. Since the brain can be permanently damaged in
three to five minutes without sufficient oxygen, it is important to note that
one of the striking features of the near-death phenomenon is that *no matter how long the person is dead, there is usually little or no brain damage
once he or she is revived; rather, there is a noticeable brain enhancement.*

Because this is true, near-death states provide a dynamic lens through
which we can continue to explore the many aspects of brain shift/spirit
shift and what such a transformation of consciousness implies.

The term "near-death experience" was coined by Raymond A. Moody
Jr., M.D., in his 1975 book *Life after Life,*[1] to describe the anomaly of

resuscitated patients who reported life on the other side of death. Five years later, Kenneth Ring scientifically verified Moody's work in *Life at Death*.[2] These two books legitimized the plethora of research papers, other books, articles, and speculations that followed—all of them based on the same model of eight basic scenario components.

These components are:

1. *A sensation of floating out of one's body,* often followed by an out-of-body experience in which all that goes on around the "vacated" body is both seen and heard.
2. *Passing through a dark tunnel or black space,* accompanied by a feeling or sensation of acceleration—wind may be heard or felt.
3. *Ascending toward a light of incredible brilliance that emits loving peacefulness,* with the possibility of seeing deceased relatives, animals, plants, scenery, and cities.
4. *Being greeted by friendly voices, loved ones, and/or beings made of light.* Conversation can ensue, and a message may be given.
5. *Seeing a panoramic, review of the life just lived,* from birth to death or in reverse order, sometimes a reliving rather than a dispassionate viewing.
6. *A different sense of time and space;* the discovery that time and space do not exist.
7. *A reluctance to return to the earthplane,* but a feeling of obligation to, so a job can be finished or a mission performed.
8. *Disappointment at being revived,* even anger or tearfulness at being back.

Few near-death episodes include all eight components. Most encompass about five. This confuses people who may have had such an experience and has given rise to a major complaint voiced by those who attend local meetings of the International Association for Near-Death Studies (IANDS) through any of its Friends of IANDS affiliates in the United States, Canada, and around the world.[3] The complaint? What happened to them doesn't match the "classical" model.

Since this discrepancy involves so many people and happens so often, the time has come to admit how the original model came into being. It is a composite of elements common to the experience that was used as a "model" by the media to sensationalize Moody's first book. My work differs because I was never privy to what others in the newly emerging field were doing, nor had I heard of Moody or his work. Today, the official definition of a near-death experience as offered by IANDS is: *"A lucid experience associated with perceived consciousness apart from the body, occurring at the time of actual or threatened imminent death."*

Right off, I isolated four distinctive types of near-death experiences in the research I conducted. I discovered elements similar to those described by Moody and Ring but different patterning from what was billed as the so-called classical version; each pattern type was accompanied by a subtle psychological profile suggestive of other forces that might be present. These four types have consistently held up throughout a quarter century of interviews, observations, and analysis regardless of a person's age, education, gender, culture, or religion. In *Beyond the Light* I used separate chapters to discuss each of the four types. What I offer here is a shorter rendition of the scenario patterns. The statistics are based on a study of 3,000 adult and 277 child experiencers of near-death states. Children's cases follow as illustrative examples of each type.

THE FOUR TYPES OF NEAR-DEATH EXPERIENCES

Initial Experience (sometimes referred to as the "nonexperience")

Involves elements such as a loving nothingness, the living dark, a friendly voice, a greeter of some kind, or a brief out-of-body episode. Usually experienced by those who seem to need the least amount of evidence for proof of survival, or who need the least amount of shakeup in their lives at that point in time. Often, this becomes a "seed" experience or an introduction to other ways of perceiving and recognizing reality.

Incident rate: 76% with child experiencers
20% with adult experiencers

Unpleasant or Hell-Like Experience (inner cleansing and self-confrontation)

Encounter with a threatening void or stark limbo or hellish purgatory or scenes of a startling and unexpected indifference, even "hauntings" from one's own past. Usually experienced by those who seem to have deeply suppressed or repressed guilts, fears, and angers and/or those who expect some kind of punishment or discomfort after death.

Incident rate: 3% with child experiencers
15% with adult experiencers

Pleasant or Heavenlike Experience *(reassurance and self-validation)*

Heavenlike scenarios of loving family reunions with those who have died previously, reassuring religious figures or light beings, validation that life counts, affirmative and inspiring dialogue. Usually experienced by those who most need to know how loved they are and how important life is and how every effort has a purpose in the overall scheme of things.

Incident rate: 19% with child experiencers
47% with adult experiencers

Transcendent Experience *(expansive revelations, alternate realities)*

Exposure to otherworldly dimensions and scenes beyond the individual's frame of reference; sometimes includes revelations of greater truths. Seldom personal in content. Usually experienced by those who are ready for a mind-stretching challenge and/or individuals who are more apt to utilize (to whatever degree) the truths that are revealed to them.

Incident rate: 2% with child experiencers
18% with adult experiencers

NOTE: I have noticed that all four types can occur during the same experience for the same person at the same time, can exist in varying combinations, or can spread out across a series of episodes for a particular individual. Generally speaking, however, each represents a distinctive type of experience occurring but once to a given person.

INITIAL EXPERIENCE

Sophia Carmien, Boulder, Colorado. NDE at age four. "I was swimming in a neighborhood swimming pool. There were two lifeguards. Mom sat me down near the pool and went to the dressing room to change. She said, 'Don't jump in the deep pool without water wings.' I had no water wings on but I thought I did. So, I jumped. Part of me was down below splashing around, not able to see much. The other part was floating up, way up higher than the lifeguards. I heard something behind me, all around me, 'speak' an unspoken question: 'Do you want to live?' I thought about that. Dying seemed somehow good, nice. Dying feels normal. And then I thought about my parents and how sad they would be. Even though it seemed nice to go, I said, 'I'll stay.' I slowly went back down in the water to the other half of me. The next thing I knew I was being held by a fat lady in a polka-dot bathing suit. I thanked her for helping me. Afterward, I thought it was normal, being as young as I was, for this kind of thing to happen to everyone."

Joe Ann Van Gelder, Newport, Vermont. Nine NDEs from age fifteen months to age ten. "My first eleven years found me challenged with both chronic and acute illnesses, including polio, plus various serious accidents. The next five years found me on a slow recovery. During each of my childhood near-death experiences I encountered a warm, supportive darkness, almost womblike, which communicated a sense of love and safety to me. This friendly darkness was not a scary place; neither was it a 'void.' It was indescribable, timeless, spaceless—where the 'real I' goes. I had many aftereffects, increasing in intensity after each experience. As a child, I took my near-death episodes as natural and normal because my mother had had such an experience as a young adult. There was no reason for me to feel strange or weird since she understood."

UNPLEASANT OR HELL-LIKE EXPERIENCE

Diana Schmidt, El Cerrito, California. NDE at age nine. "It is high noon and I am in the 'chopped' (weed-free) backyard of my paternal grandfather. I see my nine-year-old self walk across the yard and put my head down on a tree stump. A giant ax appears and splits my head open. What falls out onto the ground rather than brains are crawling, wiggling maggots! This was a terrible experience for me. It wiped out any good feelings I had about myself, as I thought I was filled with something repugnant. This 'dream' left me feeling totally frightened and ashamed. After being operated on at twenty-nine for the removal of a blood clot in my brain, I remember being so relieved. It was good news! I had a brain, not a skull full of maggots. Considering my history of blood clots and seizures, I believe this incident was an undiagnosed seizure resulting from a congenital or inherited angioma [swelling or tumor]."

Adrianna Norton, Modesto, California. NDE at age five. "I was born with a large hole in my heart, which wasn't fixed surgically until I was an adult. When I was five, I was stricken with the flu and a very high fever. During the night I found myself up in the corner of the ceiling looking down at my small sleeping body. Suddenly, I was floating in a black cube about twelve feet square with black matter, black clawlike

Adrianna Norton, NDE at age five.

hands everywhere and clawing at me. I was horrified; there was no opening for escape. Again suddenly, I was floating facedown in a 'sea' of opalescent light and felt the most warm, safe, secure, loved, comforting feeling. Waves of light tenderly massaged me. Then I was back in my body and back on the bed, exhausted. My fever was gone and I fell asleep. I thought it was a nightmare and tried to forget it. I could not. I tried to repress the memory of it *because the frightening episode overwhelmed the pleasant one,* yet it has remained vivid all my life. I've been claustrophobic ever since."

PLEASANT OR HEAVENLIKE EXPERIENCE

Gracie L. Sprouse, Keene, Virginia. NDE at age eleven. "I was swimming with my sisters when suddenly I found myself unable to reach the top of the water for air. It felt like I had just stepped into nothingness. I went down twice and was coming up for the third time when I managed to yell for help. Before I was pulled from the water, I saw a filmstrip of my life. It was just like being in a theater, as I sat cross-legged and watched the things I'd done wrong to my sisters. I was not judged by the angel who showed me this; I judged and convicted myself. The angel hovered in midair, to the upper left of the screen. I remember thinking that I was leaving my family and sisters and started to feel sorrow. The sorrow left immediately and I felt as if I'd been assured they would be fine. Then, there was such a feeling of bliss that it's indescribable. Since then, I have

Gracie L. Sprouse, NDE at age eleven.

had a lifetime of unexplained happenings. My entire outlook is different from the norm. *I see with my heart.*"

Clara Lane, Belmont, Ohio. NDE at age ten. "I was in the fifth grade when I became sick with extreme pain in my lower right side. My teacher thought it was only a stomachache and ignored it. Two hours later I was rushed to the hospital. I was terrified and begged to go home. I was fighting the ether mask when it happened. One second I was awake, scared to death, the next second I was falling straight down a dark hole as if in a well. There were loud sounds like buzzing and ringing and metal scraping together, then I was up by the ceiling looking down on myself. I felt as though I was spread out all over the room like vapor or a cloud. I watched as the doctor had a square green machine wheeled into the room by a nurse, and then worked on me using it. There were several nurses there. Suddenly I was standing alone in a room with large, heavy doors leading into other rooms. Someone came to me. I didn't see him; I only heard his voice. He led me up through what seemed like a tunnel. I seemed to be walking, but my feet didn't touch a floor. Suddenly I heard what sounded like a city-sized playground full of kids, laughing and playing. Hearing them calmed me.

Another man came to meet us. I didn't see him either. He asked the one leading me who I was, then he went away. When he returned he told the man with me that I had to go back, that they weren't ready for me yet. I was led up a sidewalk to a large building with large doors. I walked inside and saw people all around working and doing things. I was taken to a huge

Clara Lane, NDE at age ten.

iridescent white room and told to sit down on some steps that led up to a large white chair, and wait there for someone who was to talk to me. He came out a door at the other end of the steps, walked to the chair above me, and sat down. He was dressed in a white, long-sleeved, floor-length robe with a wide gold band around the midsection. He wore sandals. His dark brown hair was shoulder length; he had a long face, broad chin, dark eyes with black around both eyelids, like eyeliner pencil, but it wasn't. His skin was olive colored and his eyes were as liquid love. He communicated by looking at me. No words had to be spoken, as we could hear each other's thoughts. He told me what I had to do in life and had me go to the other side of the room and look down into something like a TV set so I could see my future. What I saw made me very happy. This man, who I believe is Jesus Christ, said that once I woke up in the hospital I would for-get what I was supposed to do in life. 'Nothing can happen before its time,' he cautioned. As I was leaving the room he said I must obey his com-mandments if I wanted to come back. When I revived, a nurse was sitting beside my bed and she said, 'Thank God you finally woke up.' I told the doctor that I had watched him work on me and the color of the machine brought into the surgery room. He didn't know what to say."

TRANSCENDENT EXPERIENCE

Cecil L. Hamilton, Palmyra, Virginia. NDE at age eleven. "My brother and I went swimming. He had a problem. I tried to get him out of the water, but in his panic he pulled me under several times. We both drowned. He died and I came back. I can remember it all like yesterday. Just as I could no longer stay afloat, a strange sound like ringing in my ears started. A peaceful feeling came over me. I felt my spirit come out of my body and I went into a black void. That was a little frightening. A long way off there was a pinprick of light. I moved toward it, slowly at first, then faster and faster as if I were on top of a train accelerating. Then I stopped and stepped fully into the light. I noticed everything—sky, buildings, glass—emitted its *own* light. And everything was much more colorful than what we see here. A river meandered around. On the other side was a city, and a road running through it to another city, and another city, and another and another. Right in front of me but across the river were three men. They projected themselves to me. They didn't walk or fly; they projected over. I didn't recognize them, yet I knew one was Lynn Bibb. (I was named after him. He died a matter of weeks before I was born.) I knew these three men were looking out for me, like a welcoming committee to escort me over the river to the first city. I had the feeling that if I went with them, there would be no coming back, so I hesitated. The first city was like first grade. People stayed there until they were ready to go to the next city—your eternal progression, from city to city. Behind me and to the left was a strong light source, very brilliant and filled with love. I knew it was a person. I called it God for lack of a better term. I could not see it; I felt what seemed like a male presence.

He communicated to me, not so much in words but telepathically, and he asked, 'Why did you hesitate?' I replied, 'Well, I'm kind of young to die.' He chuckled. 'We have babies die.' I said, 'Well, there's some things I want to know first.' He replied, 'What do you want to know?' 'What is death?' I asked. He said, 'Turn and look to one side.' As I did, I saw a bad car wreck. Several people had been killed. Out of some of the bodies a spirit came up to progress on. Some who did not believe it was possible stayed in their bodies and would not emerge. I asked if they could be reached and he said, 'Yes, some more quickly than others and some maybe never.' Death, then, is not believing in anything. I asked, 'What is hell?' He said, 'Turn and look again.' I saw an old woman in a rocking chair determined to sit and rock and worry about children and grandchildren and everything else. Hell is therefore a lack of wisdom and not moving on, choosing not to go any further, sitting there and doing nothing. Hell is not a place. I asked if there was a Devil or Satan. He said to me, 'Would God allow that?' He continued, 'If I made you God for just a few seconds, what would you do first?' I knew my first act would be to eliminate any Devil or Satan. I asked, 'How do I know right from wrong?' He replied, 'Right is helping and being kind. Wrong is not only hurting someone but not helping when you can.'

We walked as I asked about the universe and reasons for everything. All of these things were shown to me. Then he wondered if I still wanted to return to the physical world. 'I do want to return.' He asked, 'Why?' I said I would help my mother whom my father had left with four children and one on the way. God kind of chuckled and asked me for the real reason. I said I would leave the earth a little better than I found it. 'Then you may return with some of the knowledge of the things you have learned, but the rest will be veiled for a time. Live in such a way that you will not feel bad when you return here again.' I woke up facedown in the mud of the river bottom and was 'lifted' to the top. I threw up great amounts of water, then pulled myself out of the river only to discover that my brother had died."

The vast majority of youngsters have Initial Experiences, and those Initial Experiences can involve powerful feelings, knowings, and often a sense of presence, which greatly affect the child and leave a lasting impression. For instance, the warm and friendly dark experienced especially by the young is incredibly important. This darkness is similar to that of the womb, a protective love cradle, yet it somehow "voices" instructions and enjoys lively dialogue. Unlike the womb, it is *the Darkness That Knows.*

In direct contrast to adult cases, imagery is not necessarily a prime component of children's near-death episodes, nor is light.

And the dark that little ones experience should not be confused with tunnels. Yes, kids do describe tunnels on occasion, but not nearly as often as do older experiencers. Even among adults the tunnel component to the scenario is not that common. I have encountered this stereotypical element among less than 30 percent of those I have interviewed. In the original Gallup poll, conducted in 1982, only 9 percent mentioned a tunnel. Many times I've actually seen adults change their near-death accounts to include a tunnel so they could fit in and avoid the embarrassment of not matching the "classical" model.

The life review of the very young commonly consists of vivid prebirth scenarios and past-life remembrances, recounted, curiously, from the viewpoint of a seemingly "mature mind." A judgmentlike appraisal of the present life from a child's perspective usually doesn't begin until about kindergarten age.

Multiple experiences are as common among kids as they are among adults. The forty-four child experiencers who filled out the questionnaire recorded sixty-one episodes, with 27 percent experiencing another near-death event in adulthood. Van Gelder, who suffered from chronic illness, polio, surgery, and several serious accidents as a child, reported nine events between the ages of fifteen months and ten years, as already noted.

Another individual had five as a child and five as an adult, as well as a prenatal memory that was verified by her mother. The record holder in my research base is a man who claimed a total of twenty-three near-death experiences throughout his lifetime, beginning shortly after birth. The man, who asked to remain anonymous, came into the world with severe physical handicaps and was not expected to live. He was in his late forties when I interviewed him. After countless surgeries, he felt he never could have survived as long as he had without the healing strength he gained from each near-death episode.

Drowning was by far the most frequent cause of death among the children in my study. Large numbers also "died" from suffocation; during or after major surgery or during tonsillectomies; and from child or sibling abuse (in that order). Other traumas were described, like those from high fever and being hit by lightning, but what captures my attention are the tonsillectomies—a minor operation that has hardly garnered a single headline in modern medicine.

Consider what happened to Robert C. Warth of Little Silver, New Jersey, when he was five. His mother and father took him to a local doctor's office to have his tonsils out. Three other children were already there, sitting on beds with their pajamas on. He was ushered to the fourth bed. Soon after his mother told him that the doctor was going to remove something from his throat, a nurse came and took him to another room where the doctor was. She put a mask over his face. "It dripped something sickeningly sweet," he recalled. Instantly he found himself above the domed operating light looking down, and was surprised to see his body below him along with a layer of dust atop the light fixture. "I could see 360 degrees without moving," he noted. Fighting back tears, he described a scene that still horrifies him.

"My mouth was pried open and I was covered up to my neck. There was a frenzy. The nurse yelled, 'Doctor.' He swung around and said, 'Stand back.' The next thing I remember is waking up in the bed, and I couldn't talk and I felt miserable." Two weeks later Robert was taken back to the doctor for a checkup. He described for the doctor everything he had seen and heard. "The doctor winked at my mother and said, 'They tell me stories often. It's the ether. It makes them dream and hallucinate.' What else was the doctor going to say, that the little creep stopped breathing? I saw what he did, and he couldn't get me out of his office fast enough."

Melvin Morse, M.D., in his seminal work with children, noted that during the early to mid-1900s doctors regularly used too much ether for

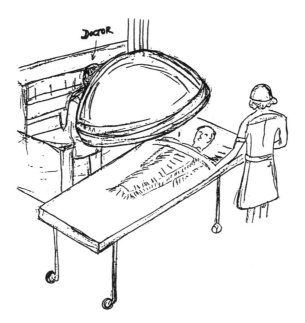

Roger C. Warth, NDE at age five.

tonsillectomies, and that's why so many show up in near-death cases during that period. This practice changed by the late 1970s (although cases like this are still reported). Apparently, *excessive* amounts of ether can trigger full-blown near-death states with some children instead of the simple hallucinations many report. My research caught the same "error of judgment" regarding the drug as Morse's did, verifying his findings, but I also discovered something else: *Medical mistakes readily surface in near-death scenarios.* They may be individual incidents, as when the patient, while out of body, witnesses what the doctor or nurse really did; or they may show up as an unusual percentage of people "dying" from a non-threatening procedure, as in the case of children across the country being overdosed with ether during tonsillectomies. The accuracy of these reports suggests that the range of human faculties is as nonlocal as the mind—something the medical community would be wise to note.

Over 70 percent of children's near-death scenarios involve angel visitations. Small children are not as explicit in their descriptions as older kids, yet the majority describe the angels as winged and either bright or dark or colored "like real folks are." The very young seldom use the term "angel"; rather, they speak of "the people" or describe loving beings made of light.

Youngsters are also met by:

- *Deceased relatives and friends,* always authentic and genuine even if unknown to the child at the time. Invariably, these are later verified.
- *Animals and deceased pets,* along with sensations of being licked, rubbed, pawed, or nosed by the animal. If not a pet, children almost invariably are greeted by smaller animals such as birds, chickens, bunnies, etc.; with adults, it is usually the larger animals like horses and lions. Critters sometimes converse telepathically or serve as guides. Occasionally, kids report having to visit the animal heaven before they can go to the heaven where people are.
- *Religious figures,* described as being more wonderful than angels. Many children were exposed to Christianity before their experiences and called this "extra special being" Jesus or Christ. Kids of other backgrounds used terms typical to their family of origin, *except* that Jesus and Mohammed were almost always described as having light brown skin and Buddha somewhat yellowish skin, regardless of the child's race or culture.
- *God,* experienced as the greatest of fathers or grandfathers (always male, never female) by the very young. Yet kids of school age and above usually saw God as a sphere of all-knowing light.
- *People very much alive,* a rarity, usually involved a favorite teacher or playmate. "Image" lasted only long enough to calm the child, then it disappeared, replaced by more common otherworldly beings such as angels.

To understand children's cases, we must keep in mind that kids are tuned to different harmonics than adults. Concepts of life and death leave them with puzzled faces. "I don't end or begin anywhere," a youngster once told me. "I just reach out and catch the next wave that goes by and hop a ride. That's how I got here."

This child, like other young experiencers, speaks in the language of "other worlds," one that is less verbal and more akin to synesthesia (multiple sensing). This ability enables them to perceive what we call reality as consisting of layered realms unrestricted by physical boundaries. Thus, they easily giggle with angels, play with ghosts, and see the future. Parents generally find such behavior cause for panic. Yet what seems worrisome may well have a simple explanation: near-death states expand faculties normal to us, hence allowing access to more of the electromagnetic spectrum.

A fascinating aspect of this is that as a child's mind begins to shift, his or her intelligence increases. Using questionnaire responses, let's take a look at what I'm implying.

Faculties enhanced, altered, or experienced in multiples	77%
Mind works differently—highly creative and inventive	84%
Significant enhancement of intellect	68%
Mind tested at genius level on standard IQ tests (no genetic markers for increase)	
main group, from birth to 15 years*	48%
subgroup, between 3 to 5 years	81%
subgroup, around birth to 15 months	96%
same subgroup as previous, but those who had a dark light experience rather than a bright one	100%
Drawn to and highly proficient in math/science/history	93%
Professionally employed in math/science/history careers	25%
Unusually gifted with languages	35%
School	
easier after experience	34%
harder afterward or blocked from memory	66%

NOTE: I found no difference between males and females with regard to enhanced intelligence and spatial and mathematical abilities. Although the percentages shown are based on the questionnaire results, they reflect what I have consistently observed with the 277 child experiencers in my study. The lone exception is professional employment. In the larger group, the figure is 40%, not 25% as shown here, which is still substantially lower than interest level and proficiency.

These figures come close to matching what I have encountered with the average child experiencer since 1978. But I want to make another observation: After a near-death experience, a child's learning ability seems to reverse; instead of continuing on along the normal developmental curve, from concrete (details) to abstract (concepts), a typical child experiencer

---

* With the majority, scores depicting genius were between 150 to 160. The exception was those who had a dark light experience by 15 months of age. Scores for these began at 186.

returns immersed in broad conceptual reasoning styles and has to learn how to go from abstract back to concrete.

The most often repeated phrase was: "I felt like an adult in a child's body."

Here are some comments from the experiencers themselves about what it was like for them to grow up this way.

Kenneth S. Taylor, Midlothian, Virginia. NDE at age seven, drowning. "I had a lust for knowledge afterward. By the time I was eight or nine I was reading adult books. I still read a lot and have a large library. The military tested me and discovered I have an unusually high and sharp degree of hearing. I never thought about it before, but they were impressed."

Judith Werner, Bronx, New York. NDE at nine days old, during surgery for infection. "I was first in my class through grade school, thirteenth out of a class of one thousand in high school, Phi Beta Kappa and Magna Cum Laude in college. Other people have always seen me as serious, precocious, [focused] inward, stubborn, and a little depressed. I was probably always psychic about the future, but it took many years to admit it to myself."

Susan Firth, Free Union, Virginia. NDE at age two from an accident, at six from drowning. "School was very difficult. From the first day, I experienced negativity in the vibrational airwaves. The sounds, clamor, and noise were dysfunctional to me, and I had to separate [from my body] for safety. I had trouble reading and comprehending, transposing letters, numbers, words. At home the broken record was: 'Won't you ever learn? What are we going to do with you? You are so stupid. Go to your room and don't come out 'til you've learned something.' Consequently, I spent more time [projecting myself] in[to] the tree outside the classroom window with the birds than at the desk where I sat. I was quite adept at being in two places at once."

Beverly A. Brodsky, Philadelphia, Pennsylvania. NDE at age seven and a half, during tonsillectomy. "I was brilliant in school and loved to learn. I read the encyclopedia from cover to cover, first the children's edition, then the adult *World Book*. I devoured books that were supposed to be far above my level. I was accused of plagiarism in the third grade by my English teacher, for spicing up an assignment with an analogy to a Greek myth. I finally convinced her it was my own work. She was stunned. I closed down to everyone except my sister and one friend. I often thought I had an inferiority/superiority complex; inferior because some connection was missing inside me, yet I was so smart I was intellectually superior to my peers."

Robert C. Warth, Little Silver, New Jersey. NDE at age five, during tonsillectomy. "I couldn't stand school. The teacher called in my mother and told her, 'Robert doesn't seem to be able to do the work. I'll have to put him back in kindergarten.' My mother was devastated. She talked to me. I don't know what happened, but within a week I was doing what the second graders were doing and so was able to skip the first grade. By the time I went to another school to finish the sixth grade, I had a miserable reputation with teachers for being the class clown. My teacher hated my guts and told my mother I shouldn't be in the sixth grade. I was sent to a psychiatrist. He said I should be skipped into the seventh grade, but my mother said no. All this time, I was frantically clipping out science articles from every paper I read. Also, I was getting precise dates when things would happen, sometimes years in advance, and I would write them down. They just 'came' to me. I was never sick or late for school in twelve years. Graduated high school with the Bausch and Lomb Science Award for top science students."

Christina Moon, Eureka Springs, Arkansas. Two NDEs, complications at birth. "I am smart. Throughout school I was told that I have a high IQ. Learning has always come easily to me. My pattern as an adult has been to get interested in something, immerse myself in it until I have learned everything I could about the subject, and then move on to something else. To some this looks like fickle behavior. To me, it is an indication of how interesting things are. I am *never* bored. I don't think linearly. I think in images, feelings, impulses. I sense things."

Carroll Cray, Atlanta, Georgia. Five NDEs due to injuries from child abuse; one prenatal experience. "My father, who had left school at thirteen, was openly threatened by an intelligent, precocious child. Other relatives were very proud but bewildered, as there was no one else in the family like me. By two and a half I could read and write, had a library card, and was reading the newspaper. Had an immediate interest in theater; saw an opera. Read *Hamlet* with some comprehension, and was performing

Shakespeare by the age of five. Learned how to fence and have had a real love of good blades and fine swords since after my fourth near-death episode. Began writing poetry at three, plays shortly thereafter. I believe my intelligence level has changed after every episode, though I can't say how. I rarely forget research, names, dates, history, but often can't remember if I've eaten or slept in the past few days. At fourteen, I tested at an IQ of 186. I have no idea what my IQ is after five additional near-death states in adulthood. I don't feel that smart, but over and over people keep telling me I am, almost to the point where they can't converse with me or understand what I'm saying. I, on the other hand, feel that I'm being perfectly clear and simple, and that anyone should be able to grasp what I'm saying."

L. S. Gordon, United States; NDE at age three, during tonsillectomy. "Suddenly began to read right after my near-death experience. Evidenced high IQ. Could think and read at incredible speed. Could think multiple trains of thought. It made a big impression on others that I could read so suddenly and without explanation. When I learned of [Einstein's formula] $E = MC^2$, I understood that the 'speed of light' was *home*—no time and infinite mass! I got it! I was dismayed that I couldn't get back to 'home.' Read physics and grasped it, even as a ten-year-old. Studied world religions and spiritual practices. Knew that 'earth school' was a Scotch-tape-and-cardboard affair. *Always* in trouble, but high IQ won me tolerance. I hated, hated, hated school—skipped, forged notes. Did my reading out in the fields. Without parents initiating the idea, I *knew* I was going to college, and I *knew* I was supposed to. From college on, I was always on the dean's list."

Lauren Thibodean, Madison, Ohio. NDE at age six, electrocuted. "I seem to pick things up very easily. Great facility with languages and math. Honor student throughout school, tested high IQ. Very sensitive to smells and tastes. Unable to tolerate light for long periods. Hypersensitive to sound. My body temperature routinely is about 97 to 97.4 degrees Fahrenheit, blood pressure lower than normal. I'm often allergic to medications. Animals and nature 'speak' to me."

Carl Allen Pierson, Hinton, West Virginia. NDE before age nine, struck by lightning. "I was an exceptionally bright child. School was a breeze for me. Made straight A's. I have had 20/10 vision and extremely sensitive taste buds—can taste something and usually tell what all the ingredients are and then can cook it. My IQ was 138 in high school. I took another IQ test in the early nineties and my score had gone up to 150."

Anthony Chipoletti, Arnold, Pennsylvania. NDE at age seven during and after tonsillectomy. "I was confident that I could predict the future, such as humans going to the moon, cures for mental and physical illnesses. I can recall saying to countless people, 'Boredom doesn't exist.' In high school, my classmates and even the chemistry teacher 'gave up' and let me teach the class—at least for a day. I became aware of a *massive* amount of scientific knowledge, specifically chemistry, without any previous studies in science."

These quotes richly illustrate the mixed blessing near-death states are to a child's development. Even those who did not test out with extraordinarily high IQs evidenced uniquely creative minds, numerous faculty enhancements, unrelenting curiosity, and an exceptional ability to know things soon after reviving. Some were unusually gifted with foreign languages.

The majority of child experiencers are natural computer whizzes, not to mention top physicists and inventors, masters of the arts and humanities, and even professional psychics. Older teenage and adult experiencers are the ones who are most often drawn to healing, counseling, and ministerial roles afterward; this is not true of the majority of younger kids. Mention math or science and they're all aglow. And history intrigues them, as well as anything to do with times past.

Percentages clearly show a discrepancy between ability and interest and career choice: 93 percent are drawn to and highly proficient in math, science, and history, while only 25 percent are actually employed in those fields (40 percent if you consider the full 277 people involved in this study).

Why the glaring difference?

I offer the following case as an example of the kinds of challenges that can derail child experiencers. Bill from Atlanta, Georgia, "died" at about two months of age when an infant chair fell over on him, cutting off his airway. Early on he tried to tell his family about his near-death episode, but was slapped down harshly by his "wrath of God" southern Baptist grandmother and shunned, ignored, or teased by other members of his family, until he learned to keep quiet. He drove his first-grade teacher crazy remembering things randomly, like the time when she was helping the class read *See Spot Run* and he up and quoted from memory a long passage from *Robinson Crusoe*.

"In my classical mechanics courses, I had what is best described as an intuitive grasp of everything I ever looked at. I would see a problem and immediately know the solution. Unfortunately, when I went to graduate school, where you have to explain how and why, I never finished my M.S. in physics. A professor in my graduate-level classical mechanics class once remarked, 'If you say once more that it is 'intuitively obvious' concerning things that I and your classmates have to work out ten pages of complex equations to arrive at, I will give you not a C but an F in this class.'

"My analytical, mathematical, creative, and scientific skills have always been very good. I examine things and solve problems as if I had a parallel-processing system instead of a brain. This is very hard to explain, but it is almost as if most problems get broken down somewhere in my brain, the various portions of each are attacked by different subparts of my brain, and the solution is integrated and put together for me with no conscious effort or control on my part. It is particularly frustrating for me to deal with other people doing joint research or brainstorming, because other people don't think like I do. Please don't laugh—I get some of my best ideas from dreams.

"I am currently able to see all sides of an object at once. I can read the 'other' side of a box of Pop-Tarts without touching or moving the box. I have seen the insides of locked objects at the same time that I saw all [their outer] sides. It's not like they are unfolded and laid out in two dimensions; it's more like looking at objects from all possible angles *simultaneously.*"

Bill has full-blown synesthesia (multiple sensing), is gifted in many languages, and is self-taught in computers.

"I once took a job at a company, and the job was operating a typesetting computer and interfacing and integrating it with the company's 'main computer.' There was no manual for it and I received no training. In two days I was making it do things the manufacturer said were impossible."

When Bill was a child his brain operated like a lightning calculator. The only other person in his family who could do anything similar was his mother, who had had a near-death experience as a teenager, but had never discussed it with anyone. He felt that heredity was not a factor in explaining his or his mother's mind—the phenomenon of near-death was. Although Bill finally became a respectable physicist, he didn't remain one, nor did he continue on with what could have been a successful career in grand opera. Instead, he became what he calls "a happy computer geek."

The bias against creative thought in the adult world, I submit, *is the reason why most people who experience near-death episodes as children seldom reach or maintain their full potential.*

And, according to my research, 85 percent of the kids with the greatest acceleration in mathematical ability also had a corresponding connection to music that was so passionate, it felt like a love affair with the embrace of celestial harmonies. Many considered it better than sex. Curiously, those who showed no particular interest in or special response to music either lagged behind in math or didn't have the skill to begin with.

The parts of the brain that process math and music are located next to each other. Near-death states in children somehow seem to accelerate both of these areas together, as if they were one unit.

There is a link between spatial reasoning, mathematics, and music, in that all three are necessary to arrange schemes that encompass the many-sidedness or wholeness of a given design. As an example, music imparts harmony, how things resonate or fit together; mathematics supplies measurement, the specifics of physical manifestation. Yet it is spatial reasoning that, through creating an overall pattern, gives meaning and purpose to the task or item at hand, while ensuring that all parts fit the whole.

This ability to create an overall valid pattern is precisely where the kids shine, for the average child experiencer becomes a spatial/nonverbal/sensory-dynamic thinker afterward—regardless of gender.

I was able to show in *Beyond the Light* how varying degrees of physiological aftereffects (especially as regard light, sound, and electrical sensitivity) are related to the intensity of exposure to light during the near-death episode. It was the *intensity of light,* not the length of exposure, that determined these effects.

Among children, I discovered some fascinating contradictions to my previous work, and they center around the issue of genius.

Near-death experiences, if sufficiently intense, seem to trigger faster and more complex growth spurts in children's brains than would be expected for children of their age. The more intense the experience, the bigger the growth spurt, including relative intelligence increases sometimes to the point of genius.

In the previous chapter, I reported finding clusters of children's near-death cases at certain ages in the overall group of 277. Birth to fifteen months and three to five years are the age groupings during which most of the events occurred. These two clusters account for most of the genius-level intelligence I found. This suggests to me that the younger the child the more susceptible he or she is to the sudden charge of intensity from a near-death episode. (Brain circuitry formation normally skyrockets in infancy; three- to five-year-olds undergo temporal lobe development as they experience the birth of imagination and creative thought. By the age of five, the brain reaches 90 percent of adult size.)

The Darkness That Knows can be a major component of scenarios for the tiniest experiencers. This unique, warm, friendly, living, loving, pulsating, and all-knowing darkness is described by little ones (as soon as they are verbal) in terms that are evocative of a passionate embrace. Their body language, facial expressions, often a shaking or quivering voice that they use when trying to find words to portray this darkness, are unmistakable. This darkness is not frightening, nor is it a state of suspension or void or lifeless nothingness. This darkness has a brilliance all its own and an enfolding shimmer that is, for them, love's fullness. Unusual healings are often associated with this dark or black light (sometimes said to have purple tinges to it), even with older children and adults.

Significantly, I found more compelling cases of genius specifically associated with infants and toddlers who experienced the Darkness That Knows, than with their counterparts who were bathed in bright light.

Because of this, I am moved to ask, What if children can have temporal lobe *enhancement* before they are old enough to experience temporal lobe *development*? Would that account for the phenomenal abstractions a child displays after a near-death experience? What if the learning reversals so apparent in child experiencers are the direct result of the brain being "charged" by the intensity of either an unusual light effect or dark effect at crucial junctures in its growth? What if there is more involved in the outworking of a near-death scenario than can be explained by the study of either the human brain or the human family?

What if the near-death experience in children is a second birth, a repositioning of brain/mind structures from regular genetic patterning to more expansive capacities and an acceleration of intellect that makes the children part of the groundwork evolution lays for the next "upgrade" in our species?

Let me go further with this.

There are three styles of learning and at least seven distinct types of intelligence. The three learning styles are visual, auditory, and tactile-kinesthetic. Most people are familiar with these but unfamiliar with the fact that intelligence can manifest in so many different ways. Psychologist Howard Gardner, famous for his insights into genius, posits that society's concept of intelligence is far too limiting. In his book *Frames of Mind*[4] he argues that Western society as a whole and schools in particular force linguistics and logic/mathematics on kids while neglecting other ways of knowing. He identifies the seven types of intelligence as linguistic, logical-mathematical, spatial, bodily-kinesthetic, musical, interpersonal (more social, outwardly directed), and intrapersonal (self-paced, inwardly directed).

It is important that we accept this broader concept of intelligence to appreciate that the genius I observed in child experiencers was not confined to linguistics or logic or even what we normally think of when we refer to visual and/or auditory and tactile learners. *What I saw was what I call "true genius," where intuition is the equal of intellect; where the brain seemed to evidence parallel-processing systems, faculty enhancements, multiple sensing, the simultaneous presence of multiple brainwave patterns, and an ability to know things unbounded by the constraints of past, present, and future, as if they could access and draw from a cosmic bank of knowledge.*

True genius is the goal of transcendental meditation, various types of spiritual and religious practices, and enlightenment; it is the idea of reaching oneness with Source. Few probationers on the spiritual path ever reach this goal, and fewer still are able to maintain the state once they reach it.

It would be an exaggeration for me to claim that children who have near-death experiences are able to maintain such a high state of brain-mind functioning, but many of them do reach this state and evidence that they did with typical aftereffects.

How many actually develop and refine what they achieved by virtue of their second birth?

Precious few.

Too much too soon may be the reason this is the case—along with the stress of readjusting back into social groups. The conundrum: How can educators be expected to teach a child who knows more than they do? Yet how can a child be expected to attend to a teacher who is utterly boring and has absolutely nothing of interest to offer?

Hence, most child experiencers go through some period of rejection afterward, both of home and of school, that leads them either to act out feelings of anger, rage, and resentment or to withdraw due to feelings of loss, abandonment, and depression. Fortunately, many are able to turn the situation around, if not in the lower grades, then by high school or in college. I find it fascinating that a third of those who filled out the questionnaire had another near-death episode in adulthood that they said healed the confusion of their earlier one. This underscores another force at work—a spiritual dimension.

Theresa Csanady of Glenview, Illinois, suggested that I investigate the field of gifted children in my search for links to the spiritual dimension of intelligence. What I found has a direct bearing on the uniqueness of near-death kids, for those qualities that identify a gifted child are amazingly similar to those that describe child experiencers.

Linda Kreger Silverman, Ph.D., a psychologist and director of the Gifted Child Development Center in Denver, Colorado, is a leader in this field, and she has given me permission to list the characteristics of gifted children that she has identified in her research:[5]

- Gifted children often have unique learning styles; they learn in different ways from other children.
- They also learn at a faster pace. They solve problems rapidly.
- They are usually developmentally advanced. They learn to talk, walk, read, etc., earlier than usual.
- They may appear healthier, physically stronger, and better coordinated than their agemates.
- They are very curious and tend to ask complex questions.
- They also give complicated answers. Their detailed explanations show that they have greater depth of understanding of topics than their classmates.
- They are quick to recognize relationships, even relationships that others do not see.
- They organize information in new ways, creating new perspectives.
- They often see many solutions to a problem.
- Their thinking is more abstract than their classmates', involving hypothetical possibilities rather than present realities.
- They often see ambiguity in what appears to be factual information.
- *They have large vocabularies and tend to express themselves well.*
- They have unusually good memories.
- *They may be natural leaders. They may initiate and organize activities for others.*
- They also enjoy working independently. They easily become absorbed in the mastery of skills.
- *They may prefer the company of older children and adults.*
- *They may like to be best at everything, and may refuse to participate in activities in which they might fail.*★
- *They are often perfectionists, becoming very upset if things don't turn out as they expect. Sometimes they compare themselves and*

their achievements to great persons they have read about rather than to others their own age.★

- *They are not necessarily gifted in all areas.*
- They usually don't want their giftedness pointed out.

Italics are my own and indicate areas of deviation. Regarding large vocabularies, natural leadership, a preference for the company of older people, and limitations in gifts, these traits were true with some child experiencers, but not true overall. The starred items signify a definite "no." I say this because I have seen only a few kids out of all of those I have interviewed who were competitive or perfectionists by Silverman's standard. These two missing traits are significant.

The average near-death survivor, child or adult, couldn't care less if goals are fulfilled, deadlines met, or awards won. What motivates them is quite different. Silverman included in the material she provided me a monograph about Dabrowski's theory of emotional development.[6] Kazimierz Dabrowski, a Polish psychologist and psychiatrist, based his theory of emotional development on the study of sensitive, nonaggressive, highly intelligent, and creative individuals. Through neurological examination, he documented that creatively gifted individuals had more pronounced responses to various types of stimuli. He called this "overexcitability" and equated it to an abundance of physical energy, heightened acuity of the senses, vivid imagination, intellectual curiosity and drive, and a deep capacity to care. The greater the strength of these traits, the greater the potential for an ethical, compassionate path in adulthood.

His discovery dovetails with what I have consistently seen in child experiencers.

Truly, youngsters who have undergone a near-death episode stand out. I call them the "second-born" because of the following telltale characteristics:

ELEMENTS OF A SECOND BIRTH

- Those hardly born can undergo a second birth.
- Temporal lobe expansion can precede or accelerate natural development.
- The learning curve can reverse itself, placing abstract conceptualizing before foundational understanding.
- IQ enhancements and faculty extensions can accompany heightened

spatial/nonverbal/sensory-dynamic thinking, giving rise to creative problem-solving skills.

- An awareness of future can clarify the earth world of time and space, by engendering "rehearsals" that provide for advance preparation in meeting life demands.
- Sensing multiples can open up whole new worlds of possibility and new dimensions of what is real.
- Brain shifts can jump-start the engine of evolution, enabling the human species to adapt to ever-changing needs and pressures.
- Spirit shifts can advance attitudes and behaviors toward social justice and moral integrity, as compassion and caring replace the obsessions that drive greed.
- The higher mind can emerge as the higher brain develops, thanks to structural and chemical changes that occur in the brain after a brain shift and in the heart because of its realignment after a spirit shift.

It is my belief that the formula evolution uses to guarantee renewal and rebirth in the human family, and the continuous cycling of *the Second Coming* (that transcendent enlightenment that lifts us to the next vibratory octave of existence) is brain shift/spirit shift—the engine that drives evolution . . . the mechanism that enables us to make quantum leaps in our development as a species.

FOUR

@

Jumbles of Good and Evil

All have their own personal ways of acting according to their visions. We must learn to be different, to feel and taste the manifold things that are us.

—LAME DEER

THE GRANDIOSITY OF THEORIZING about a child experiencer's possible second birth is unconscionable if we ignore the reality behind the theory—the positive and negative aspects of how kids really respond to transformational events: *what they think.* By taking a few moments to see through their eyes, we can begin to appreciate the fuller scope of our subject. This will prepare us for an in-depth look at the impact of aftereffects, covered in the next chapter.

Here is a brief sampling of comments that should dispel any notion that a baby's mind is a blank slate:

Margaret Evans, Roscoe, Illinois. NDE-like experience at age seven, dramatic death dream. "As a baby I was very observant. I 'knew' certain things. I understood what death was and could tell when each of my two grandparents who lived with us in the same building were going to die."

Dorothy M. Bernstein, North Olmsted, Ohio. NDE at ages ten months and three and a half years, both suffocation. "The tiny person perched at the head of my crib said, 'You're a baby.' I remember glancing up at a nearby mirror and catching my reflection, that of a baby lying in a crib, then of grabbing a foot and sticking it in my mouth and biting down. 'Yup, this is me,' I replied. 'This is real. I really am a baby. Wow, isn't this something!'"

Some children's memories begin *before* birth, as in the case of Carroll Gray of Atlanta, Georgia: "Red, warm, wet fear. Voices raised in anger somewhere nearby. Not a childlike perspective, but an adult awareness of what anger is. Voices were male and female. A sense of alarm. Something drastically not as it should be. Male accusing female of killing his son."

Two weeks previously, the doctor had informed Gray's mother that there was no heartbeat, that the baby was dead. At the moment of this particular memory, Carroll's father, screaming and enraged, grabbed his wife and sent her flying across the room, right into the corner of a large table, causing her amniotic sac to rupture. The mother was rushed to the hospital, where a "dead" baby girl was delivered via an emergency cesarean section. To everyone's astonishment, the child began to breathe.

The case of Carroll Gray typifies something that I've found to be commonplace among children's near-death experiences, and that is the jumbling together of good and evil. For kids, the prospect of "wearing" a body, even the act of breathing, lacks definable edges. What we regard as a blessing may be horrific to them, or vice versa.

Carroll went on to have numerous near-death scenarios, starting twenty-four hours after her emergency delivery. The fragmented speech pattern she uses is how she remembers thinking at the time.

"Looking down at the baby from above, through the glass of the thing it's in [the incubator]. It's tiny. Unfinished. Its head open from forehead to base of skull. Brain under something like gelatin. Skin yellow. Fingers and toes blackened. Purple blotches. Body fur, more like an animal than a human. Tubes, needles. On its back. It can't breathe—no one has noticed that it can't breathe. It's me. I recognize the hands and feet as mine. But this is wrong. Anxiety. Alarm. I'm not supposed to be here. A mistake. Fear. Sorrow for the baby. Born too soon and already traumatized by the loud anger it absorbed in the red stuff. That kept it small, too. Head the size of soap ball, eleven inches long. Two pounds and dropping. It's not going to make it. I can't fit into something that small, and I'm not supposed to. Sense of being in the wrong place. Supposed to be somewhere else. Late for . . . something." The attending physician warned Carroll's parents that the baby could not possibly survive, and thus obtained permission from them to try thirty-one experimental procedures on the infant.

Carroll remembers looking at "the baby" in the glass thing three days later and determining that its heart and lungs were working but its stomach wasn't. "Little lashes. Eyes moving under thin lids. Not my face. After all, it's a baby and I'm not. It might just make it. Is that good or bad?" The attending physician reported bad nights followed by rallies, though nothing hopeful. Yet against all odds, the child lived.

Eight months had passed when Carroll Gray's father took a sharp pencil and drove it through her stomach. It entered below the right rib cage and exited to the right of her spine. She floated free of her body. "The living room is in disarray, a heavy platform rocker and two lamps knocked over. The man, disheveled and apparently intoxicated and angry, leaning over the baby, screaming for it to stop crying. The baby lies on an end table, impaled on the pencil, gasping jerky breaths, gushing blood, its right little finger facing toward its shoulder. No feeling of pain, or connection to the baby at all. Realization that the pencil has missed major vital organs but that it may die anyway. No wish to return to its tiny body." The pediatrician, a drinking buddy of the father, never reported the abuse to the authorities.

On a snowy winter day two years later, Carroll's father strapped her by the waist to a sled and set out on a brisk hike to the home of a friend. He went inside to visit. Hours later he remembered that he'd left his daughter outside. By then, she had contracted pneumonia and was in the first stages of hypothermia. Her near-death scenario this time was lengthy and focused on a walk she took along a curving wall of white light to the right of a mist. A grown-up soon accompanied her. He was tall and slender, with a kind face and thinning hair. He wore a shirt, pants with suspenders, practical shoes, and a vest with something shiny on it—a watch chain that glinted light. He allowed her to pick his pocket and pull on the chain. A gold watch slid out. "For a moment I am me and the toddler at the same time. The toddler cannot read, but I can. The watch is not running; it stopped at 1:17. I smile. He smiles. I put it back and pull on the other side of the chain. On it is a small gold shiny thing. It has curlicues on it. The curlicues on one side are writing in English, the toddler's first name, on what I recognize as a small, two-bladed pocketknife. On the other side, a little shield surrounded by a flower garland with the year 1917 on it. I look up at him. 'That's my name.' He smiles, nods. 'It's all right, I'm the other Carroll.' He smiles again. 'It's yours. Remember.' I nod. The shiny thing is mine. Neat. I'll remember." The man let her choose the direction in which she might continue to walk. She looked both ways, shrugged, then returned the way she had come, into a dark, peaceful, unscary tunnel.

At the age of two and a half, in front of both parents, Carroll Gray repeated back to her father *every word he had said when he threw his pregnant wife into the table. She also described the situation and furniture placement.* You will recall that Carroll wasn't born yet when she "saw and heard" what her father did. Nor was her heart beating. She had been pronounced dead in her mother's womb by the physician ten days prior to her delivery. Her parents were dumbfounded. No one knew the full story of what had occurred, nor had they discussed it between themselves. A short time later, she detailed what she had once looked like and how she had been cared for "in the glass thing," her impalement with the pencil, and her ordeal on the sled.

Afterward, she told her grandmother about the man who had walked next to her along the white wall. Her grandmother, suspicious of who it might be, opened the family album to a page with numerous pictures of many people. Carroll immediately identified the grandfather who had died two years before her birth, and for whom she had been named. She then related with great accuracy every facet of his watch, chain, and gold pocketknife, including the time the watch had stopped and the date on the pocketknife, but was unable to convince anyone that the grandfather had given those treasures to her. They remained tucked away in a glass case until, twenty years later, her mother, while sorting through papers, happened upon the grandfather's will. In reading it, she was flabbergasted to learn that he had bequeathed his watch, chain, and gold pocketknife to his granddaughter and namesake. At the time of his death he had no granddaughter or namesake, nor did anyone have any inkling that he expected to have one, or that through perhaps an act of precognition he was privy to futuristic knowledge. Carroll finally got the treasures her grandfather had promised her when she "died" at the age of two.

At twelve, Carroll survived death yet again when she had a severe attack of asthma. She then "died" five more times in adulthood from varied health crises, each time experiencing another near-death scenario, making a total of ten, in addition to the prebirth incident. Her father, resentful that she lived, continued his villainy until she was forced to seek legal protection. "The monster died last year," she confided to me. "At last, I'm free."

Throughout Carroll Gray's story, regardless of her age at the time, we can recognize the workings of a decidedly mature mind that is stunningly accurate in what it perceives. This oddity was displayed by every child experiencer I ever had sessions with, irrespective of age. It's as if consciousness can function quite apart from personality, and, in so doing, is aware of other agendas—perhaps the mission of the soul. Carroll's case, though, implies that the traditional understanding of soul plans as being divinely guided may not always be true.

Children do not process their near-death states as do adults, nor do they regard them in the same fashion. A case in point: "I was very small when I had my near-death experience. When I could run and play like the other kids again, I'd go from room to room. I'd look under the beds, in the closets, behind the doors and furniture—from the top of the house to the bottom—other people's houses, too. I'd look and look but I never found them [the beings of light who had visited her]. They loved me. I know they did. They were warm and wonderful and bright with light. They came to me when I died and they left when I breathed again. I looked for years and years. Sometimes I'd curl up underneath my bed and cry. Why couldn't I find them? Where did they go? Why did they leave me in a place where no one cared and no one loved me? Was I that bad that they couldn't return?"

The teenager who spoke these words was four years old when her heart stopped and beings made of light came to get her. She recalls walking hand in hand with them into realms of music and joy and beauty, and so much love that she wanted never to leave. Then, suddenly, without choice or warning, she revived and found herself back in a body racked with pain. Surrounded by strangers, she was forced to deal, alone and frightened, with the aftermath of major surgery. She has yet to recover from the shock and the anger at feeling abandoned, *not by her parents or the medical staff*, interestingly enough, *but by the "bright ones" who loved her and then left her behind.* She now sees a counselor and has requested anonymity.

A young man from New Zealand, with tears flooding his eyes, told me about a time, when he was barely seven, that he died of a high fever from pneumonia. He had disobeyed his parents about playing outside, overdoing it, when he had not sufficiently recovered from a previous illness.

Confined to bed, alone, frightened, and guilt-ridden, he left his painfully hot body and went in search of help.

He described "walking" through the house and seeing his father enter through the front door. He ran to his father with arms outstretched, believing that help had been found. His father looked him in the face, then ran right past him, ignoring his pleas. The boy was invisible to his father, but he didn't know it at that time. He was heart-broken by what his father did and decided that, because of this, he wasn't good enough to be loved anymore. He never saw how panic-stricken his father was once the boy's lifeless body was discovered nor the heroic efforts made to save him. When he revived in the hospital, all he remembered was pleading for help and being refused. He withdrew from his family after that and remained estranged from his father for many years. No amount of counseling made any difference until we spoke, and he could finally understand what had happened to him and why.

Stories of children's near-death scenarios are compellingly heavenlike, innocent renderings of a greater reality and the pure lands our hearts know must somehow exist on the other side of death's door. The cases of little ones, we say, confirm that we are more than just a body and that life is everlasting. Yet the foregoing experiencers I have quoted are examples of what I keep hearing from the young, especially those who "died" as preteens and can compare "before" with "after."

Clearly, children can be and often are more confused and disoriented by their near-death episodes than by any life-threatening event that precipitated them. Listen to these voices:

Laura, San Francisco, California. NDE at age three and a half, child abuse. "For many years, I simply wanted to die again and go back."

Emily, Seattle, Washington. NDE at age two, high fever; at five from complications during surgery. "I wanted to go back in my dreams. I looked for The Light in the hall closet downstairs. I felt loved there. I was saddened when I could not find The Light. I missed The People. I liked them very much."

Regina Patrick, Toledo, Ohio. NDE at age four, pneumonia. "Afterward, I was concerned that 'they' would be mad at me for forgetting the instructions they gave me."

Janet Blessing, Pittsfield, Massachusetts. NDE at age nine months, pneumonia. "I felt so homesick afterward. I regretted being in the flesh again, cut off from the Voice of God/Source of Guidance. I oscillated between periods of great elation and creativity and deep suicidal depression as a teenager."

Mary Cosgrove, San Francisco, California. NDE at age thirteen, severe meningitis. "I recall not really wanting to 'wake up' or 'get well.' My initial reaction was confusion, guilt, even some anger during my recovery. I told no one about it. I was in a quandary of sorts, feeling different, as though I was from another place or family. I wanted to return, and finally tried to by slashing my wrists at twenty."

P. Ann Baillie, Ann Arbor, Michigan. NDE at age three months, hypothermia; at five months from drowning. "Being sent back into this mess of a family has often felt like a betrayal. Being loved and welcomed briefly on the other side and then returned into a loveless world was sometimes more than I could bear, especially because I could not seem to kill myself and I wanted to."

Lois Bradford, South Dakota. NDE at age four, complications during surgery. "Psychologists were telling me my problem was a projection from my parents, yet I had come to terms with my inadequate human parents. As horrendous as my history of sexual abuse is, and the ongoing abuse by my family members, *nothing* is as traumatic as the spiritual implications of being rejected by God. You can't believe the horror of this. I was bad and God confirmed it."

Tom Meeres, southern New Jersey. NDE-like experience at age fourteen, severe reaction to death dream. "I was so disassociated from ordinary perception afterward that I couldn't even imagine how to live the rest of my life. Something as ordinary as getting out of bed and leaving the relative safety of the bedroom seemed frightening. I had no idea how to relate to other people anymore, leading to long periods of depression during the next twenty-odd years."

All of these experiencers had positive, uplifting scenarios. All of them! They found their true "home" and wanted to stay there, but couldn't.

The result?

One-third of those in my study of childhood near-death states turned to alcohol for solace within five to eight years of their near-death experiences (the incidence rate with adult experiencers is about one in five). Over half dealt with serious bouts of depression afterward (adults have a slightly higher incidence). Twenty-one percent actually attempted suicide within about twelve years of their episode (this is an exceptionally high rate, compared to less than 4 percent of adult experiencers). None who sought to re-create their episode through the use of drugs was successful (the same is true of adult experiencers).

Among adults, the near-death experience is, for the most part, a suicide deterrent. Unfortunately, the same cannot be said of children.

Numerous experiencers have admitted to me that they became alcoholics as children because they couldn't handle the aftermath of coming back from where they had been. Those who tried to kill themselves did so as a way to return "home." Kids who had their episodes while they were of school age were much more likely to be affected by such extremes than those who "died" in infancy or as a toddler. Among the experiencers I interviewed, *how the episode ended,* especially if abrupt, proved to be the deciding factor in their response. We need to realize that children tend to personalize whatever happens to them. Hence, if they are left with a sense of:

Loss	It's their fault "everyone went away," and they feel guilty.
Rejection	They're bad, and they feel ashamed.
Betrayal	They're unworthy, and they feel abandoned.
Acceptance	It's okay to leave "home," and they feel satisfied.
Joy	They're trustworthy, and they feel confident.
Love	They are extra special, and they feel secure.

Child experiencers tend to repress their feelings until some unexpected incident (usually in adulthood) triggers what lies tucked away within their deepest self. Delayed aftereffects are commonplace. Regardless of the challenges adult experiencers face, kids have it tougher. Adults can at least speak up for themselves or exercise a fair degree of choice. Should a child say anything about an experience, he or she is usually ignored or hushed. Although many youngsters are able to integrate their near-death experiences successfully, the reverse is also true.

Good and evil can indeed jumble together with children, as is further evidenced by the next two cases. Nathan Kyles III of El Campo, Texas, was almost eleven when, with his brother Dale, he was given permission to splash around in a motel swimming pool while an older cousin applied for work.

"I got out of the water and walked inside to where my cousin was. When we were ready to leave, my cousin asked me, 'Where is Dale?' The first thing that came to my mind was the pool. I ran back to the deep end and saw my brother looking up at me from the bottom. I bent over and somehow grabbed his hand, but he pulled me in. Now I am on the bottom with my eyes closed, scared, trying to call my cousin, thinking I am about to die. Every time I opened my mouth I swallowed more water. Then I felt my life leave me. To this day, before God, I swear that everything good or bad that I had ever done passed right before my eyes. I felt a hand grab my shirt collar and snatch me out of the pool, but nobody was there. When I opened my eyes, I saw that my brother was already out. My cousin didn't know how to swim, so he didn't save us. Years later, we were talking about it, and the other two told me a white woman saved us. Nobody knew her. After she pulled us out, they said, she just disappeared."

Nathan's next comment echoes what is said by many child experiencers: "Afterward, I blocked all of this from my mind."

In Nathan's case, once he returned home after his close call with death, his mother told him to shut up before he could offer a single word, then she whipped both boys for leaving the house. His later attempts at communication were also rebuked. Guilt and shame came to overlay the miracle of his experience, not because of his episode, per se, but because of the way his family treated him after he came home. Certainly his mother was worried about her children and, to that degree, her reaction was understandable. Still, the question remains: Would Nathan have turned out differently if she had let him speak? After the whipping, Nathan didn't care anymore. His grades immediately plummeted. His teacher became alarmed and called on his mother, but she couldn't get him to listen, either. Within the span of one year, he turned from a positive, studious, happy, thoughtful child to a sullen criminal who didn't give a damn about anything or anyone.

Nathan explained: "Before it happened, I was never in trouble with the law. After it happened, I started stealing, burglarizing houses and buildings. My whole way of thinking changed. I was about twelve when I went to jail for the first time. I got caught stealing some old coins out of a lady's purse while playing with her son. The judge kicked me out of town for a year, and I had to live with my father nine hundred miles away.

When I returned, I went downhill further." A long litany of difficulties followed, beginning with a prison term at the age of nineteen for parole violation. Charges of burglary, terrorist threats, and harassment were later dropped because it was proved he had not committed them. When he was released, however, he promptly stole again and wound up back in prison. "I stayed in prison this time for nine years and two months. I was sent to a halfway house because my mom had died earlier and my parole plan was all messed up. I started smoking marijuana, I guess for comfort at my mom being dead. So, while in the halfway house, I was written up for violating their rules, which was also a violation of my parole. Again, my parole was revoked, and here I sit in prison for the fourth time."

It would take some digging to determine if Nathan, an African American, was a victim of racial prejudice, as his punishment seems outlandish considering the crimes he committed. But it wouldn't take any digging at all to pinpoint the moment he underwent a personality change that radically altered his life for the worse.

Nathan's case opens the door to the topic of family reactions and how deceptively complicated they can become. The following account, although filled with miracles, dramatically illustrates the extremes kids can face when family members feel threatened by the near-death phenomenon.

Lynn from Michigan underwent open-heart surgery at thirteen to correct a condition she had had almost since birth. She was unable to run and play with the other kids, and she would on occasion turn blue and get sick. A large black Great Dane named Harvey was her constant companion and best buddy.

"The last thing I remember in surgery was a male voice saying in a very matter-of-fact way, 'Uh-oh, we have a problem here.' The next thing I knew I was floating around the ceiling looking down on my body. My chest was open wide and I could see my internal organs. I remember thinking how odd it was that my organs were a beautiful pearl gray, not at all like the bright red chunks in the horror flicks I loved to watch. I also noticed there was a black doctor and an Oriental one on the operating team. The reason this stuck in my mind is that I was brought up in a very white middle-class neighborhood, and I had seen black schoolteachers but never a black doctor. I'd met the operating team the day before, but they were all white.

"Suddenly, I had to move on, so I floated into the waiting room, where my parents were. My father had his head buried in my mother's lap. He was kneeling at her feet, his arms wrapped around her waist, and he was sobbing. My mother was stroking his head, whispering to him. This scene shocked me, as my father was not prone to showing emotions. Once I realized they would be fine, I felt myself pulled into a horizontal tunnel.

"The ride through the tunnel was like nothing else. I remember thinking, 'So this is death.' The tunnel was dark, and every once in a while something that looked like lightning would flash across my path. These flashes were brilliant in color and didn't scare me. At the end of the tunnel was a bright light.

"From the light came two dogs of mine. One was a collie named Mimi who had died three years previously from an infection, and the other was a boxer named Sam who had died two years before after being hit by a car. The dogs came running and jumped on me and kissed my face with their tongues. Their tongues weren't wet, and I felt no weight when they jumped on me. The dogs seemed to glow from a light that was inside them. I recall saying to myself, 'Thank you, God, for letting my dogs be alive.' I hugged my dogs as tight as I could.

"I then called my dogs and together we started walking toward the light. All colors were in the light and it was warm, a living thing, and there were people as far as the eye could see, and they were glowing with an inner light—just like my dogs. In the distance I could see fields, hills, and a sky. The light spoke and it said, 'Lynn, it is not time for you yet. Go back, child.' I put my hand up to touch the top of the light. I knew then that I had touched the face of God. I told God that I loved him, and I wanted to stay with him. Again the light said, 'Lynn, go back. It is not time for you. You have work to do for me. Go back.'

"I know this sounds silly, but I asked the light, 'If I go, can I come back and will my dogs still be here waiting for me?' The light said yes, and then told me there were people who wanted to see me before I left. From out of the light came my maternal grandparents. I ran to them and embraced them. They were going to walk me part of the way back. Just as I was turning to leave, a man stepped from the light. He wore a full dress uniform, U.S. Navy. He was very tall and very blond, with blue eyes. I had never seen the man before, but he knew me and smiled.

"'I am your uncle Franklin. Tell Dorothy that I'm okay and that the baby is with me. Tell her I never stopped loving her and that I am glad she got on with her life. Tell her that when her time comes, I will come for her. Remember to tell her I love her.' As I turned, the man shouted, 'Tell Dorothy, tell her you met Franklin and I'm okay and so is the baby.'

"My grandparents told me if I stayed any longer I might not make it back. But I wanted to talk with Jesus. I had a very important question to ask him. A beam of light, different from yet similar to the first one, covered me. I knew this light was Christ. I leaned against it for one moment and then asked my question. 'Dear Jesus, is it true that you gave me this heart condition so that I would have a cross to carry like you did?' (Sister Agnes, my sixth-grade teacher, had told me that my heart condition was my cross to bear for Christ.) I heard the voice of Christ vibrate through me as he said, 'No, this heart condition of yours is not a cross from me for you to bear. This heart condition is a challenge to help you grow and stay compassionate. Now, go back.'

"As I walked back, my grandmother told me that my father was going to leave my mother and that I would be my mother's strength. I saw people hiding in the tunnel, people who were afraid to come into the light or who were disoriented about where they were. I expressed concern for them but was told not to worry, as a guide would be along to help them. Some of these people looked like soldiers. Then I remembered Vietnam and I knew where the soldiers were coming from."

Lynn detailed what it was like to be resuscitated and then wake up hours later hooked up to a myriad of tubes. She recalls being unable to speak and being fascinated by shadows moving among the medical staff, shadows she came to realize were people who had died there. She claims it didn't take long before she could watch death take place—to see the soul as it exited the body. Her doctor released her after a month because he was afraid that all the time she spent talking to dead or misplaced souls would drive her crazy. Her early release pleased her father, as if it gave him an excuse to be cold and unemotional again.

"The day I left, in front of my parents, I asked Dr. Davidson who the black doctor was in the operating room. Dr. Davidson said he had been called in at the last minute when one of the team members became ill. He wanted to know if this doctor had been by to say hi, but I said no, I saw him during surgery. Dr. Davidson stopped smiling and told me to go home and forget everything."

Once Lynn returned home, her life changed. Light bulbs would pop if she got angry, and formerly inanimate objects would move around of their own accord (the research term for this is psychokinesis). She would see images whenever she touched anything (synesthesia). From touching jewelry, she could tell who owned it and where it had been worn (psychometry). When she looked at a person, she could see their life in flashes, including their future (clairvoyance). School became easy, as she no longer had to study to get really good grades (intelligence enhancement). But sunshine bothered her, and so did loud noise (increased sensitivity to light and sound).

"My father left us. In front of the whole family, he told me he thought I was crazy and belonged in a mental hospital. It was Thanksgiving Day, one year after my surgery. I told my father I could prove I wasn't crazy. I turned to Aunt Dorothy and said, 'Who is Franklin?' There was silence. Every eye at the table was on me; mouths were wide open. Uncle George, who was married to Aunt Dorothy, looked at me with tears in his eyes and said, 'Lynn, if you wanted to hurt me, you've done a good job.'

"Everyone went home early and my father left us. A few weeks later my aunt wanted to know how I knew about Franklin. I told her exactly what had happened during surgery. Then my aunt led me up to her attic and unlocked a large trunk. (I had never been in her attic before, nor had I seen the trunk.) She pulled out pictures of the man I had seen in the light. My aunt told me that she had married Franklin during World War II, after a brief twenty-four-hour courtship. She had been engaged to Uncle George at the time, but left him for Franklin. My aunt started to cry as she told me that she and Franklin were very happy together for two months, and then he was shipped out. After he left, she discovered she was pregnant. When she was seven months along, my aunt received word that Franklin had been killed in the invasion of Italy. He was on the lead ship dropping off troops. The news caused her to miscarry. She hemorrhaged so badly that a complete hysterectomy had to be performed to save her. The next year Uncle George married her and destroyed all pictures of Franklin, requesting that everyone in the family never speak Franklin's name again. The only pictures to survive were those Aunt Dorothy hid in the trunk."

With this final verification of what she had seen during her near-death experience, Lynn became openly confident and trusting, although she preferred solitude to a social life. She lost all fear of death, changed her diet to include less meat, began to exhibit steadily increasing displays of psychic abilities, and became a friend of ghosts.

Yet the guilt she felt about her father's actions and what he did to her Great Dane still haunts her.

"He took my dog when he left, and he'd call me on the phone and accuse me of being possessed by the devil, saying I had to become a Christian or he'd kill my dog. And while we'd be talking he'd beat my dog so I could hear him cry out in pain. He did this with phone call after phone call until he killed my dog with me on the line listening. I couldn't believe my father actually did it until that night, when Harvey's soul came to say good-bye and let me know he was okay. For years afterward I'd have coughing fits where I could hardly breathe. It wasn't until I reached adulthood that I connected the coughing to my pent-up emotions about my dog's death."

After years of counseling, Lynn has yet to release the grief she feels about her near-death experience. "My father walked out on our family because of me, because of how I changed after my episode, and my relationship with my uncle was never the same again. My family was badly hurt and my dog was killed, and it's all my fault."

Here's another case of how a child's near-death experience changed not only the child, but the entire family. Unlike the case of Lynn, the Mendenhall family managed to overcome the challenges they faced in dealing with their "strange" daughter, Denise. What happened to Denise became a "shared event" everyone could benefit from. It is important that the family dynamics be presented as they occurred. For this reason, I include the full report submitted by the father, Doug Mendenhall.

"In the summer of 1999 our little ten-year-old daughter, Denise, was literally counting the weeks, days, hours, minutes, and seconds until school started. Denise was always a happy, sweet little girl. Soon after school started her personality changed. She was unhappy all the time, claiming how much she hated school, her friends, everything. Then she started going to the bathroom all the time and drinking tons of water. She would get sick and just not feel well. We asked several medical people that lived in the neighborhood about the symptoms she was displaying, and were told it was probably just a virus. One even was a diabetic nurse and another one was a medical doctor! It was like they were shielded from seeing that it was diabetes. Her personality change was so dramatic, that we talked about getting her to see some mental health professionals.

"It progressed to the point where she felt real sick on Friday, November 5. She played in the morning with her mother, ate lunch, and asked if she could lie down for a nap. My wife went in to check on her an hour or so later and she was asleep. Then after another hour she checked on Denise again and found she hadn't moved and was breathing really strangely. She called me in and we found that her eyes had rolled back in their sockets and she was unresponsive. I called a doctor friend and he said to get her to the hospital immediately, also he would call ahead and have them ready for her. So we took off to the hospital. I literally drove over one hundred miles per hour and hit every light green.

"At the hospital they descended on her. As they pulled her clothes off, I was shocked at what a skinny little girl she was. She had always been skinny, but now she looked like a little child from a third world country, skin and bones. I stared in disbelief.

"They put an IV in her immediately and started checking. They told us it looked like she was in a coma and wanted to do many more tests. We sat and waited as they wheeled her off to do a CAT scan.

"Two hours later a neurologist took us to a room and told Dianne and me that Denise was in a coma, from the diabetes she has. But the most devastating thing was that she had suffered a stroke. It was at the base of the left side of her brain, the main artery. He then said that the left side of her brain, more than two-thirds of it was destroyed by the stroke. The blood vessels and capillaries had fragmented like tissue paper and the blood had flowed freely. Normally they would put in a shunt and drain off the blood, but she was so far gone, they saw no reason to do so. All of her organs were shutting down. She would not live past the next twenty-four hours we were told. If by some miracle she did live, she would be a vegetable the rest of her life, never to walk or talk again.

"They had put a tube down her throat to breathe for her if she quit breathing. Later we would learn that they had wanted to harvest her organs for donation, but had never brought out the forms. A 'bolt' was put into her brain to monitor the pressure, as the liquids they had to give her would make the brain swell, cutting off the circulation at the base and that also would kill her. It seems like there was no way she could live.

"She stayed in the coma for three days and never quit breathing. After two days they took the tube out of her throat. At the end of the third she woke up, looked at Dianne and me and said she was hungry. The nurse looked up, startled, asking if she had just talked. I said she had and they descended on her as she went back to sleep.

"The next day she woke up and stayed awake. They moved her from ICU to the third floor where we could learn to give her insulin shots. I remember that she really was a vegetable when she woke up. She was taught to do everything all over again, from talking, reading, writing, even going to the bathroom. Within three days she had progressed to the point where she walked one thousand feet that day. She truly was a miracle! The doctors really didn't know what to make of her. They would come into her room, look at her, shake their heads, and walk out. We left the hospital on November, 30, 1999, twenty-five days after going in.

"We figured that life would go on as normal except that we did have a miracle child with us. Though we now had to give her two injections of insulin each day for her diabetes.

"One day I was trying to give her a shot of insulin and she kept fighting me. She wouldn't let me give her the shot. After forty-five minutes I was upset with her, and let her know it. She yelled, pointing her finger above my head that I 'was mad and I was red.' I asked what in the world she was talking about. 'You're mad, you're red,' she said again. I had read enough that I knew about the energy field around our body, called the aura.

"'You can see auras?' I asked.

"'What's that?' she responded.

"I told her it was the energy around our body. She said that she could see them, since she woke up from her coma. This was the start of our family entering a world we did not know existed.

"Over the next month, Denise displayed many gifts or abilities and told us many things. She not only could see the aura of a person, she knew what the color meant. At this point she only saw the first level of the aura. She is able to see 'spirits' as we call them, or people that have passed on (died). She sees Christ and her Heavenly Father. She can tell what kind of person you are; she sees into your heart.

"The most fascinating thing she told us was that while she was in the coma for three days, she had spent that time with Jesus. She told me about his birth, life, his suffering in the garden, the cross. It was in detail, all the colors, smells, and sounds. She told me things that I knew a little ten-year-old could not know.

"All of this changed our lives significantly. My wife and I have six living children, five were at home during this time. The events polarized our family somewhat. I knew in my heart that Denise was telling me the truth of what she had experienced. Yet it was hard for others to understand and accept. We learned many 'lessons' from our little ten-year-old daughter.

"She taught us not to judge: anyone or anything. We learned of God's unconditional love for all of us. One of the biggest lessons was to be grateful for all things. Gratitude is a huge lesson we were to learn over and over. We learned that after a person dies, he or she can move on to God, or some become 'earthbound.' Such was the individual (spirit) that was in our home at the time. She even encountered some who would not believe they were dead! We learned that evil is real. There are dark spirits who do work for Satan or the Devil. She sees them also.

"We learned through our experiences with her that we all have a guardian spirit(s) or angel(s). We had several experiences where our lives were saved by them and she saw what they did to save us. She thought it was 'cool.'

"I guess the main spiritual impact on our lives was the fact that she spent three days with Jesus and still sees him and interacts with him on a daily basis. This has had the biggest impact on our family. One person asked Denise who her best friend is and she said, 'Jesus.' We ended up going out and talking to people one-on-one for the next year. All during that year she kept telling me, 'Dad, you are supposed to write a book about all of this.' I told her that I didn't write books and that I didn't want anyone to know about all of this. I felt that it was just too weird for most people to accept, and didn't want to invite persecution into our lives.

"Finally at the end of the year 2000, I agreed to do a book about it. We had a friend help us write it. It was published some seven months later. We then went around and did 'book reviews' where we gave them away. The book is called, *My Peace I Give Unto You,* and we gave away over seven thousand copies over the next eighteen months. From the e-mails we get it has changed many lives and helped many people find their Savior, Jesus Christ.

"In May of 2002, we were prompted to write a second book. You see our experiences with Denise never quit. We are continually being taught things and are having experiences. So we published the second book in November of 2002. We have since printed over one thousand copies of it. It is called *Possibilities . . . Lessons from the Spirit.* Since we have been asked to travel all over the country telling our story, we now sell both books. That defrays our expenses somewhat, since we do not charge when we do book reviews. The books are available on a website at: www.publishinghope.com. At one time we had them available in some bookstores, but now we sell them at book reviews or ship them from our home or people can order from the Web site.

"Doing the book reviews has changed our lives. We have met many people with similar gifts as Denise. We have met many children and adults who see the spirits of dead people. There are dozens we've met who see auras. Others 'fly' at night when they sleep as Denise does. These people have told us our books have helped them to realize that they are not freaks, that there are many others out there similar to them, with gifts. There are others who can see into you and determine where an illness is. They have come to understand that these gifts come from a loving God and are to be used for his work. Whether they are to be used or not is the will of God, and not that of Denise or those with similar gifts.

'Today, our family has learned to live with a daughter/sister who lives in both worlds, the one the rest of us see and the other one that few others see. She enjoys meeting people that have lived before. When she sleeps she can go back in the past and see events. She has witnessed all of the Bible. She fell in love with the movie *Titanic* when it aired on television and went back to see what it was really like. At first, being able to do this made it difficult for her to attend our church. When people put their own interpretation on biblical events she would turn to me and say, 'Dad, that's not how it really happened.' Now she goes to enjoy the people and be around kids her own age.

"She prefers to be a normal kid, yet knows that she is not. She likes to be around friends who 'know about' her, yet treat her as any other friend. Being a fourteen-year-old, she loves to talk about the cutest boys, etc. Individuals who look at her as 'special' or gifted she doesn't like to be around. Or those who want to continually ask her questions.

"We are now used to having others that have passed over, from the other side of the veil, 'hanging' around. There are some special friends she has made on that side who hang around a lot. Others come when thought of. Some come because they know she can see them. Most of the time they are only known to her when they are there. At other times, the rest of us have 'experienced' them at our home. After three plus years of having her live in both worlds, it has become old hat for our family. There are many occasions when we do have fun with it and interact with those who are passed on, through her. I guess to some people that may seem a bit odd or weird, yet to us now it is quite normal.

"As for the future, we will continue to do book review meetings when we are invited and share our story with those that want to hear about it."

What happened to Lynn and Denise speaks volumes about the phenomenon called near-death, and how it can be both a blessing and a nightmare. What these two went through as children shows us that integrating the experience is *a very sensitive issue for the young and their families,* one that has never before been adequately addressed.

FIVE

The Impact of Aftereffects

Deep in their roots all flowers keep the light.
—THEODORE ROETHKE

IT TAKES A CHILD EXPERIENCER to understand a child experiencer. A young man, preferring to call himself A Child from Minnesota, was suffocated at the age of three and a half by an older brother. He has this to say about the challenge of experiencing the near-death phenomenon as a youngster:

"Children react differently to near-death episodes than adults because the set of experiences they have to compare them with is smaller. To an adult, such a phenomenon is only one of many life occurrences. But to a child, a near-death experience is the world itself, or 'all there is.' A child has a more difficult time 'drawing the line' between what is eternal and what is earthly. Children are forced to rely on the experience more, simply because they lack what adults can draw from. This colors everything children think, say, and do.

"Speaking for myself, I have come to understand that the long-term effects of this phenomenon have been very large indeed. These effects include (1) an ability to desensitize the self from physical sensations; (2) an ability to communicate through nonverbal and nonauditory means; (3) a partial loss of ability to communicate verbally and auditorily; (4) problems reintegrating the ethereal self back into the physical self; and (5) challenges interacting socially.

"My experience of being out of body enabled me to learn very young how to perform the separation of body and spirit. My understanding of the process, however, was unconscious. I did not know what I was doing or how I was doing it until much later. This first experience arose as a result of intense pain, so, in the beginning, I used this skill simply to avoid pain. Since the skill itself was unconscious, it quickly became a knee-jerk reaction to discomfort of all sorts. Eventually, I came to remain in that state as much as possible. This led to an inability to function socially. As I desensitized myself to my own feelings, I was equally unable to feel the pain or joy of others. And—as I explored this state—emotions, people, and all of social life grew ever more foreign to me; I grew ever more withdrawn. I have come to believe that body and spirit need to nourish each other, and cannot remain separate indefinitely."

Almost every child experiencer becomes adept at dissociation, as did A Child from Minnesota. The term "dissociation" was formerly used in the field of psychiatry as a label to describe an individual who withdrew or severed any association with his or her body and/or environment. It was considered an aberrant, unhealthy mental state. Current thinking on the subject has shifted considerably as more mental health professionals are now recognizing that dissociation may actually be a natural by-product of consciousness as it develops along new lines of thought and creative imagination,[1] that it is more a sign of adaptation than insanity. But, as A Child from Minnesota finally learned, even positive skills that enrich our lives can become crutches.

Without a supportive framework of understanding in the wake of a near-death episode, a child experiencer can easily feel as if he or she is either stupid, crazy, or suddenly "foreign." Family and friends who are unaware of what such an experience can entail may find the child's sudden behavior changes either frightening or perhaps an attention-getting ploy, maybe even the product of an overactive imagination.

The full profile of physiological and psychological aftereffects appeared early in chapter 2. What follows are more questionnaire results to give us a deeper look at how these aftereffects impact a child's life:

Significant increase in allergies	45%
Became vegetarian	18%

Unusual sensitivity to light	
decreased tolerance	59%
increased tolerance	20%
Unusual sensitivity to sound	
decreased tolerance	74%
enhanced desire for classical music	41%
Electrical sensitivity	52%
Health	
still dealing with handicaps from death event	32%
went on to have major illnesses in adulthood	30%
blood pressure substantially lower after episode	27%
feel as if bodymind was rewired/reconfigured	41%
direct improvement in health after episode	45%
state of health now	
excellent	77%
challenged	23%
Psychic enhancements	
more intuitive	64%
more precognitive	73%
more knowing	48%
more of an active, vivid dream life	66%
conscious future memory episodes	34%
visible manifestations of spirit	27%
Unusual connection to nature/animals	66%
Spiritual inclination	
mystical	66%
religious	25%
Relationship with parents/siblings after	
better	30%
alienated	57%
Relationship with friends/strangers after	
open/friendly	27%
became a loner	57%
Marriage	
once, long-lasting	41%
twice, second one long-lasting	16%
divorced, never remarried	23%
single, never married	20%

Attitude toward money
    careful and responsible   30%
    disinterested, doesn't "give a hoot"   66%
Attitude toward job
    loves to work   80%
    doesn't like to work (or unemployable)   16%
Homeowner   68%
Mission
    knows exactly what it is and is doing it   45%
    has a sense of what it might be but no details   32%
    doesn't have a clue   23%
Immediate response to episode afterward
    positive   34%
    negative   61%
Desires to return to the Other Side
    yes   41%
    no   43%
    learned how to return at will   9%
Regrets about the near-death experience
    yes   32%
    no   57%
Aftereffects
    decreased with time   9%
    increased with time   73%
    remained the same   18%

NOTE: Concerning counseling, only 27% ever obtained any. Of that number, only a little over half were helped to any degree.

COMPARISON WITH ADULT EXPERIENCERS

If we compare research results between child experiencers and adults (as detailed in *Beyond the Light*), we will see some startling differences. To begin with, 57 percent of child experiencers who filled out the questionnaire went on to enjoy long-lasting marriages once grown (combine first and second marriages that were long-lasting). Adult experiencers, on the other hand, report having tremendous difficulty afterward forming or maintaining stable relationships. Of the three thousand in my research base, 78 percent of the marriages ended in divorce.

Both groups experience unusual increases or decreases in light sensitivity: about 79 percent of the kids (this includes both tolerance-level changes), which is close to the adult range of 80 to 90 percent. Whereas 73 percent of adults evidence electrical sensitivity, only 52 percent of the kids claim to exhibit the same anomaly—perhaps more a reflection of who has access to technological equipment than a true deviation. Older experiencers are four times more likely to become vegetarians than the younger crowd (even "near-death" kids snub veggies).

Afterward, parent-sibling relationships tend to be strained for child experiencers. Additionally, kids are more likely than adults to suffer socially and to report having regrets about what happened to them. An astounding number would go back to the Other Side, even if that meant suicide. Child experiencers, whether still young or grown, seldom see a counselor and receive less help when they do. This is not true with adult experiencers, contrary to how loudly they may contest the fact. Because the disparity between children and adults in this area is so enormous, it begs further exploration.

Family/Friend Alienation

One-third of the child experiencers in my overall study and with the questionnaire group admitted to having problems with alcohol within five to eight years after their episode. Almost to a person, they claimed that undeveloped social and communication skills were the culprit, along with an inability to understand what motivated the behavior of family members and friends.

Unfortunately, 42 percent of the child experiencers I had sessions with in the overall group underwent the tragedy of parental and sibling abuse. And note the *sibling* abuse—big brothers and sisters can pack a mean wallop or give a nasty squeeze when they're roughhousing or angry. The worst of all horrors, always, is parents who mistreat their children. While such abuse is rampant throughout the general population, the additional stresses inherent in the near-death phenomenon and its aftereffects seem to exacerbate situations that are already less than ideal.

Still, there's another aspect to the issue of alienation that, for the child, may be even more profound. Completely aside from any abuse or peer pressure from family or friends, and whether or not parents are supportive, the most significant factor is *who or what greeted the child on the other side of death*. What parent, no matter how wonderful or loving, can compare with the Holy Spirit? What person, friend or foe, can interest a child who has visited the bright realms and become buddies with an angel? For the child experiencer, connecting with such transcendent love, then abruptly losing that connection, can be very confusing, sometimes devastating.

The Issue of Suicide

Children reason differently than adults. Unaccustomed to a consideration of cause and effect, they tend to act on impulse; hence the high degree of alcoholism, suicidal tendencies, and even actual attempts at suicide. It seems perfectly logical to a child that the way to rejoin the light beings met in death is to die and go back. This is not recognized by them as self-destructive. *Yet it is the children, not the adults, who are the most likely to leave the heaven of their near-death experiences and return to life so their families won't be saddened by their deaths.*

Parent-child bonding is initially quite strong. These kids want to be with their families. That bonding brings them back, time after time. When I speak with youngsters, their common retort is, "I came back to help my daddy" or "I came back so Mommy won't cry." The parent-child bond doesn't begin to stretch thin or break until after the child revives. The climate of welcome or threat they are greeted with, as well as how the episode ended, directly impinges on everything that comes next.

The story of Nadia McCaffrey, now of Sunnyvale, California, gives us an example of what can drive a child experiencer to attempt suicide. While spending her vacation from convent school at her grandparents' estate in France, seven-year-old Nadia was playing in a meadow of wildflowers when she stopped abruptly. She had disturbed a red asp viper, a deadly snake. "It stayed perfectly still for a long moment, curled on its tail in a perfect circle, the upper body standing straight up, two piercing eyes staring deep into my soul. I am petrified. I want to scream. I can't move. A horrible pain suddenly flooded my senses. The snake left very fast; two tiny spots of blood appeared on my left ankle."

Nadia struggled up the steep hillside, but collapsed before her grandmother found her. First aid was immediately applied; her grandfather pedaled his bike to reach the only public phone in the village to summon a doctor. Here is Nadia's account of the crisis.

"I left this dimension and was gone for about a week. It was then that I saw her. She introduced herself, saying, 'I am your little mother of the sky.' She was beautiful. I still see her so clearly, as though she were standing in midair, glowing with an extremely bright and powerful light, so loving and warm and comfortable. Leaving my body in my bed, I floated in her direction. She smiled very softly and opened her arms, holding up the palms of her hands to help me understand that I was not to come any closer as I listened to her. She visited me twice. Each time the message was the same and each time I did the same thing—slipped out of my gray skin. The sight of this puffy form was unbearable to the spirit I had become.

"The last time I saw her, she wore a long white gown with a cord knotted at the waist. Her head and shoulders were draped in blue material. There was a live green snake at her feet and a tear-shaped drop of blood on her right foot. Both her arms were extended toward me, with her palms up. Her head was slightly bowed, but I can't remember seeing her eyes. I wanted to curl up in her arms, to remain with her rather than return to my body, but I had no choice. My body claimed me, and I was overwhelmed by pain and sadness, and unable to completely understand what had happened to me. I had to stay in bed for a couple of weeks. My leg was three times its normal size and of the same mottled color as the snake. I refused to talk with anyone. I hated being back in this dimension. I was filled with resentment, and longed to slip out of my painful and disfigured body."

Later Nadia learned that an adult will survive for only twenty minutes after being bitten by an asp, yet she had lived for over two hours without the antidote. People said it was a miracle that she had survived. It took months for her to learn how to walk with a cane, but her spirit didn't heal as quickly. "I started asking my grandmother about the beautiful lady. I desperately needed some information about my experience. She seemed to be startled by my account, full of fear, and horrified at what I was saying. She cautioned me— 'People would not understand. They would put you away forever if you told anyone about this.' From then on, she thought that I was possessed and never let me forget it until the day she died.

"The rest of my childhood was not happy or good. I became a rebel, fighting everything and everyone. The sisters at the Catholic school I attended didn't know what to do with me. When I turned seventeen, people said I was beautiful and bright, yet no one knew I did not want to live. Although [I was] very popular, I pushed people away and isolated myself. I was not able to share the way I felt and ended up hurting people as I rejected their offers of friendship. After seeing the Lady of Light, being back was not easy. At first, I thought she would return. When she didn't, I wanted to be where she was, in the light, with the love. There was a hollow spot in a park tree where a limb had been removed, and into it I placed a statue of the Virgin of Lourdes. It comforted me to visit her there.

On the wall of my grandmother's bedroom was another picture of Mary that reminded me of her and I talked to it, keeping hope alive, wishing that she would speak to me or give me a sign."

Soon after, Nadia decided to go back to the light. She made two suicide attempts. The first time, she swallowed pills marked "poison." She became very sick, vomited, lost consciousness, and was rushed to the hospital, where her stomach was pumped. Visits to a psychiatrist began.

"The second time I became more sophisticated, calculating the [number] of pills required to end my life. It worked but, unfortunately, a girlfriend from the village came unexpectedly to borrow a schoolbook and she found me wearing a beautiful ball gown, with no sign of life except a feeble pulse. The hospital was forty minutes away.

"I was out of my body, looking down at myself. I lost interest in nurses and doctors trying to revive me and was attracted to a long tunnel. I could see a very bright light at the end of it. I floated inside and with what seemed to be extraordinary speed, reached the light. Oh, the light, the peace, the great feeling of love. Once more I was there. Then a voice, extremely powerful, a man's voice, said I had to go back, I had work to do. Sadly I returned to my body, finally understanding that I had to stay. This experience totally changed my life. Once I knew I could not go back, I stopped fighting the world and began to pass on the love that I had once received."

Today, Nadia McCaffrey is dedicated to "Changing the Face of Death" (the name of her organization). She has worked many years in hospice care and now seeks to establish a center for both children with developmental disabilities and the terminally ill who cannot afford medical costs for their condition.[2]

Another case involves Debi of California: "When I was about eight years old, I was in surgery for kidney stones and guess what? I died on the table. The life I was leading at that time was so filled with abuse and negativity that I embraced being able to 'leave.' I went through the dark tunnel, found the 'light,' and tried to race into heaven. I was stopped by a very wise, older man—tall, flowing beige-colored robe, long gray and white hair and beard. He seemed to be one 'adult' I was unafraid of. I looked up in confusion when he looked at me with sadness on his mouth and in his eyes, and he said, 'No, little girl, it is not time yet. You have to go back.' I awoke coughing up blood in the ICU. From that moment until just this year I *hated* my life. I tried suicide at sixteen and when that didn't work, I went to great lengths to sabotage my life. My life was lived on the 'other' side of the mirror, so to speak. No matter what I did, I was not allowed to die.

"When other people walk ahead in life, toward something, if I walk with them it turns out not to be right for me. This is what I mean by living on the 'other side' of the mirror. I have to turn around and go 'backward' in order for things to be 'right.' I am continually ostracized for this because, to most people, it looks like I am being silly walking 'backward' instead of reaching a destination going forward. The only people who seem to understand what I am really doing are children and those who had a near-death experience. I 'see' things others cannot. I 'hear' things others cannot, and, to a degree, I can read minds. I am not lying. I have not told this to anyone because I cannot seem to find a group of people 'like' me. I am forty-eight years old. Since I have quit fighting the inevitable, I am now able to approach the rest of my life with kindness and love for myself. The integration of my inner child to who I am today is actually being allowed to happen. Pretty exciting stuff!"

Obviously, Debi had many problems to contend with long before her surgery. Still, in her case, her near-death experience only served to deepen her despair, not lessen it. As adults, we make our biggest interpretive mistake in assuming that the way we might respond in a given situation is how a child would respond. Not so. Debi's life was greatly complicated by the contrast she experienced between the heaven of her near-death episode and the hell of daily fare. It took her a long time to make peace with having been "rejected" from the bright world on the Other Side of death.

Money, Mission, and Home

Look at what occurs once child experiencers mature: job satisfaction 80 percent, home ownership 68 percent. Add these to those long-lasting marriages and you get a picture of contentment adult experiencers can't even begin to match, and one that the general population might envy. Maybe it's the added years, the extra time children have to experiment with what works and what doesn't as they grow up. In fairness, adults are on the opposite end of the developmental curve, with the bulk of their lives behind them. It is interesting to note, though, that salary motivates neither adult nor child experiencers, as the majority tend to eschew money and materiality, possessions, and awards. Why is it, then, that so many child experiencers put such strong emphasis on home ownership? Adults can't wait to be rid of their mortgages; kids can hardly wait to have one, and once they get a home, they keep it. Their attachment to home, I believe, is a direct result of losing their "real home" when they were children. This wound appears to create a subconscious need to make certain that no one can ever take away their home again.

Youngsters seldom do anything about their mission (the reason they believe they came back to life) until they are older, even if they know what their mission is. Adults seem almost driven to communicate theirs and mobilize necessary energies quickly. Yet it is the kids who wind up doing more and making a more positive and lasting contribution to society. Perhaps this is another finding that simply reflects the age difference, but maybe not. I have observed that child experiencers tend to mature rapidly after their episodes, while adults become more childlike. Thus, while the kids cogitate and plan, their seniors take all manner of risks and "run with the wind." Emotionally, the kids come back as the grown-ups; the adults revert to being more like children.

Judgment

The nonjudgmental aspects of near-death episodes are touted by almost everyone, a result of the very real presence of unconditional love and forgiveness most adult experiencers report. But with children, another story emerges: many are met on the other side of death by a being whose role is that of a critical or caring parent-type. This parental figure either gives orders, judges them for past deeds, or in some manner prepares them to meet and fulfill their destiny by instructing them in advance on what to look out for and how to behave. Images of a critical or caring parent are most often found in cases from Asia and various indigenous cultures like those of the Native Americans, yet child experiencers from the industrialized nations describe similar "lecture" episodes as well.

It is not unusual for children to face an array of judges who have animal forms, not human, or to be sharply criticized for actions few adults would ever take seriously. If you consider how a child's mind works, you can better understand why small infractions would loom large and have far-reaching effects. Children personalize everything. The consequences of their behavior are important to them.

There is a counterpoint to the judgment issue among adult experiencers, and I would say it is the life review. Older children, teenagers, and adults have a lot of these—opportunities to witness or relive their past experiences in this life and see how their actions affected others. Even though some report a tribunal arrangement (with human-appearing judges actually judging them for past indiscretions, errors, or mistakes), most claim that it was "me judging me." And many were also subjected to fully experiencing the end results of deeds and decisions, even undergoing the pain and suffering they caused others to endure, so they could learn from what previously occurred and make significant change for the future.

On the subject of judgment, then, the most prevalent manner of disclosure for children seems to be the instruction they are given; for adults, what they are shown or must relive. The impact of judgment, or the lack of it, strongly interweaves itself throughout whatever comes next in the experiencer's life.

CHARACTERISTICS TO BE ALERT FOR IN CHILDREN

- A powerful need to have a "home," even if it is only their own bedroom.
- An equally important desire to have an "altar" of some kind in their "home." Anything on the altar is holy.
- An intense curiosity about God, worship, and prayer. Many insist their parents attend church afterward—any church is fine.
- An unusual sensitivity to whatever is hurtful or to lies, especially as reflected in world events and the "white lies" parents and siblings often tell.
- Loss of boundaries, as if they have "no skin." They may have to relearn social courtesies and common rules and regulations.
- An ability to merge into or become one with animals, plants, or whatever is focused on. Borders on self-identification in multiples. Can ease back to normal self-image with age and increased socialization.
- Heightened otherworldly activity and psychic displays. Drawn to mysticism and the paranormal.
- A change in sleep patterns. May forgo naps entirely in favor of increased flow states.
- An awareness of the life continuum and anything "future," including future memory episodes.
- A shift toward being a fast talker and fast thinker, with a driving need to create, invent, read, and learn. May be misdiagnosed as having attention deficit disorder (ADD). Explore alternatives first before considering drugs.[3]
- Behavior changes in school. Just as many become disruptive as withdrawn. This can carry over into family life, with authority figures merely tolerated.

According to Diane K. Corcoran, R.N., Ph.D., a former army nurse and leading proponent of educating medical professionals about the near-death experience and its aftereffects, especially in kids:[4] "Children may not realize that the things they are feeling are common aftereffects. They may be able to see things others don't, or they may at special times know things that are going to happen but find that nobody believes them. We need to listen to children. And we need to let them know they're okay.

"Just last week, in a workshop of nurses," Corcoran added, "a young mother said she had a two-year-old who had a near-drowning incident. She emphasized that they were not a religious family and she and her husband did not teach about God or church; however, since the incident, she said, the child has been talking about angels and wants to be one when she grows up. She drags the family to church now, and is very involved with all that happens at Sunday School. 'It's as if her angels are *personal friends*,' the mother remarked. 'What do you think is the matter with her?' Even after the lecture I gave on near-death states, she still was not sure that her daughter might be an experiencer."

HEALTH

For 73 percent of the child experiencers, aftereffects increased over the years. Participants were emphatic about making that claim, stating that the older they became the more exactly they fit the profile of characteristics, trait for trait. Some became ambidextrous afterward or switched handedness. A number of them showed me how their handwriting had altered as well. Changes could be that profound! Not everyone was so affected, though. A few participants noted only slight changes and tossed off their episodes to overactive imaginations when they were young.

Intriguingly, however, I found a correlation between those who reported the fewest aftereffects and those who were the most challenged healthwise as they aged. They were the same individuals.

I'm not indicating here that a lack of aftereffects means poor health. Rather, what I have observed is that there seems to be a link between a childhood repression of aftereffects and the profusion of health problems that can occur later.

The child who is expected to be "the same as always" after a near-death event can block the experience as well as some of its aftereffects, even to the point of denial that anything so ridiculous could ever have happened. Yet all too often there is a price to pay for such repression, not only in the increased probability of health challenges when older, but also in the individual's feeling strangely empty or lost, agitated that something important seems to be missing from his or her life that can't quite be identified or understood.

There are some experiencers who are permanently crippled or handicapped after their episodes, or are weakened to the extent that they go on to endure severe or chronic illnesses once grown. Nevertheless, the pattern of aftereffects is still apparent in most of them. Dealing openly with the impact of near-death states casts a decided advantage in how happy and healthy an experiencer can become.

Like adult experiencers, child experiencers show a preference for alternative approaches to medicine as they mature. All of those in my study who claimed now to have excellent health (77 percent) credited their good fortune to a more spiritual reverence for life, along with having turned to things like herbs, homeopathy, massage, and vitamin and mineral therapy for healing. As they aged, most found pharmaceuticals difficult to tolerate.

One particular case worth noting is that of Cheryl Pottberg of New York, who had her near-death episode at age thirteen during heart surgery. In her late thirties she suffered a cardiac arrest, which damaged her liver. She could not metabolize normal doses of heart medication, and it poisoned her system, necessitating the insertion of a temporary pacemaker. Two months later, while having open-heart surgery to correct the original heart defect, she had her second near-death experience: a reunion with her grandmother, who had been dead for thirty-three years, and a session involving "God's Word" and predictions for "the end of an age."

Millennial prophecies emerging from an adult scenario are rather common, but an experiencer as critically ill as Cheryl turning to a medical physician for help and receiving exactly what was needed via holistic means is nothing short of miraculous. Unable to endure further surgery, yet far from well, she discovered Gerald M. Lemole, M.D., one of the most respected heart surgeons in the country, who had shifted his practice to embrace a wide range of alternative healing techniques. Lemole is known to send patients with complex heart conditions to local health food stores before considering surgery. His success rate using holistic treatments is so high that it has become an embarrassment to his surgical colleagues.[5]

Part of the vitamin protocol he gave Cheryl Pottberg was the herb milk thistle, which is known to benefit the liver. Six weeks later, blood tests showed that she had near perfect liver function. Also, her heart condition has improved to the extent that she is back in college earning a degree in social work, determined to complete her mission of committing to paper "the prophecies of God."

SPECIAL HEALTH PRECAUTIONS FOR CHILD EXPERIENCERS

BLOOD PRESSURE: Although more adults than children exhibit a substantial drop in blood pressure after their experience, all should be aware that current medical opinion considers long-term low blood pressure a major component of chronic fatigue syndrome and therefore a disease that should be treated chemically. Experiencers who continue to be hale and hearty and energetic should let their doctors know that low blood pressure is *normal* for them.

LIGHT SENSITIVITY: All well-meaning adults shove children outside. Fresh air is healthy. Kids need it. But if the child is a near-death experiencer and the schoolteacher or coach or parent forces him or her to practice or play in bright sunshine for long periods of time, day after day, the results could be troublesome. Because of their unusual sensitivity to light, they can be subject to allergic reactions to bright sunshine or unusual states of fatigue followed by a weakening of the body's immune system.

SOUND SENSITIVITY: Peer pressure is hard for youngsters, and especially for teens, to contend with. Types of music listened to and decibel level comprise the mark of allegiance to whatever is "in." At dances, proms, parties and gatherings, even school-wide assemblies in the auditorium, sounds are blasted out, tuned "way up" or "far out." If the teenager is a near-death experiencer, any type of loud music or noise can be painful—even injurious. Most prefer nature's sounds, classical music, or the broad range of New Age music now available.

DECREASED TOLERANCE OF PHARMACEUTICALS: When a child is ill, he or she is rushed to a doctor or maybe the emergency room in a nearby hospital, where a shot is administered or pills are prescribed. This is standard procedure. But if the little one is a near-death survivor and suddenly more sensitive, possibly even allergic, to the type of pharmaceuticals normally administered to a child of his or her weight and age, the treatment can be more dangerous than the illness. Alert the physician.

The public, for the most part, is unaware that near-death states engender aftereffects or that youngsters are often affected in special ways. Thus, when child experiencers complain of strange headaches or manifest a series of colds or flu-like symptoms when there seems to be no good reason for such ills, they are told, "Toughen up, kid," or, "It's just your imagination." Considering the range of their new sensitivities, the wiser course of action may be to investigate their complaints.

PHASES OF INTEGRATING THE AFTEREFFECTS

The child you get back after a near-death episode is a remodeled, rewired, reconfigured, refined version of the original.

Whereas it takes the average adult experiencer about seven years to integrate the full range of aftereffects, it can take children two to three times that long. Why? Because of the extraordinary lengths they can use to deny, ignore, or block the reality of what happened to them and is continuing to occur. Fitting back into the family of origin is a survival necessity for children. And, *whatever the family suppresses, the child represses.* Comments such as these are typical:

Clara Lane, Belmont, Ohio. NDE at age ten, appendicitis. "I never felt free to talk about this when I was younger. People didn't and still don't believe things like this. But I know the truth, and that's what's important."

Carol Jean Morres, Long Beach, California. NDE at age fourteen, extreme distress in epigastric area. "Because others cannot accept my experience as real, I have had to keep it locked up inside me for the most part, and that creates a feeling of isolation and loneliness and of 'being different,' all of which is ultimately depressing. I guess the one word to describe others' lack of belief is anguish."

Beverly A. Brodsky, Philadelphia, Pennsylvania. NDE when nearly eight, during a tonsillectomy. "I had no childhood after my near-death experience. I felt cheated."

The process of integration, at least among those I have studied, takes place in four distinct phases. Some zip right through all four in rapid fashion, and with few distractions. Others take many more years than might seem reasonable. Each person responds to the phenomenon in unique ways. The following chart highlights what is average for most.

BRAIN SHIFT PHASES OF INTEGRATION MOST EXPERIENCERS GO THROUGH

Phase One—First three years

Impersonal, detached from ego identity/personality traits. Caught up in desire to express unconditional love and oneness with all life. Fearless, knowing, vivid psychic displays, substantially more or less sexual, spontaneous surges of energy, a hunger to learn more and do more. Childlike mannerisms in adult experiencers, adultlike behavior in child experiencers, a heightened sense of curiosity and wonder, IQ enhancements, much confusion.

Phase Two*—Next four years

Rediscovery of and concern with relationships, family, and community. Service and healing oriented. Interested in project development and work environment. Tend to realign or alter life roles; seek to reconnect with one's fellows, especially in a moral or spiritual manner. Unusually more or less active/contemplative. Can resume former lifestyle, but more desirous of carrying out "mission."

Phase Three—After the seventh year

More practical and discerning, often back to work but with a broader worldview and a confident attitude. Aware of self-worth and of "real" identity. Tend toward self-governance and self-responsibility. Spiritual development an ongoing priority along with sharing one's story and its meaning. Dedicated. Strong sense of spiritual values.

Phase Four†—Somewhere between twelfth and fifteenth year

Immense fluctuations in mood and hormonal levels. Often discouraged or depressed while going through a period of grieving—reassessing gains and losses from the experience, while fearful that aftereffects are fading. Many problems with relationships, money, and debts. A crisis of "self." If able to negotiate "the darkness light can bring," a depth of maturity and confidence emerges that is unique to the long-term effects of a transformation of consciousness.

---

* Child experiencers in my study who turned to alcohol for solace (33%) began drinking during this phase.

† Child experiencers who attempted suicide (21%) did so in this phase.

The seventh year is like a marker, a first birthday that celebrates the experiencer's ability to "bring to earth the gifts of heaven" in practical and meaningful ways. Somewhere between the twelfth and fifteenth years, maybe up to the twentieth, there is another marker—a second birthday—and it catches most experiencers unawares. *It is a second drop, a second shift.*

The second drop is like a second death, in that it heralds a time of life reversals and the need to ask some tough questions: Were the sacrifices I have made since my experience worth it? Am I capable of carrying out my mission? Is it possible to live a spiritual life in the earthplane? Have I been honest with myself? Are my aftereffects fading? If the experiencer can successfully negotiate the challenges of this second drop, a second shift is possible—a major advancement toward "the peace that passeth all understanding."

Every one of the child experiencers in my study who ever had a serious problem with alcohol started drinking during phase two—a period when relationships of varied types become primary and the pressures of pursuing further education or a job versus the need to launch their mission tend to overwhelm. As to why they drank, the majority said it was to ease the pain they felt or to escape the ridicule of their families and friends.

Of those who attempted suicide after their episodes, almost all of them did so during phase four. Also, most of those who had another near-death experience in adulthood had it in phase four. Example: a young boy drowned at the age of five, miraculously revived fifteen minutes later, and immediately began to "see through" people and act in "odd" ways. As he matured, what interested his agemates bored him. Behavior problems resulted. Once he turned eighteen, he joined the army, hoping he would die. He did, in an accident. He had another near-death scenario during resuscitation that explained the earlier one and gave him the courage he needed to transform his life.

The second drop that occurs is not always as perilous as it was for the young man just mentioned, but, unlike the "first birthday," this is a time of *reckoning* and *reassessment* when experiencers make major decisions that require new commitments. The first shift can be linked to the original near-death state. The second shift seems more dependent on choice, on the experiencer's willingness to surrender to a greater plan. Regardless of how integrated and spiritual an experiencer may appear to be after the seventh year, all pales by the power unleashed if the second shift occurs.

OUR TINIEST EXPERIENCERS

I want to emphasize that anyone at any age can have a near-death experience. That includes tiny ones still in the womb, babes being born, infants, and toddlers. Once they are verbal, our smallest experiencers do their best to convey what happened to them—through speech, drawings, words on paper, or actions. The way in which their attempts to share their story are received, determines, to a large extent, whether or not their episode has a positive influence on their life or is tucked aside, ignored, or repressed. Although the pattern of aftereffects cannot be denied, the experience can be.

These tiny ones, via their expressions and language, show signs that suggest they may have identified with the otherworldly imagery and behaviors they were once exposed to, rather than, or in addition to, that of earth and their earthly human family. Their temporal lobes, as they form, seem to build their "libraries" of shape, size, sound, smell, color, movement, and taste *to accommodate the otherworldly models provided by their near-death experience.* (The temporal lobes function as "libraries" in how they alter the input we receive—from the day we are born until we die.) This imprinting is augmented by sensory response and intuitive knowing to the extent that the child can seem wise beyond his or her years when, in fact, the youngster is simply responding to what feels natural.

Frequently, family and friends cannot account for the child identifying in this manner, or in having models of life and living different from their own; nor do psychologists have training in how to interpret what has happened to the little one.

With this in mind, here is a summary of the differences I have seen between how adult and child experiencers (especially the very young) tend to handle the aftereffects of near-death states:

Adults—deal with changes afterward, and the necessity of finding new reference points. They are challenged to redefine themselves and the life they live from another perspective. Before-and-after comparisons can be made.

Children—deal with the strangeness that what they encounter in the world around them does not match what they know and identify with. They are challenged to recognize the source of their uniqueness and accept the validity of what they have gained from the experience. What happened to them is the basis of all they know.

Adults integrate. Children compensate.

Contrary to my work with adult experiencers—where I found that it took most of them up to seven years to integrate their episode—I discovered that child experiencers can take twenty to thirty years or more to integrate theirs. This is not necessarily a gloomy thing, as compensating is the major way children have of adjusting to the changing conditions in their lives. Once they make such accommodations, though, it usually takes until their middle years before they question "why." A child is perfectly capable of balancing two differing worldviews in a healthy manner if they have supportive parents or relatives who are good listeners as well as talented at creating boundaries with an invisible "fence" around them, so that the child can explore and experiment without ridicule or feeling "foreign" or bad. This is done by being open and encouraging while still maintaining basic disciplines so necessary for healthy growth. There are gentle or thoughtful ways parents can hold their ground without "squashing" or inhibiting the child (much information is now available, through books and magazines, to teach parents how to do this).

MUTUAL PARENT-CHILD EPISODES

Occasionally in my work, I have come across cases where both a parent and that parent's child were experiencers. Some of these parents readily shared their accounts with their families and were especially sensitive to the needs of their child experiencer. Most, however, were not this communicative, nor did they attempt to determine if any of their children might have had near-death experiences, too—even when it was obvious that a child of theirs could have. Sons and daughters, then, were often left to fend for themselves without benefit of the guidance and understanding their parents could have provided. Two such cases follow.

L. S. Gordon had her episode at the age of three during a tonsillectomy. Like typical child experiencers, hers was the Initial type. She never labeled her episode growing up because it wasn't as detailed and experientially complex as descriptions she had heard of her mother's. She and her mother never discussed this. Forty-seven years later, she was finally able to re-experience her own scenario's radiance and allow all of the aftereffects to manifest—due to the manner in which her mother died. As she tells it, "Bette Gordon, like an NDE Medicine Woman, with intent calm, was reading Betty Eadie's book *Embraced by the Light*[6] when she suddenly propped it up in the crook of her elbow, looked at the book, and exited. Incredible! She died with the reassurance that what she had always known was true." L. S. Gordon wrote a book-length manuscript of poetry as a way to reconcile what had happened to her. An excerpt:

> *If we could see as God does,*
> *we might find legions of angels surrounding us,*
> *legions of souls upholding us, learning*
> *from us, humbled and amazed*
> *by what we dare. Do we lose hope sometimes, give in*
> *to fears that make us monsters? We do: To bear*
> *the dense, particulate fruits of this world,*
> *we must be capable of anything.*

The second example is that of Michael and Ralph Kelley of San Antonio, Texas. Ralph, Michael's father, contracted typhoid fever at age thirteen. The illness was so bad that when his ordeal was over, he had to relearn how to walk. During the high fever, he experienced a scenario that so overwhelmed him that it shaped the rest of his life. Although his legacy was the Light's Perfect Love, which he showed in the caring and forgiving way he treated people throughout his many years, he never discussed his episode until just before his death, when his son Michael insisted that he "fess up." It was important for Michael to hear his father's story, since he had also experienced a near-death state when he was just two years old. He had opened the car door during a family outing and had fallen out, suffering a brain concussion and other injuries.

According to Michael: "I distinctly remember watching from outside of my body as my father picked me up from the street and put me in the car. I also remember a city bus stopped in traffic and seeing a brilliant white light that seemed to surround everything." Michael often revisited the scene in his mind. "My school grades always suffered because the message from those replays was more profound than anything offered by my teachers." Another car accident and brain concussion in adulthood brought on a second episode. Afterward, Michael was so shaken that he lost control of his life. It wasn't his father, but near-death research that he read, that finally made an important difference for him. Since his confrontation with his father, Michael has been more in touch with the truth of his own experience. He says:

"Why life? We live to execute a properly conceived life plan whereby each human being becomes an artistic genius. The light's knowledge and love are the paint and the inspiration that we, God's little brushes, apply to Earth's giant canvas, allowing each of us to add our few, unique brush strokes to God's Grand Painting of Life."

In both of these examples, the children went through needless periods of confusion because their parents, for whatever reason, never invited dialogue about otherworldly journeys—neither their own nor those of their children. What happened in these two families underscores the fact that just because one has shifted to a more loving and spiritual way of living does *not* mean that new reality is translated into every aspect of one's life.

Those who have undergone a brain shift/spirit shift still make mistakes and ignore, without meaning to, the very loved ones most in need of their understanding and their care. This happened to me with my own children, and I've seen the same thing occur with ever so many others.

SOME ADVICE FOR PARENTS

- Sleep patterns for the young alter abruptly afterward. Children may experience less nap time, increased flow states (where they "blank out" into nothing, and end up feeling refreshed and invigorated as a result), and restlessness. Some may fear sleep and suffer nightmares; others seem exhausted on waking, as if they had "toured the universe" or attended some type of school while asleep. Reliving the near-death episode in the dreamstate is commonplace. Encourage the child to share this. Listen.

- Love changes for child experiencers. It is *normal* for them to lose the parent/child bonding. That doesn't mean they cease to be loving and thoughtful, but it does mean they tend to act more distant than before. The child switches gears and begins to mature faster, become independent. Interests change from those of the family, sometimes radically.

- After their experience, most kids have a marked decrease in their ability to express themselves and socialize. Since language is the most critical skill anyone has, stimulate the child's speech with your own. Promote dialogue with question/answer games, group storytelling, reading out loud, and speaking on "pretend" microphones. Encourage the child to participate in community projects as a volunteer.

- Writing and drawing are just as important as dialogue. Ask the child to make a special book about his or her near-death experience. Have lots of paper handy for pages that cover: newspaper account of death event (if any), drawings of each aspect of near-death episode, description of what occurred, information about dreams afterward, sketches of any "beings" that continue to appear, poems, ideas, thoughts, and extra pages to record more things later on. Choose a title and bind book with ribbon. A project such as this validates the experience . . . *as well as the child's feelings.* The parent(s) should keep a journal of the whole affair, too. This helps to stimulate parent/child bonding and can serve as an invaluable resource once the child matures. Consider giving the journal to the child when he or she becomes an adult. I would encourage a child experiencer of any age to create such a book. Aafke H. Holm-Oostenhof of Holland did, and the exercise changed her life. I am lucky enough to have a copy of Aafke's book. She may yet have it republished.[7]

- With newborns and infants, if there is any chance their life could have been at risk or if there was birth trauma, do this as soon as possible: outline the baby's body with gentle hand or finger strokes. Repeat several times each day until they can turn over and are more active. Practice baby massage, gently exercising their limbs and pelvis, along with gentle back and shoulder rubs. This will help to bring them back from "the otherworlds" in a healthy and positive way should they have had a near-death experience. If they did not, well, it's a good exercise for any parent to use with "new arrivals" as it promotes trust and self-confidence.

- Child experiencers of any age tend to withdraw, can even reject hugs and cuddles. Recenter them in their bodies using techniques such as: patting their shoulder when you pass by, touching their hand if you speak to them, nudging a knee from time to time, or rubbing their back. Smile. Teach them to pat and nudge you like you do with them. Pets are wonderful for touch therapy, as are plants and gardens, making things with clay, perhaps cloth and paper sculpture. Make cookies that the child can help prepare, then turn him or her loose shaping the cookies *by hand* into imaginative designs. Do food sculptures (you can find more inspirations in books like *Play with Your Food* by Joost Elffers).[8]

- Speaking of food, watch sugar levels. Child experiencers are more sensitive than the average child to chemicals and excessive sweets, especially refined sugars and "replacement" sweeteners/products. Practice good nutrition; use veggies and maybe a piece of fruit or cheese and crackers for snacks.
- Since most near-death experiencers exhibit electrical sensitivity after their episode, avoid over-exposure to electrical items (especially electric blankets). Full-spectrum lights are preferred to fluorescent ones. Limit the use of computers and television and make certain plenty of water and fresh air are available during use of technological equipment, and in general.
- Child experiencers of near-death states are sensitive to their environment. Here are some more tips: cottons usually work best for clothes and bedding. At meals, have a burning candle for a centerpiece, and say the type of Grace where each person in turn can offer his or her *own* prayer. This is especially meaningful to the child. Flowers put kids at ease. Let them pick and arrange the flowers, if possible. Be careful of too much exposure to bright sun (midafternoon), and music turned too high (loud volume is often painful to them). Recheck former medication as it may now be too potent.
- Visualization techniques are a must for the child to learn, as well as some kind of focusing exercise, so they can revisit the "other worlds" at will. Wherever one has once been in consciousness can be returned to and re-experienced. A child experiencer does *not* have to attempt suicide to go back (nor does a teenager or adult). This can be done through desire and intention and the "magic" of visualization (there are suggestions for this in appendix 1 at the back of this book).
- Child experiencers, even in the early years of grade school, are perfect candidates for the study of philosophy, of morals and integrity, especially if using the Socratic method—where asking questions inspires deep probing responses and critical thinking. They can easily engage other students and promote class discussions. Talk to the teacher and/or school administrator to see if such study can be done as a part of class enrichment.

SIX

Many Types, One Pattern

Probably a dozen times since their death I've heard my mother or father, in an ordinary, conversational tone of voice, call my name. They had called my name often during my life with them . . . it doesn't seem strange to me.

—CARL SAGAN

JUST AS THERE ARE many ways in which one can undergo a transformation of consciousness, numerous are the types of conditions that can trigger a near-death state. Whether the initial experience can be recalled or not, the pattern of aftereffects remains the same, and what occurred is recognizable *more by that pattern* than by any memory of the episode. The reason is straightforward: the aftereffects validate the phenomenon.

Two particular aspects of this are rather curious: how a near-death experience can occur *without* the individual being clinically at risk of dying, and how an experiencer can display the aftereffects pattern, yet have no recall of a near-death scenario. By taking a look at these factors, we can gain a better sense of how truly widespread the incidence rate of the phenomenon has become and how dynamic its reach.

WHEN NOTHING THREATENS

It is possible to have a near-death experience that has as great an impact and the same patterning of aftereffects as the worldwide phenomenon, and not be in the throes of physically dying. No one can explain why this occurs; we just know it does. Officially, the research term for the anomaly is *near-death-like experience*.

How many people have had such an episode? Well, in 1992, the International Association for Near-Death Studies discovered that, of the 229 experiencers attending their annual conference that year, 37 percent had their episodes in settings unrelated to anything that could be construed as life-threatening.

Children have near-death-like experiences, too, especially after they have formed concepts of death that are meaningful to them and pondered the question "Can I die?" I've noticed that powerful shifts in their awareness take place once they consider this. Many go on to dream about dying afterward; some have nightmares. Similar to mini-rehearsals, a child's death dreams can actually be healthy explorations of mortality. There are times, though, and always without provocation or warning, when a simple death dream can suddenly escalate into a deeply involved experience resembling near-death, and with the same far-reaching consequences. The three dreams that follow illustrate this.

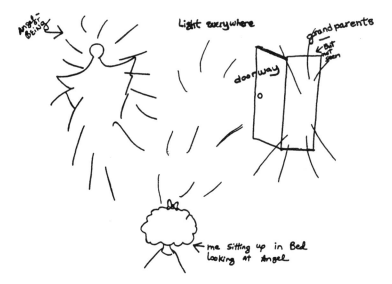

Margaret Evans, NDE the night before her seventh birthday.

According to Margaret Evans of Roscoe, Illinois, the night before her seventh birthday was a life changer. She and her twin sister were sound asleep in the same room when, for no apparent reason, Margaret sat bolt upright. Actually, only half of her did—the half that projected out of her body. "I looked straight at this being of light just a little off to my left but in my line of vision. The being generated the white-gold light I was bathed in—a very soothing, accepting, loving light. It was very bright but not hard on my eyes. The angel was neither male nor female and had no distinct features, just the sense of them. Communication between us was telepathic. My first thought was a remembrance that this moment had been prearranged between us before my birth. It was an opportunity for me to leave this life if I so desired, and the angel was there to offer me that choice. To my right, coming out of the light, were my dead grandparents. They seemed to be on the other side of a doorway. I knew they were there but I couldn't see them. I wanted to go to them so badly. I was happy about the reunion waiting for us, but then I turned and somehow saw my sister and myself still asleep in bed. I thought of my parents in the other room and how I would miss them if I left. They would be very hurt. I decided to stay."

Margaret claims that as soon as she made the decision, the angel told her she would live a long life and then disappeared, along with her grandparents and the light. Never once did she regret her decision to stay, as "the angel and my deceased grandmother have protected me throughout the years since."

Muriel E. Kelly of Chandler, Arizona, had rheumatic fever at age six and was left with a serious heart murmur that necessitated a lot of bed rest. At the age of twelve, still very sickly, she fell into an unusually deep sleep when suddenly "I found myself standing on a cobblestone road with people around me dressed in bright robes—red, blue, pink. Everything was so bright and sunny. Birds were singing. Baby angels were smiling and flying around. I saw all different sizes of angels. The music was hauntingly beautiful."

Hearing her name called, Muriel turned to see Jesus beside her, dressed in a white-and-red robe. "He knelt down and gave me a hug and I hugged him back. He told me we were going somewhere to talk. When he held out his hand, I noticed the hole in the middle of it from the nail." As the two walked along, people nodded and smiled, and children played. "When we arrived at the building, we went inside and walked on a red carpet to a throne where Jesus let me sit on his lap. We talked and he let me hug and kiss him. He had long brown hair, brown eyes, a wonderful voice, and skin darker than mine."

Jesus told Muriel that someone was waiting for her, so the two walked out the door to the street and over to an apartment with many doors, laughing all the way. He told her she would know which door to knock on. As he watched approvingly, she found a door that seemed somehow special. A voice inside beckoned her to enter. It was her mother, who had died when Muriel was nine, leaving behind five children. Their reunion was love filled. "I asked Mama where Daddy was, and Cecil, Willie, John, and Paul. Mother told me they weren't here 'cause it wasn't their time. I had no idea what she meant, so she took me to an area where we sat on a cloud and looked over the whole world. My mother located my dad and brothers riding in a car. We could see right through it. Dad was driving, and we heard my brothers and Dad crying, saying, 'I wish Muriel was still here. We miss her. If she were here we wouldn't be mean to her.' My dad said I was in heaven with Mama and I'll never be back. I didn't know what was going on. I started crying for my dad and brothers. I remember really sobbing and wishing I was back with them. Well, I got my wish. I woke up in bed."

Muriel healed completely soon afterward and went on to live a normal life. She even passed the navy's physical when she enlisted—no heart murmur was detected, nor has any trace of her early health traumas ever reappeared. Her doctor was as surprised about this as she was.

Tom Meeres of New Jersey was fourteen when, on a summer night, his peaceful sleep turned into a terrible fall through a spiral or tunnel

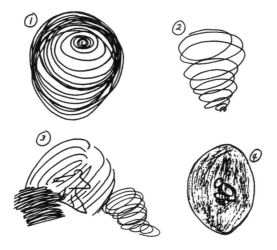

Tom Meeres of New Jersey, NDE at age fourteen.
(1) First view of the spiral (tunnel). (2) Perspective while falling.
(3) Slowing down near the wall of the tunnel. (4) Velvety black void.

(image 1). He had had falling dreams before and had experienced a similar sensation under anesthesia, so the thought "here I go again" was of some comfort—yet this "dream" was to be unlike anything before or since.

Falling was fast; (image 2) he heard undulating noises and garbled voices. He slowed enough to recognize that the tunnel walls were ribbed, (image 3) but the falling continued until he became nauseous. Just as he wished for death to stop the terror of it, he suddenly found himself in a velvety dark void, feeling totally supported and cared for. He curled up in the fetal position (image 4), but panicked with the thought that this isolation might last forever. No sooner did he think that than he discovered he was in a dark cave.

"To the right is a beautiful light coming from a round opening above me. I am drawn in and through the light (image 5) until I find myself look-

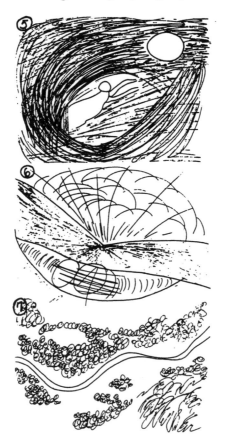

(5) I am drawn through the light. (6) An immense cliff. (7) Perspective from high above a landscape.

(8) Seeing many openings in the cliff.

ing out over the sheer drop of an immense cliff. (image 6)." Fear struck once more, but the light helped him float, then fly: "I'm high above a strange landscape with a river valley that seems to stretch out forever (image 7). The light suffuses everything so that forms are discernible only in shades of gray. All fear is gone and there's just a wonderful lightness of being. I am myself, yet there is no feeling of separateness from the light."

Sensing a city and people beyond his view, he wondered who they were and what they were doing. He noticed his arm as he flew toward them, expecting to see a shadow. There was none, for light shone everywhere. Before he could think of a question, his grandparents appeared before him. "I can't tell you what they look like or how I hear them, but they say who they are, that they care about me, that I must go back, that I have a purpose. I don't want to go. They strongly urge me to, and I agree." As he turned around, he recognized that he had gone too far. The openings in the cliff were too numerous to count, and he couldn't tell which one he had emerged from. Getting back became a struggle, like swimming against the tide. He started to panic. Finally, he saw the right opening and fell through (image 8).

"The euphoria upon awakening," said Tom, "was greater than anything I have ever felt. Was it a dream? No, it was too real. Were the people my grandparents? They said they were, but what's important is that they care about me and that I have a purpose in life. Who can I tell about this? No one. That's why I suppressed it for twenty-seven years."

Other types of conditions can foster a near-death-like experience. Here is one that involves a blow to the head during a rock fight; another concerns a tumble down flights of stairs, as well as a "visitation" from a ghostly dog.

At the age of ten, Timothy O'Reilly of New Jersey happened to get caught in a rock fight between two groups of kids. The empty lot where the fight occurred was long and like a big pit, with swampy water about a foot deep at the bottom. To cross the swamp, Timothy had to negotiate a walkway of wooden planks laid atop discarded tires that zigzagged through high weeds. Three-fourths of the way across, the opposing group began throwing rocks at him.

"I started to run back to my friends," explained Timothy, "but when I was about ten feet from dry land I looked up and saw this kid holding a huge rock over his head. I think the rock was about the size of my ten-year-old skull. As he let go of it, I remember thinking, 'This thing is going to hit me.' I turned my head to the right just before the rock hit me square in the back of my head."

He was knocked unconscious by the blow and fell into the swampy water. "Although I felt like I was still standing, everything went black. My arms were stretched out to either side and I heard a buzzing sound. I couldn't see my body as it seemed transported elsewhere, but I had one. I began to flail back and forth as my legs started to sink or melt. They disappeared, and I had no torso and there was no gravity. I wasn't afraid. All I thought of was the buzzing sound. It reminded me of a science-fiction movie about a dinosaur that I had seen on TV. A bird would send an electrical charge from his long beak to destroy cities in Japan, and whenever the bird sent out that charge, it made a buzzing sound like the one I experienced. Later, I had to go to the hospital for a few stitches."

Round Trip, the touching forty-minute video that captures the transformations undergone by people who have had near-death experiences, is the creation of Timothy O'Reilly.[1] He never connected his interest in the phenomenon with what happened to him as a child until he researched the video. Filming *Round Trip* did more than assist him with recall; it seemed to be the stimulus he needed to release long-suppressed aftereffects. "I had a spiritual growth spurt doing the project," he chuckled, "and all kinds of intuitive flashes and synchronicities occurred. They haven't quit."

Laura Hanner of Redding, California, was at her wits' end at age thirteen. She had been repeatedly raped by a close family member, yet when she asked her alcoholic mother for help, she was beaten and accused of lying. Upset, she fell down five flights of stairs in the apartment building where she lived. "I do not remember how I ended up at the bottom of the stairs. Somehow I did. As I was sitting there crying, I became aware of this clicking sound. I looked in the direction of the sound and saw a dog coming to me. He was built like a German shepherd but as white as snow. That dog came up to me, sat down, and spoke via mental telepathy. *He spoke to me in my head.* It scared the heebie-jeebies out of me. I did not know what to think, but I was spellbound. He told me that I would never again have to feel fear, and that I was going to be watched over from then on. Well, I was astonished. *Dogs don't talk.* But that one sure did!"

Afterward, Laura, who had been failing in school, suddenly excelled, with new and exciting ideas flooding into her mind day and night. People seemed to come out of the woodwork to protect her whenever she needed them. The appearance of Space Dog, as she called her mysterious visitor, signaled a complete change in her life. "I am just a little four-foot, ten-inch Puerto Rican woman. Ever since Space Dog, I've had visions and they come true. I'm not trying to impress anyone, and I have nothing to gain by making this up. It happened."

Laura's talking dog did not act like a mental projection or a hallucination. He behaved as if he was a messenger of hope from the Other Side, who validated her sense of worth while inspiring her to transcend the poverty of her life.

Near-death-like experiences defy the reference points established in near-death research. But the fact that they do match the overall pattern of the near-death phenomenon, both in experience types and in their aftereffects, demands that we entertain new possibilities of thought.

A particularly exciting possibility is that perhaps death is auxiliary, *not causal,* to the phenomenon. Perhaps the real orchestrating force of near-death and near-death-like states is that of the soul as it journeys through the human condition, making course corrections along the way, revamping and revitalizing itself whenever necessary.

TUCKING IT AWAY

"The incident is probably my most vivid memory, and I can 'play' it back step by step, without change, as I did when I was a young child. It is doubtless the most profound and distinct experience of my life." Larrick Stapleton of Wynnewood, Pennsylvania, spoke those words. He was only four when death came to call, and he's in the minority. Not because he died and had a near-death episode, but because he has never forgotten it. Children are *six times* more likely than adults to tuck away their experience, lest it interfere with the demands and expectations of growing up.

Because of this tendency, child experiencers are subject to recurring dreams or nightmares about what happened to them, or such behaviors as an excessive need for attention or privacy, reckless activities as if they had a "death wish," or a haunting sense that something's missing.

Here is just such a case, and it involves a lifetime of strange occurrences until, at last, family secrets were revealed. Greg Smith of Kansas City, Missouri, speaks for himself:

"In the forefront of my consciousness has always been my earliest memory. I doubt most people think of their life in chronological order, but my earliest awareness was the equivalent of an intense, wonderful, mystical, heavenly LSD trip, although LSD hadn't been discovered yet. It turned out not to have been caused by drugs, but something even more sinister. I had always assumed it was a vivid, intense childhood dream that for some odd reason just stuck with me throughout life. What confused me, however, was the fact I remember little of my early childhood except that 'dream.'

"I recall, without any type of incident or 'introduction,' the feel of those 'footsy' pajamas I wore as a toddler, slowly, in child-time and child-steps, climbing a marblelike, translucent stairway that gradually circled to the right. My left hand reached up and slid along the smooth balustrade. In the sky were millions of twinkling light-stars emitting sounds similar to thousands of wind chimes, underscored by choirs of beautiful voices in perfect harmony and unison. Normally I was a fearful kid, but this was a journey of confidence. I only hazily remember being guided by someone on my right, perhaps more of a force, or only a partially visible being. I know I was the only flesh-and-blood human on that lovely stairway.

"As the stairway curved around more tightly to the right, I came to a landing. There, on a plain, but thronelike chair sat a feminine entity, a 'good fairy,' as perceived in my child-mind. She was in a dress sort of like the good witch in *The Wizard of Oz* [movie] but without any crown; and, rather than pink, she wore a shimmering gown with a bluish-white cast to it. She also didn't carry any magic wand!

"The fairy/angel/being took me on her lap, and I recall about six beings standing in a half-circle to my side, her front. My attention was focused on her, however. They played no conscious part in my experience.

"We talked for a few minutes—about what, I don't think I ever knew. I just knew it was a pleasant experience. Then, for a forgotten or never known reason, I had to leave. With her assistance, I slid off her lap with no urge of wanting to linger. I felt complete, wonderful, and loved. And with my right hand on the railing, after a few steps down, I just seemed to dissipate, this memory joining into the fragmented memories of a normal childhood. And I remember nothing else of the strange, yet very real experience.

"As I mentioned, I always believed it to be an intense, colorful, childhood dream that was continually in the forefront of my mind, kind of like a song you can't get out of your head. As I grew up, I was drawn, more so than any of my friends, to spiritual things, especially things to do with heaven, but never making a connection to my always-conscious 'dream.'

"Years and years later, as an adult, I was told in the course of discussing family history, that my grandmother, who lived with us for the first few years of my life, had to be institutionalized after she began exhibiting bizarre behaviors. She had threatened my mother (her daughter) out of the blue one day with a large knife; one morning my dad found her frying eggs still in the carton! And early one evening my mom heard a commotion from my room and found her mother trying to suffocate me with a pillow in my crib. Fortunately, a pediatric resident (at the University of Kansas Medical Center) lived across the street, happened to be home, was summoned by my frantic mom, and revived me. The blueness left my face and was replaced with a healthy pink glow.

"My grandmother wasn't so lucky. She no doubt had Alzheimer's disease, although the term wasn't known then. She was deemed a threat to our safety and, still a Colorado resident, was sent to live the last two years of her life at the Colorado State Hospital in Pueblo, where she died.

"The missing piece to my puzzle of what had happened to me was finally solved. I'd had a brief, childhood near-death experience and have longed to return to that wonderful place all of my life. Many times I've felt 'homesick' while sitting in my home! But I take comfort in the knowledge that where I am is not my real home. Someday I'll be able to reach the top of that beautiful staircase and step into the Land where Love has Its Eternal Day."

Amanda Csanady of Glenview, Illinois, also does not remember having had anything like a near-death episode when she was two and a half. Her mother was informed six hours after she was rushed to the hospital that she had suffered a febrile convulsion caused by an ear infection. Her ear troubles necessitated numerous surgeries over the years that followed, finally reversing her 40 percent hearing loss. Today, she is an active young woman who happens to exhibit the profile of brain shift/spirit shift aftereffects.

Her mother sent me a collection of her childhood drawings, which are

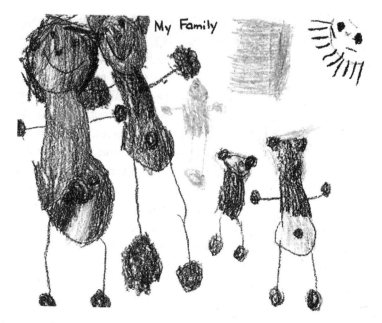

My Family

Amanda Csanady, NDE at age three and a half, drew this picture (1) of her family a year after the experience.

full of rainbows with tunnels through them and mysterious yellow doors leading to secret places. I have included a sampling of her artwork to show how effectively children can communicate the deeper truths of their lives without words.

At the age of three and a half, a year after her brush with death, Amanda drew a picture of her family (image 1). Shown are Mom and Dad, her older brother and herself, and a small, featureless, yellow non-entity close to a yellow door, both barely visible in the middle to top placement. A contemplative white sun, outlined in yellow, shines black rays from the upper right and frowns sadly (its features are also black).* Mom

---

*Always notice what young children do with the color yellow. They often use yellow to depict spirit beings, new life from the womb, souls leaving bodies, and affirmations of spiritual truths. If engaged in frequent out-of-body episodes or feeling detached from their body for whatever reason, it is not unusual for kids to draw themselves as a featureless, yellow nonentity. In Amanda's case, however, she depicts herself hovering midway between her connection to the spirit being from the world behind the spirit door and her living brother and parents. The sun is blackened, unable to help her, and looks sad. Suggested here is a conflict Amanda could have been feeling at the time about which world she should inhabit.

(2) Amanda's drawing at age four and a half.

has a broad streak of yellow drawn across the area of her uterus, as if Amanda was somehow acknowledging that her mother was pregnant.

At four and a half, as a kindergarten assignment to make placemats, Amanda did another drawing (image 2). The faint, almost invisible door to the spirit worlds is on the left this time, with a happy self-portrait in the middle. On the right, there is a small rainbow with a tunnel through it. All three central figures are suspended in air and outlined in yellow. (Notice a richness of detail, showing she is adjusting to her life, but still connected to and part of the otherworld readily available through the mysterious door. As is true with most near-death experiencers, she is awash in feelings of love and loving thoughts.)

At age seven, she won a Fun-velope contest held by Mead Johnson (image 3). Her drawing was used for the month of June in their 1987/1988 Enfamil calendar.[2] A tunnel leads into the large rainbow on the right; a swimming pool is below it (both are suspended). The train-track sidewalk goes to the far right from a rainbow door on a happy red house filled with windows. There are a canopy of hearts, much yellow, many details, and the sun, finally full strength and at the upper left. (Note lavish, uplifting elements and a bright sun where most children draw it, upper left. Lots of yellow, but only behind structured outlines. Although mysterious openings

(3) Amanda's drawing at age seven and a half.

abound, the picture illustrates a joyous return to family bonding and the confines of Earth.)

Amanda's use of yellow and the imagery she drew is significant. Youngsters who have undergone near-death scenarios often tend to picture themselves suspended between worlds as Amanda first did, or as a featureless yellow nonentity—and many times with a mysterious yellow door nearby—until parent-child bonding is re-established or at least of more importance. When I ask those young ones who use yellow and these images why they do this (not all child experiencers do this, but the majority do), they usually shrug, smile, and say, "It's a secret." Additionally, I have been privy many times to drawings done by children shortly before they died. Not only did their artwork depict foreknowledge of their coming deaths, but the majority *drew the continuance of their lives in yellow*—as streamers, bubbles, circles, wispy clouds, or butterflies, winding upward to the left-hand corner of the paper, *where they had told their par-*

ents God was. (Remember Amanda's sun? It was strong and bright *only* at the upper left.)

The color yellow is an important aspect of near-death states in general. Of those experiencers who saw a light during their episode, kids and adults alike usually describe it in terms of yellow-gold-white, with yellow predominant initially, as if it were a kind of filter or lens.[3] Interestingly, yellow, as a color in the light spectrum, cannot be seen or captured on film directly. Since there are no color cones for yellow on the human retina, to us it is a product of brain chemistry. In photography, it emerges from the chemical processing of film images. One way or another, yellow results from chemicals. Considering the force of its light during near-death states and transformations of consciousness, I suspect yellow usually heralds extraordinary accelerations of chemical activity in the brain proper—another clue to the validity of the brain shift/spirit shift theory.

Amanda Csanady's drawings, then, along with her peculiar use of yellow and the fact that she displays the aftereffects pattern, convince me that she had a near-death episode at the age of two and a half . . . irrespective of "missing memory."

People like Amanda are nonexperience experiencers, those who claim nary a glimmer of memory about anything so exotic as a near-death experience, yet live out their lives as if that's exactly what once happened to them. This situation is especially pronounced among the very young.

Here is a brief presentation of four such cases of adults trying to make sense of why they have always been oddly different from their fellows.

Debi Canon, Fair Oaks Ranch, Texas. "Died" at age ten months during surgery on a tumor formation in the nervous system that had left her paralyzed from the waist down. Her death was expected; her survival wasn't. "I grew up 'knowing' there was something special about my being alive. I knew I had a specific job to do, yet I resented being here and being denied my 'assignment.' People thought I was weird. They would nod and change the subject whenever I was around. I was unusually intuitive, could read minds and see into someone's soul. I had a strong sense of being guided to where I was needed."

Debi's IQ tested out at the genius level. She has an abstract mind, a master's degree in nursing, is proficient in science, and has "healing hands." Animals seek her out. She is like no one else in her family. A

Debi Canon, NDE at ten months of age.

homeowner with a long-lasting marriage and no particular regard for money, she is exceptionally healthy and totally devoted to spiritual growth and learning. The older she gets, the more pronounced the characteristics become that would identify her as a child experiencer. As her "mission," she is actively integrating spiritual healing into traditional medicine.

Randi, California. Serious health condition at age six weeks, not expected to live. "Growing up I always knew that God was real. From my earliest memories I felt very close to God. As a child, I would talk to God frequently. When I needed comfort I would picture myself in God's lap and feel secure. I have never had a good relationship with my mother. She has always treated me coldly, as did my brothers. My father was distant but there if I needed him. I felt as if I did not belong in my family. Until the ninth grade, I struggled academically in school. I couldn't seem to learn as fast as the other children. Then it was as if a light went off in my brain and learning became easy and fun."

Randi had a serious case of eczema until she was fifteen, when it finally cleared up. Her mother used to say that she was allergic to her own skin. She has since begun using herbs and homeopathic remedies. Randi is a homeowner with a long-lasting marriage and no interest in money. She has an unusually bright, intuitive mind with enhancements in math and a love of history. She had "trauma-memory" nightmares as a child. She is a natural at interpreting dreams and sensing the future. She looks much younger than her years, has a glow about her, and exhibits electrical sensitivity and what she calls "gifts of the spirit" (the spiritual extension of psychic abilities).

Virgil Rinquest, Montana. "Died" at age six months after being suffocated by his older brother. "I started having psychic experiences as a young child. I remember loving to see rays of light coming through the door window and imagining that the light took me to Jesus. My guardian angel was always helping me. I felt connected to strangers and would walk down the street 'sending' love to people I never met. A beautiful white dove landed in front of me while I was praying once. That kind of thing often happens to me."

Virgil was both religious and spiritual at a very early age and eventually became an ordained minister. There were more instances of sibling abuse from his older brother, making life difficult for him. He endured four decades of traumatic nightmares, all linked to his "death" as a child. He is a homeowner with a long-lasting marriage. Money does not motivate him; a deep desire to help others does. Missing any math and music enhancements, Virgil did receive a Ph.D. in psychology and is fluent in numerous languages. He has a quick and agile mind, is highly intuitive, and remains to this day in communication with angels. The ethereal messages he claims that angels give him enable him to balance his double career of minister and psychologist. He looks younger than his years and is currently writing a book for African American men like himself, concerning how to handle conflict successfully and heal the wounds of racial discrimination.

Sandra S., Los Angeles, California. Received too much ether during a tonsillectomy when she was nearly five and "died" of the pneumonia that resulted from the surgery. "People commented on how smart I was. I learned to read right after my experience and was reading books beyond my chronological age. I was a 'whiz' at math and spelling. Elementary school was lonely; I felt different, probably because I was too smart and overweight. Animals seek me out when they're injured and I can heal electrical things, too, except watches—they don't last. I love mythology and had a facility for languages, but I gave up the idea of becoming a mathematician or a linguist to study comparative religions. That satisfied me for many years."

Sandra involved herself in Christian doctrine when young but converted to Judaism after experiencing Shabbat (the day of peace and completeness). She felt she had "come home." After one divorce, she married a child survivor of the Holocaust, and now teaches in a Jewish community. A homeowner who has been married a long time, she finds money utterly distracting. Considered a genius with "tons of energy," she wonders if her eating disorder is the result of having blocked out what happened to her during the tonsillectomy.

Nonexperience experiencers such as those mentioned are a growing phenomenon. Considering the 70 percent experience rate estimated for children by Melvin Morse, M.D. (85 percent with children who have a cardiac arrest), and today's increasingly efficient resuscitation techniques, it is highly possible that near-death episodes in childhood far outnumber those among adults.

With this in mind, I offer the following eight clues that might be helpful in identifying child experiencers, irrespective of what they do or do not remember.

1. A life-threatening illness or accident sometime during childhood, or an unusually stressful delivery at birth.
2. Behavior changes immediately after this incident: becoming appreciably more somber or gregarious; exhibiting increased intelligence or a hunger for knowledge; tending toward abstractions and a maturity beyond one's age; having an intimacy with God or otherworldly companions; acting aloof or estranged from most family members and friends; suddenly more sensitive or allergic; disinterested in activities "normal" for one's age group while drawn to topics like history, mythology, and language or math and science; infinitely more creative and inventive; vivid psychic and visionary displays; an awareness of future.
3. If still young, doing nearly everything earlier than agemates— drawing or writing poetry about other worlds, other realms, other ways of looking at things beyond what would be expected for the child's age.
4. Evidence of a learning reversal once in school; having to go from abstract thinking on the conceptual level back to concrete, practical details on the physical level. This can confuse or threaten teachers.

5. Drawn to anything that feels like "Home," and will tend toward homeownership even if money is scarce.

6. Motivated by service to others or somehow making a contribution to the greater good, rather than getting rich. If married, apt to stay married.

7. While maturing, the profile of brain shift/spirit shift characteristics (in chapter 2) fits better and better, as if the aftereffects are on the increase or expanding.

8. An inordinate attraction to material about near-death states and to people who have had such experiences, combined with a sense or feeling that something important is missing in their own lives or somehow forgotten.

Morgan J. Blank of Pleasant Hill, California, is typical: "I have been searching for thirty-three years to try and understand why I am the way I am. There were many times when I felt I was crazy or delusional. I knew that the experience I had when I drowned in our family pool at the age of two affected me. It has affected the way I view the world. It has affected the way I view people, humanity, love, our purpose on this planet. It has affected me down to the core of my being and on the cellular level. It has affected every aspect of my life and I never knew why . . . *I just knew!*"

Sooner or later, as in the case of nonexperience experiencers like Morgan J. Blank, the power of the near-death phenomenon tends to reassert itself. Spontaneous recall is common. One man was simply surfing the Internet when he happened upon an account that caught his eye. In an instant, a memory of his own experience returned to him, complete with those aftereffects he had managed to repress. It happened so fast and with so much power that he fell off his chair.

As children age, full recovery of their episode (be it near-death, near-death-like, or nonexperience), and the subsequent integration of the many aftereffects into their daily lives, becomes paramount. The majority turn to God for the assistance they need, or ask their angel friends for guidance. Others initiate rigorous programs of study and self-analysis, while a few practice specific yoga breathing techniques that they claim help them to surface the dormant aspects of themselves. For those who go to therapists, counselors, psychologists, or psychiatrists, benefits or lack thereof have a lot to do with the professionals' sensitivity and training.

The difficulty both child and adult experiencers have with professionals relates more to prevailing notions of what is culturally acceptable than it does with the judgment factor of whether or not the experiencer is mentally or emotionally fit. Lily Tomlin, the famous comedian, used humor to focus on this disparity: "Why is it when we talk to God we're said to be praying, but when God talks to us, we're schizophrenic?"

Sometimes an experiencer is lucky enough to find a therapist who is also an experiencer. When this happens, there is instant rapport, and miracles follow. To the extreme, I know of people who were involuntarily committed to psychiatric hospitals simply because they exhibited the normal aftereffects of the average near-death survivor. A few were later released when a new therapist assigned to their case, who happened to have had such an episode, recognized "who" they were. Those professionals who consistently have the best record working with experiencers are the ones trained in transpersonal psychology.

Joseph Benedict Geraci, an adult experiencer who is now an administrator of the New Britain School System in New Britain, Connecticut, wrote a Ph.D. dissertation titled "Students' Post Near-Death Experience Attitude and Behavior Toward Education and Learning."[4] He made some comments in his proposal that are pertinent: "Transpersonal psychology addresses those human experiences that take consciousness beyond the ordinary ego boundaries of time and space. Experiences include unitive consciousness, cosmic awareness, mystical experiences, and maximum sensory awareness."

Transpersonal psychology, as a legitimate field of understanding and exploring varied states of mind, is by its nature geared to experiencers. Other ways to "touch" memory are also effective, including art therapy, vision quests, philosophical counseling, and consciousness coaching (refer to appendix 1 at the back of this book). Reconnecting the heart with the mind, not just "remembering," is the true goal.

SEVEN

6

Cases from History

Only those who can see the invisible, can do the impossible.
—THOMAS JEFFERSON

POWERFUL SUBJECTIVE EXPERIENCES are the outworking of a force capable of causing life-changing aftereffects. The strength and intensity of this force determines the experience. And this force is spirit and spirit is real. How we respond confers value and meaning.

When spirit intervenes, it is physically felt. Some describe this intervention as a sudden "bolt of light," akin to an electrical charge. Others report a calmer energy like a force field that glows with a brilliance unique unto itself. The energy is always powerfully present, and the association made is usually to that of a light that is alive, intelligent, all-knowing, and all-loving. The very young who encounter the Darkness That Knows use similar terms—"sparkle," "shimmer," "pulsate," "radiate"—describing a soft, inviting "bright dark."

Thus, the presence of spirit is perceived as that of a force. What effect might incidents like this have had on the history of civilization? Have any of these child experiencers, once they matured, made a significant impact on society? My answer to both questions is a resounding *yes*.

While the near-death phenomenon has not been noted historically in the phenomenon's now-familiar vernacular, what is recorded does offer tantalizing hints that many of our revered historical figures may indeed have experienced near-death episodes that presaged their greatness.

Use the following guidelines, as well as the eight clues suggestive of how to recognize a child experiencer given in the preceding chapter, to identify such people.

- *A serious illness or accident between birth and age fifteen that nearly claimed the individual's life.* Any record of an otherworldly vision or dream connected with the event will be highly unusual, unless he or she lived in a "primitive" social structure that honored spirit.
- *Marked differences in behavior afterward.* The subject may be ahead of or different from agemates for that historical period, becoming more so as the years advance, with a nontraditional or nonconformist attitude. He or she may be possessed of a charm or charisma that attracts people, animals, etc. He or she could be considered socially retarded when young, yet unusually creative and bold; unafraid of death; highly intuitive; aware of things future.
- *Presence of the cascade of aftereffects.* Although it is difficult to find existing records that register such characteristics, personal letters, journals, and even poetry can reveal a great deal. Electrical sensitivity seldom applies, but a unique sensitivity to the sun, sound, and the types of medication used at the time are often noted. Be alert for excessive complaints about stomach upsets, numerous colds, or serious bouts with the flu. Even though most are blessed with robust health, increased sensitivities, allergies, and occasional fits of depression may have made health issues a concern.
- *An almost obsessive drive to accomplish a particular task or project.* Most will have been workaholics with no sense of time or money, yet inclined to have property or be aligned with distinctive places or groups, whether or not they ever married.

Using these indicators, it is possible to find historical personages who so closely match the profile of aftereffects and behavior characteristics that it is extremely likely they underwent near-death experiences as children.

Most of the saints in the Catholic Church had their first experiences of God as children, and many conform with the indicators. Great visionaries and prophets of all persuasions often match, as well.

For a specific example of perhaps a quintessential child experiencer, consider Abraham Lincoln.[1] When he was a child of five, Lincoln fell in a rain-swollen creek and drowned. His older friend Austin Gollaher grabbed his body and, once ashore, "pounded on him in good earnest." Water poured from Lincoln's mouth as he thrashed back to consciousness. Although there is no record of the young boy's confiding an otherworld journey to anyone, ample remarks were made by friends and family who observed his sudden craving for knowledge afterward, his insistence on learning to read, and his going to exhaustive lengths to consume every book he could find. Five years later, just after his mother's death and before his father remarried, he was on a wagon driving a horse and yelled, "Git up," when the horse kicked him in the head. He hovered at death's door throughout the night, with his sister Sarah in attendance. On reviving, he completed the epithet aimed at the horse: ". . . you old hussy." Little more can be gleaned about the incident until, as an adult, and referring to himself in the third person, he is quoted as saying, "A mystery of the human mind. In his tenth year, he was kicked by a horse, and apparently killed for a time."

Among the characteristics suggestive of a brain shift/spirit shift that Lincoln came to exhibit: the loss of the fear of death, a love of music and solitude, unusual sensitivity to sound and light and food, sensing in multiples, wildly prolific psychic abilities, a preference for mysticism over religion, absorption tendencies (merging), dissociation (detachment), susceptibility to depression and moodiness, increased allergies, regular future memory episodes, hauntingly accurate visions, the ability to abstract and concentrate intensely, clustered thinking, charisma, moral upliftment, a brilliant mind, perseverance in the face of problems and obstacles, and a driving passion about his life's destiny.

Certainly the argument can be made that Lincoln's many idiosyncrasies were the result of his extreme poverty as a youth coupled with a relentless determination to succeed. Yet nothing during his early years indicated genius; none of his unusual talents appeared until *after* he had survived two close brushes with death. As an adult he nearly died again, and once more he displayed signs that he might have had yet another near-death episode—with additional aftereffects.

The same could be said of Albert Einstein. At the age of five, he nearly died of a serious illness. While still sick abed, his father showed him a pocket compass. The fact that the iron needle always pointed in the same direction no matter how turned, impressed upon him that something existent in empty space must be influencing it. Although speech fluency did not occur until around the age of ten (perhaps because of dyslexia), family members recall how deeply he would reflect before answering any question—a trait that made him appear subnormal. Interestingly, he learned to play the violin at six (later delighting with the mathematical structure of music), taught himself calculus at fourteen, and enrolled in a Zurich university at fifteen. Like Lincoln, he was plagued with nervousness and stomach problems and nearly died from these afflictions as an adult. Also like Lincoln, the unusual characteristics of his temperment and talent trace back to the age of five and afterward. [2]

J. Timothy Green, Ph.D., a fellow near-death researcher, has a fascinating notion as to how Einstein may have been inspired to produce a theory of relativity. He notes that Einstein was seventeen when he was a student in Zurich, Switzerland, of Albert von St. Gallen Heim, a distinguished professor of geology. Heim had once fallen while climbing the Alps and described a most peculiar death experience. Following this incident, he collected similar accounts over a twenty-five year period from others who had fallen or had similar accidents. He presented conclusions to his research in 1892 and published his findings that same year. In so doing, Heim became the first person in modern history to publish a collection of what would later be referred to as near-death experiences. [3] According to Green,

> It is of record that Einstein was a student of Heim in the years immediately after the publication of this paper, and was privy to comments like: "When people fall from a great height, they often report that time seemed to slow down or stop completely—as it expands." Years later, when Einstein was interviewed as to how he came to work on the relativity theory, "He had been triggered off . . . by seeing a man falling from a Berlin rooftop. The man had survived with little injury. Einstein had run from his house. The man said that he had not felt the effects of gravity—a pronouncement that led to a new view of the universe."

There is no question in my mind or in Green's (and he stated this to me) that it is important that these two men knew each other, and that Heim had an influence on the young Einstein. It is reasonable to suppose that the professor's near-death experience and his subsequent research paper on the subject had a profound effect on his curious student, laying the groundwork for Einstein's famous theory and maybe even validating what had previously happened to him when a lad of five.

Similar patterns can be observed in the lives of Queen Elizabeth I, Edward de Vere the 17th Earl of Oxford (who may well have been the *real* Shakespeare),[4] Mozart, Winston Churchill, and Black Elk.

A Lakota Sioux, Black Elk witnessed the Battle of Little Bighorn and participated in the Battle of Wounded Knee. But that's not why we know of him. He is famous because a white man by the name of John Neihardt interviewed him in 1930 and 1931 and forever captured his visions in the singular triumph *Black Elk Speaks*.[5]

Black Elk first began to hear voices and see spirit beings coming from the clouds as early as age five, but this confused him and caused many complications. At age nine, however, he fell seriously ill, his legs and arms swollen, his face puffed up. A disembodied voice spoke to him: "It is time. Now they are calling you." Two men appeared from out of the clouds, holding spears that flashed lightning. "Hurry," he was told, "the Grandfathers want you." With that, he left his body behind and flew away into the cloud realms, joined by the men he "knew" were Thunder Beings.

The imagery in this, a full-blown transcendent near-death experience, is among the most spectacular I have ever come across: flying horses, flaming arrows, forests, mountain peaks, cloud realms, explosions of color, beings of various types. Featured in his scenario are the Six Grandfathers (great powers), who taught him many things and both told and showed him his future, which would include hard times ahead for his people and special powers he would be given to help them. Then, his mission was revealed to him: he must *save the world* (a pretty tall order for a nine-year-old). Astride a bay horse and from the highest of mountains, he gazed upon the whole of the world he was to save and saw more than he could tell and knew more than he could ever say. All knowledge was his.

Beings he "knew" as the Riders of the Four Directions came to him and he saw in a sacred manner the spirit shapes of all things, and he knew that all people must live together as one people. "And I saw the sacred hoop of my people was one of many hoops that made one circle, wide as daylight and as starlight. And in the center grew one mighty flowering tree to shelter all the children of one mother and one father, and I saw that it was holy." A spotted eagle took him back to his home and became a life-long "messenger" for him.

"I could see my people's village far ahead, and I walked very fast, for I was homesick now. Then I saw my own tipi, and inside I saw my mother and my father bending over a sick boy that was myself. And as I entered the tipi someone was saying: 'The boy is coming to. You had better give him some water.' Then I was sitting up and I was sad because my mother and my father didn't seem to know I had been so far away."

Black Elk remained as if half-dead for twelve more days. His experience replayed repeatedly in his mind, but he could not share it. If he tried, "It would be like a fog and get away from me." Too young to understand, he felt like he no longer belonged to his people. Feeling himself to be a stranger, he hardly ate and longed to be back in the spirit world.

Black Elk began to hear voices and have visions on a regular basis, including warnings of troubling times in the future. A medicine man recognized a powerful light coming from him. He seemed to levitate at age thirteen as he was prepared by his father for the Battle of Little Bighorn. By age seventeen, he was warned in a visitation from the Thunder Beings that a penalty of death by lightning would be meted out if he didn't share what had happened to him when he was nine. He finally told his story to a medicine man, who arranged for the whole tribe to make costumes and then act out each element of his story in ceremony, to benefit the whole tribe. Realizing that saving the world really meant healing people, he became a medicine man and began to heal the sick.

Black Elk was very much aware that it was not he who cured people, but the Great Spirit. This humility lasted throughout his lifetime. He lived a rather active and colorful life, but in the twilight of his years and nearly blind, he became a recluse. His conversion to Christianity was a mere convenience, for he knew that God was the God of all. Biographers were discouraged from writing about him, as it was against federal law at that time for Indians to discuss Old Ways or the religion of their past.

Nevertheless, John Neihardt, who was familiar with the Lakota Sioux and was accompanied by his interpreter, Flying Hawk, went in search of Black Elk. Why the old man was waiting for him as if he was expected, and then broke federal law in trusting this white man and sharing with him his greatest vision, is a mystery—until you know something about Neihardt. At the age of eleven, Neihardt had "died" of a high fever and had a dramatic near-death experience. Never the same again, he became as Black Elk . . . one of those who *know*. The recognition and camaraderie between the two were instantaneous, and they became as family. Published in the thirties, the book Neihardt wrote went out of print but was rediscovered by Carl Jung and republished in the sixties. It became a best-seller and has sold well ever since, hailed, even by Native Americans, as the Rosetta Stone of authentic Native American spirituality.

A less familiar name, perhaps, is that of Walter Russell. He had his first near-death experience at age seven, and it prepared him in a strange way for the financial disaster his family would soon suffer. In 1881, at age ten, Russell was pulled from school and sent to work, keeping "a good heart" because of the unfailing faith he had gained from his otherworld journey. A musician since infancy, he secured a church organist position at thirteen and thereafter became entirely self-supporting and self-educated, earning his way through five years of art school. When he was fourteen, his plans were interrupted by black diphtheria and another near-death episode, in which he was officially pronounced dead by an attending physician. He claimed to have discovered the secret of healing during this event, as he felt he had entered into "at-one-ment" with God.

These two near-death experiences set the stage for dramatic periods of illumination that would occur every seven years throughout Russell's life. According to Glenn Clark in his biography of Russell, entitled *The Man Who Tapped the Secrets of the Universe,* "He escaped encyclopedical educational systems of information-cramming and memory-testing which filled other children's lives until they were twenty-five. He used his precious youth to find out the secret mysteries of his inner Self. His whole life has been used in the search of the real Self and the relation of this real Self to the selective universe of which he knows himself to be a vital part."

Russell excelled in whatever he turned a hand to, and won lasting friendships and lucrative art commissions. He had a studio in Carnegie Hall in New York City, became a commissioned sculptor for President and Mrs. Franklin Delano Roosevelt, was a longtime friend of Mark Twain, and painted and sculpted Thomas Edison. Walter Russell's motto was "Mediocrity is self-inflicted. Genius is self-bestowed." At age forty-nine, he suddenly was enveloped within the fullness of cosmic consciousness. This state lasted for thirty-nine days and nights without abating. "My personal reaction to this great happening left me wholly Mind, with but slight awareness of my electric body. During practically all of the time, I felt that my body was not a part of me but attached to my Consciousness by electric threads of light. When I had to use my body in such acts as writing in words the essence of God's Message, it was extremely difficult to bring my body back under control."

Once he regained use of his faculties, he set about to record the experience in *The Divine Iliad* and then spent six years penning *The Universal One,* a text containing the drawings and revelations given to him of the universe and how it worked, covering such subjects as chemistry, physics, and electromagnetics. He later corresponded with Albert Einstein about his own theory that this is a "thought wave" universe created for the transmission of thought. His second and lasting marriage was to English-born Lao Russell, herself a visionary since childhood, who grew up knowing she was here "to change the thinking of the world." Together they established the University of Science and Philosophy and published many books, including a home-study course on spiritual principles. Although both have long since passed on, the University continues their work in offices located near Waynesboro, Virginia.[6]

A final example is Valerie V. Hunt, Ph.D. Very much alive and vigorous, although retired, Dr. Hunt was the very first researcher to objectify electronically the aura of light around people, places, and things, which, she showed, does indeed exist and has specific color frequencies that register consistent and measurable waveforms. I have seen some of the films taken of her experiments, especially those of the human aura, showing how it expands and contracts according to mood, attitude, and interactions, and I can attest to the impact these films have on people—entire crowds have been moved to tears. To actually *see* the electromagnetics of aural energy fields play out right in front of your eyes is an awe-inspiring privilege. Her work is a scientific milestone.

Her early years were rather difficult, though. She was in a coma at the age of three, with dire predictions for her survival. Not until she was an adult working in the field of psychotherapy was she able to revisit that harrowing time and recover her childhood near-death experience, complete with the sensory world she had once known. Considered a mystical child by her mother, she early on had a reputation for being so far ahead of other kids that most avoided her. She escaped by composing poetry, drawing, singing, and thoroughly indulging in the spirit realms around her. Before the coma she had been an outgoing, exuberant child. Afterward, she became serious, quiet.

According to Hunt: "One day, quite by surprise, my parents took away my paints, my paper, my crayons, and my books. No one wanted to hear about the fun things my mind created. My frustration mounted daily—my world had rejected what I found exciting. I mumbled to myself angrily with little satisfaction. My parents didn't listen. Finally, I started 'multiplying words' with God, for real. I flashed back to my months in a coma when I experienced being with God in a beautiful land of flowers, sweetness, and love; quiet serenity. I wanted to stay forever, but I recalled that God had said I would go back to the world to bring it beauty. I complained because I did not like the world, and besides I had no talents for beauty. I was just a little girl who sensed beauty but didn't know how to create it. I remembered God assuring me that I would be given ample talents to do my 'beauty work.' It was then that I became aware of people, the room, and things I had known before. I had returned from my distant journey.

"At first, adults praised my pictures and writings, expecting I would grow to be an artist. But also I sensed that despite my new gifts, the world wanted me the old way—a little, ordinary girl, doing what normal little girls my age did. It was then that I hid in a deep, dark hall closet . . . where I sat feeling quite protected, so that I could argue with God. I knew it was all God's fault. He had pushed me out of Heaven, given me skills that no one would let me use. In spite of my anger, God was kind and understanding with a new solution—if I couldn't bring beauty, I could bring knowledge."

Hunt continued, "To this frightened, angry little girl in a dark closet, the answer seemed strange, although also sustaining." Hunt expresses a common lament of child near-death experiencers when she says, "Although I had been enthralled at my post-coma skills, there was also a haunting suddenness to my change that was scary, particularly when adults said that it was not 'real.' "

Her full story, and her twenty-five years spent as one of the foremost researchers in the science of human energy fields, is chronicled in her book, *Infinite Mind: Science of the Human Vibrations of Consciousness*.[7] As director of the electromyographic laboratory in the physiological science department at the University of California, Los Angeles, and as a researcher in the shielded "Mu" room of the physics department, she was able to document scientifically the light, color, and sound of "invisible" energy networks and how they relate to human health. She evidenced what psychics see and healers sense, as well as the common perceptions of those who have undergone a brain shift/spirit shift. She explored the energy patterns of light and spirit, and proved them real.

History is replete with stories such as those I have just relayed. What happens to children is significant, for it directly engages evolution's nod. Our science, art, culture, our discoveries, and the multitude of decisions and acts that make up our history, all are profoundly affected by little ones who flit around the edge of death's curtain, then return, forever different.

Raymond A. Moody Jr. believes that the near-death phenomenon itself is a primary factor in stimulating the growth of culture throughout the ages. He bases his finding on the fact that the entire tradition of intellectualism in the West can be traced back to sixteen men, among them such scholars as Pythagoras, Democritus, Socrates, and Aristotle, and that eight of the sixteen had experienced a near-death or out-of-body state. Records exist that suggest all sixteen used a single near-death experience as a central model in their formulation of the concepts for matter, reason, and truth.

He publishes a newsletter that goes into detail about these sixteen men, as well as other aspects of near-death research, including what he calls "the empathic death experience."[8] He has found that bystanders, be they loved ones or medical personnel, can "co-live" an individual's death in the sense that they can subjectively join in consciousness with the dying to help escort the individual into the light, perhaps experiencing elements of departure that may mimic the classical pattern of a near-death state, and/or sharing in some indefinable way the power of forgiveness and love.[9]

Moody feels that once people realize how easily they can participate in life's fullness, and make a profound difference in their own lives and the lives of others by doing so, there will be a spiritual revolution like nothing the world has ever seen.

EIGHT

⑥

Evidence for a Life
Continuum

We are all islands in a common sea.
—ANNE MORROW LINDBERGH

WHEN DOES THE SOUL enter the body?

Most traditions claim at first breath. But what if that's wrong?

Challenging the age-old assumption that first breath heralds the entry of the soul are both a recent medical discovery and an observation I made while interviewing child experiencers of near-death states.

The medical discovery is that the fetus at twenty-six weeks, or six months in gestation, can feel and respond to pain like an infant. This means that surgery on fetuses and newborns or, for that matter, third-trimester abortions, can no longer be performed without consideration of the pain threshold and welfare of the new life, not just those of the mother. Nor can physicians and religious leaders continue to justify withholding anesthesia for newborns during circumcision; the excuse "It's traditional" is now null and void.

In my overall study, I observed that prebirth memories usually began at around the sixth or seventh month in the womb, with fully one-third of my participants having such memories still intact years later. Recall of the actual birth event was commonplace overall, although greater detail was given by experiencers born prematurely or exposed to trauma or extreme mood swings from the mother within three months of birth.

Some had recall as a fetus earlier than month six, even of their conception and of actively taking part as a spirit in choosing their own DNA. Most of those who spoke of remembering their conception, however, said they "floated" in and out of their mothers' wombs until finally "settling in" when fetus formation was more complete.

Thus, medical research of fetal awareness and responses to pain directly overlaps with the period when the majority of children in my near-death research reported the beginnings of memory as a soul resident within a human body.

This unexpected link suggests that by the third trimester the fetus has a developed consciousness with faculties in place—that it is an inhabited body undergoing the final touches necessary before birthing from a water world to one filled with air. How we regard and treat a fetus, therefore, has less to do with mother or medicine than with how we feel about the reality of spirit.

Most birth and prebirth memories are clear and coherent, yet will quickly fade or be repressed if the child, once verbal, is ridiculed or silenced when expressing those memories. If child experiencers are allowed to be themselves without pressure, doors to their world swing wide open. What they say may seem senseless unless we remember that, with kids, *how they feel* about what they perceive matters more to them than any logic, imagery, or detail. Most of what they report, though, is not only accurate but startlingly mature, as if they, as souls, were comfortable with leaving and reentering a life continuum existent beyond that of the earthplane.

The idea of a life continuum, of life before birth and after death, has been broached repeatedly. Here's what I noticed in a quarter century of research about the varied aspects of this most important of all mysteries.

CHOOSING TO BE BORN

Not everyone I interviewed who had birth or prebirth memories claimed to have had a choice in the process of leaving where they were to come into form, but the majority did. I examined the adult case of Berkley Carter Mills in *Beyond the Light* to establish a sense of how experiencers tend to remember this. He was "killed" attempting to load compressed cardboard into a truck at his job. His life review, conducted by Jesus, started at conception. An excerpt:

He relived being a tiny spark of light traveling to earth as soon as egg and sperm met and entering his mother's womb. In mere seconds he had to choose hair color and eyes out of the genetic material available to him, and any genes that might give him the body he would need. He bypassed the gene for clubfootedness, then watched from a soul's perspective as cells subdivided. He could hear his parents whenever they spoke, and feel their emotions, but any knowledge of his past lives dissolved.[1]

In the same book, I also spoke about Alice Morrison-Mays, who has become something of a celebrity for giving public concerts in her home despite dealing with the pain of emphysema and a collapsed adrenal system (Addison's disease).[2] Besides near-death states, she could also recall prebirth memories, but chose to remain quiet about them until recently.

Alice remembers operating from the viewpoint of the soul in deciding which parents to choose before incarnating. A candidate for family that resonated with her was a musically gifted couple who were eager to have another child after having lost a baby son soon after his birth three years earlier. Feeling especially welcomed by them, she made the choice to be their child and basked in joy and anticipation for most of the nine months. "About the time of my birth, my peaceful and happy gestational existence was shattered. I found myself being 'hit' with and immersed in terrible shadow and dark mistlike clouds. The impact of this gave me sudden pain and despair. I seemed to be swimming in agony. I didn't want to go on with the birth but I couldn't return to where I had come from."

The death of Alice's maternal grandfather was the cause of the problem. "The unexpected shock of it was a blow to my mother, who absolutely adored her father. She suppressed this shock, along with the depths of her grief. What she 'held in' hit me with full force. She was determined not to express her feelings because of her fear that doing so would jeopardize the birth of her second child, now at full term. An additional impact on me was the medication the doctor gave to hold off my arrival. So, in effect, I received a 'double whammy' and was lost in the trauma of it all. Four days later, birth was forcibly induced, and with great reluctance, I was born, apparently in good health."

Alice believes that her mother's decision to suppress grief directly affected her in her unborn state, leading to, on the positive side, an unusual emotional sensitivity that helped in her career as a symphony cellist and, on the negative side, a rare and severe form of emphysema that was genetic in composition and slowly crippled her.

EMBRACING A BIRTH AFFLICTION

Arvin S. Gibson, in his paper entitled "Near-Death Experience Patterns from Research in the Salt Lake City Region,"[3] wrote about the case of a young man named DeLynn who was told during his near-death episode that he, as a soul, had chosen to be born with a debilitating disease. Quoting DeLynn: "The specific choice of cystic fibrosis was to help me learn dignity in suffering. My understanding in the eternal sense was complete—I knew that I was a powerful, spiritual being that chose to have a short, but marvelous, mortal existence."

But with Christina Moon of Eureka Springs, Arkansas, the issue of choice differs. She had two near-death episodes: one stemming from the emergency cesarean section performed on her mother (she was too large for a natural birth and "got stuck"), and the other at three months of age during plastic surgery to correct a deformity (she was born with a harelip and cleft palate). "I had an angel around me all the time," Christina recalls. "She passed her finger over my mouth before I was born and left me with my harelip. But I never felt anger about it because I was always aware of her love for me." Christina received the "gift" of a handicap without complaint but has no memory of actually choosing it. She harbors no regrets about it, as the compassion she has gained from dealing with her deformity has become a tremendous advantage for her in hospice work and midwifery.

LETTING THE MOTHER KNOW

Expanding on the idea of the child remembering life before birth, it is a well-known fact that women throughout the world who are about to become pregnant typically either somehow meet their baby's spirit in advance of conception or dream about their child early on in what is termed an "announcing dream." This phenomenon has been investigated by numerous researchers over the years, among them Robert L. Van de Castle, Ph.D., an expert who authored *Our Dreaming Mind*.[4] The consistent accuracy of these announcements implies that the soul is not only capable but also interactive when making itself known.

N.T.A. of Omaha, Nebraska, provides us with an example. Now an adult, she experienced a near-death scenario at age thirteen months when she bit an electrical cord. "With my first pregnancy, I knew it was a girl. She came to me in my dreams several months before conception, a totally wonderful nature girl who loves the outdoors. With my second pregnancy, sunshine came shining through and a boy spirit appeared in my mind. I heard him say, 'I'm here.'"

A mother from Portland, Oregon, offered: "Before my last child (a daughter) was born, I saw her twice, once in a small child's body, looking at me, and once right after her birth, as a wonderful sort of butterfly-shaped light flash—extraordinarily beautiful and bright." She continued, "The whole mental state of pregnancy is one big altered state of consciousness. It's like a *'near-life experience'*—you get a little peek behind the veil."

REACTING TO A CHANGE OF PLANS

How does one explain toddlers who detail in graphic terms their mothers' attempts to abort them when they were still in the womb? Or little ones who inform their parents that they chose to kill themselves *while still babies* because they didn't want to stay here? Yes, I have encountered many such cases. Here's one that incorporates both extremes.

Dorothy M. Bernstein of North Olmsted, Ohio, had a total of four near-death events, two in childhood and two as an adult. Her childhood accounts centered around the cessation of breath because of her choice to die. Today, we would say that she was a victim of sudden infant death syndrome, or SIDS. But her understanding of what happened to her is quite different from how we might interpret it. She claims, "I knew the truth about how my mother tried to abort me, and even again at five weeks before I was born, me, the seed of an alcoholic, a rapist, an adulterer, an abuser. Who could blame her?" While still a virgin, her mother had been raped. Dorothy, as a fetus in the womb, said she was aware and knew all that had happened. "I never cried as a young child. I remember being wet and hungry and thinking, 'Don't cry or she'll kill you.' My mother thought I was such a good baby, but I remembered the pain."

Dorothy noted that her crib was kept in her parents' bedroom after her mother married. One day, at the age of ten months, she witnessed some sexual behavior she was not meant to see and was punished by her father. She can vividly recall the painful confusion that preceded her decision to "go home," and then knowing exactly how to kill herself: by expelling all the air from her lungs and constricting her chest muscles to make her heart stop. Her last remembered thought was, "Oh, God, how could he hurt me like that?" and God's mysterious reply, "Perhaps he was trying to protect you." As she explains it, that "voice" so startled her that she gasped, which restarted the breathing process. Her account is filled with descriptions of a brilliant light, focusing on the mirror's reflection of an angel picture, having a spirited dialogue with a tiny person perched at the head of her crib, and promising God: "I will never forget from whence I came, nor will I ever deny you."

Nonetheless, at the age of three and a half, badly traumatized by the neglect and abuse she received from her mother after the birth of her mother's "love child" (her half-sister), she recalled once again making the decision to "go home." She used the same method, with the same results. Only this time, Dorothy said, feelings of warmth and love coming from the crown of her head convinced her that God wanted her to live and to help her sister. Breath returned, but, sadly, the situation with her family worsened. When I spoke with Dorothy about her two bouts with breath stoppage as a child, she mentioned reading a newspaper article about sudden infant death syndrome. "The doctors suspect the infants die because they just forget how to breathe. Not true! *I chose not to breathe!*"

Sally Dunn, a grandmother from Gila, New Mexico, gives us another way to view "a change of plans." "My daughter Jennifer's first child, Sashena, drowned at eleven and a half months. Jennifer 'knew' Sashena would not be here long. Very unusual day when it happened. The soul returned in her brother, Jasper, four years later." Sally noted that Jasper seemed to be in a hurry to grow up, yet he made strange sounds. "I puzzled over the sounds for months and then, Aha!, realized what it was. It was the noise a person would make when trying to close off passages to water coming in through the nose and throat. I knew Jasper would stop making those noises once I told his mom, and that's what happened." When Sally shared her revelation with Jennifer, she had one of her own. "Mom, when you had an abortion, that was the same soul that was in Sashena and is now in Jasper."

REMEMBERING PAST LIVES

The plan of the soul seems to encompass multiple dimensions of existence, as well as countless lifetimes. Children speak of this as casually and confidently as they might inquire about dinner. What follows are a number of accounts from my files.

The father of five-year-old Gregory Buxton of Montreal, Quebec, tells about his son's close call at birth. "Gregory did a loop loop in his mother's womb and got the cord tied around his neck. Every time he would try to come through the birth canal, the cord would tighten and he would retreat back into the womb. When he was finally delivered, he was blue and unmoving for quite some time. Today, Gregory looks at people with a depth of love that is inexplicable. He claims to remember heaven and past lives. He told me in detail how he had been a fighter pilot during World War I and had been shot down in Europe. He went through his death, telling me how long it took him to die because 'there weren't any doctors around.' He told me how he had lived in New York in an earlier life and that he had hung around his present sister before her birth so, through her, he could experience where we were living in Brooklyn. He said he was disgusted to see how New York had gone downhill since the day when he last had lived there."

Margaret Evans, a near-death-like experiencer, explained: "I have no memory of being inside my mother; neither does my twin sister. Just previous to birth, I was very high up above the planet with other spirits. There was quite a group of us and although we couldn't 'see' each other, we all knew we were together on a mission. A terrible thing was about to happen on earth that could not be stopped and we were needed to help out." Margaret described seeing a gigantic mushroom cloud coming toward them in the sky, a cloud that meant instant death to many people, and recalls how busy she and the other spirits were, assisting the dead in "crossing over." Years later, she finally learned what had occurred—it was 1945 and atomic bombs had been dropped on several cities in Japan. She remembered dying before the mushroom cloud incident, as a little girl of about five or six in a small village in England. "I was riding in the front seat of a car with [a man] who seemed to be my uncle. He was speeding and lost control. We slammed head-on into a stone wall. The split second before impact, I shot out of my body. I was very happy with the family I had then and wasn't supposed to die as young as I did." In her present life, she was frustrated as a child to discover that the father she had now looked similar to her previous father in England.

Rhona Alterman-Newman of Cherry Hill, New Jersey, who was pronounced dead at the age of six months after surgery for a strangulated hernia, began having past-life memories as a youngster. Feelings of horror and fascination were often triggered, for instance, when she was driven past a large stone mansion that stood between her two grandparents' homes. "I could 'see' kids playing outside on swing sets and seesaws. I'd tell my parents this and they would tell me to shut up. I knew it was an orphanage. I knew the layout of the house, and I could 'see' a green tiled bathroom. Either my little brother, or I myself as a little boy, got hung in there. My older sister in this life was there, too. I contacted one of my grandmothers and asked her about the house. She said it wasn't an orphanage, but I insisted. It took her a long time to find out that in the late 1800s it had been a Jewish orphanage. None of us could have known that."

Denise Grover of Lansing, Michigan, recounted, as so many parents do, that "because of rather stifling religious limitations, I had no concept or belief system to accommodate ideas about reincarnation. However, my son Neil, at the age of three, began that introduction. While sharing a meal with myself and his older siblings, Neil boldly announced, 'I was dead before, but now I am alive again!' We all found this amusing, to say the least, since there appeared to be no context for it. But, for years, he maintained that he had been here before. At about the age of eight, Neil would wistfully express an interest in seeing pictures of how he looked before. No, not the baby album photos, but he would voice his desire to know what he looked like the last time he was here. By nine, Neil explained to me how the idea of parallel universes works. Additionally, he often dreamed (and still does) of events that play themselves out in the near future (future memory). He is an impeccable judge of a person's character, seemingly 'seeing through' facades with ease."

One case that already has extensive verifications and is currently undergoing clinical study is that of Rand Jameson Shields.[5] Rand speaks directly: "In August 1962, when I was eight years old, I was wading in a swimming pool when a man dove on my head. Dazed, I ventured out into deeper water and drowned. In the minute my face was underwater, my soul joyfully left my body. The ceiling of the sky above me rolled back to reveal an infinite light universe, the earth below me dissolved away, and I intuitively understood my soul's purpose and the nature of the spiritual universe. Two wonderful light beings, long familiar to my soul, then appeared before me. Just as I was about to leave with them, my soul was snapped back into my body. A woman had pulled my face from the water, and I resuscitated.

"During the following year, however, my soul was again pulled away from my body, about eighty times, each time going to a sky of loving white light. There I was made to physically 're-experience' sixty-eight events from previous past lives. Thirty-four of these experiences, it turned out, were of my most recent past life, including the entire period my soul spent between my last death and my birth in this life.

"My re-experiences were so many and so vivid that I have remembered them all my life, unchanged. They were so unique that when I became an adult, it was easy to locate where I had lived in my past life, and identity and verify who I had been. I even discovered that people I had known and loved in my re-experiences actually lived—in the very same houses of my memories! In the eight casual visits I have made to the town over the past twenty-five years, I, and others, have uncovered 114 precise pieces of evidence verifying that every one of my thirty-four unique childhood re-experiences occurred to this man who died twenty-eight months prior to my birth, to the day. I have not found one piece of evidence that contradicted any of my past-life memories. So far, I have identified thirty-six precise buildings and locations in the town that were part of my memories, situated around each other exactly as in my memories. Many of the verifications are one-of-a-kind, occurring to nobody else in the world. "Professionally, I am a medical writer. I have a fair sense of statistics— enough to know that the possibility of my past-life memories being someone else's are astronomically small. Currently my case is being analyzed by Dr. Jim Tucker, in the Department of Psychiatric Medicine at the University of Virginia.

"For most of my life, because of my past-life memories induced by my near-death experience, I have known there is no death. I do not fear the experience of dying, as I already experienced it in this life, as well as re-experiencing it in previous lives. My past-life memories have helped me come to understand the story of my soul. Even more important, in my experiences of being in pure soul, I gleaned an intuitive understanding of the spiritual universe, and of heaven. Ultimately, my soul was permitted to 'see' heaven. My soul has been vibrating ever since, and I have come to understand exactly what it is my soul needs to do to move forward. I ache to tell the world."

ENCOUNTERING THE UNBORN

If the cases I have submitted thus far seem beyond evidential credibility, here are two that demand serious attention.

Four-year-old Jimmy John drowned in his parents' backyard swimming pool. He was an only child. His mother was in her late twenties, his dad in his early thirties. Emergency crews arrived within minutes. CPR was administered. Nothing happened. Fifteen tension-filled minutes later, the professionals managed to resuscitate the boy. His distraught mother, beside herself with relief that her precious son was back among the living, suddenly turned chalk-white as Jimmy John blurted out for all to hear, "I met my little brother. He's 'over there,' where I just was, and he told me all about Mommy having him pulled out of her tummy when she was thirteen." The boy went on to correctly detail his mother's secret abortion, an event she had never discussed with anyone. In fact, she had long since forgotten about it. Jimmy John was absolutely elated to discover he had a brother; their reunion had been laughter filled. Both vowed to remain in contact now that they had finally met. Neither parent could handle Jimmy John's report of his newfound sibling. Embarrassed, frustrated, confused, and horrified, his mother nearly had a nervous breakdown. His father, feeling betrayed by his wife's secret past, sued for divorce. Jimmy John's joy was lost in the shuffle, as was the communication I had established with the family. How this incident resolved itself, I do not know.

Note, that in this case, what should have been a much older brother was described as being a "little" brother. I have encountered this type of imagery "accommodation" countless times. It's as if initial greeters on the Other Side of death's curtain serve to relax or alert the experiencer, and will not necessarily match any notion of what they ought to look like at that moment. Sometimes this is uplifting (afflictions are healed, body appears younger and healthier), and other times it is confusing or strange (as with Jimmy John's "little" brother who really should have been about sixteen). It can be argued in this case that meeting a child appearing younger than the boy would be much less disorienting than being greeted by the larger body-type of a teenager.

Still, children's near-death scenarios that feature the youngster being greeted by an *unborn* sibling, as happened to Jimmy John, are not that uncommon. In most cases the unborn were either miscarried or aborted, and the amount of time that passed seems to make no difference. But, occasionally, the unborn are *future* siblings yet to be conceived. The next story is one such episode.

Merla Ianello of Thetford, Vermont, recalls that as a child she saw a guest in her home who was about three or four years old choke to death trying to eat a plastic-wrapped frozen juice treat called an Ice Pop. She insisted on naming them "Death Pops" after that, and one day she asked her mother who the child was. Her mother, staring in disbelief, said, "It was you." Merla remembers standing in the kitchen doorway looking into the dining room when the incident occurred. "My mother was screaming and shaking a kid upside down by the ankles. My father was leaning over, helping her. My younger brother sat in a chair at the table, watching. *I was so scared!* Boy, that kid must have been really naughty. I would never be so bad as to make Mom shake and scream like that! She yelled *my* name. I cringed and was upset that maybe I had something to do with her anger. Before I knew it, my mother took away my Ice Pop and my brother Lou washed it down the drain. I wanted to protest but was too scared to ask for it back. She might get mad again and this time shake me by *my* ankles."

Merla witnessed this episode from several feet *outside of her body.* Guilt prevented her from associating "the kid" she saw with herself. The extra child in her drawing (to the right of her mother's shoulder, indicated by an arrow) she unmistakably identified by name as her brother Michael, whom she could clearly see, even though her mother insists that this was impossible, as *Michael wasn't conceived until the following year, nor had any mention been made of a future child or what name any such child might be given.*

Merla Ianello, NDE from choking on a "Death Pop."

(Remember, children personalize everything, and will tend to blame themselves if incidents/behaviors do not correspond with what they were taught. It took Merla many years to accept that *she* was the child who "upset" her parents so much. She had misinterpreted their panic and grief for anger and disapproval.)

SEARCHING FOR THE "MISSING" TWIN

From the very beginning of my work, experiencers have pulled me aside and whispered things like, "I'm not all here. There's another one of me. I have a twin, but my twin doesn't have a body." This "missing" twin was occasionally a participant in prebirth awareness states or during a near-death scenario at birth. Sometimes individuals did not discover that a twin had ever existed until years later when that twin appeared in a near-death episode of theirs. Hardly anyone will speak openly about the subject. Because several "twinless twins" filled out my questionnaire, in addition to those who submitted to interviews, I feel that I must tackle the subject of the "missing twin" phenomenon.

Although it is unconnected to near-death research, the story I am about to relate is typical not only of what I keep finding but to the discoveries of other researchers, as well. A woman (who requested anonymity) had an abortion after discovering she was pregnant. Shortly afterward she learned that she was still pregnant. Unbeknownst to anyone, she had been carrying twins—one was removed but the other remained. The woman took this as a "sign" that she must keep the second baby and raise it, so she refused another abortion and later delivered a healthy baby girl, who grew up a fast friend of her invisible twin sister. This camaraderie exacted a heavy price for a number of years, as the mother, fearful that her daughter was going insane, took her to one psychiatrist after another for evaluation. Nothing abnormal was ever found. Currently, the two sisters enjoy each other's company by communicating telepathically and through dream states. The mother has finally accepted that she has two very real daughters: one with a physical body, and the other with a spirit body.

Perhaps the most famous case of a missing twin is that of Elvis Presley, whose twin died at birth. Presley went on to communicate with his "bodiless" brother all his life. Maia C. M. Shamayyim, in her article "Elvis and His Angelic Connection,"[6] quoted at length from a conversation she had with Mary L. Jones, a close friend of the Presley family: "I remember Elvis saying so seriously (in 1966) . . . that he thought he was instilled into his mother's womb along with her natural son (Elvis' twin, Jesse), and that Jesse chose to die giving Elvis a path to an earth life. He always had visions even as a child. He felt that he was somehow different and not of this earth and was held to earth to bring some new understanding and love to its people—to guide them to a higher realm of spiritual awareness through music—and that he was doomed because he could not adjust to earth's gravity and pressure; it was burning him up. (Elvis' normal temperature was over 100 degrees.)"

Regardless of how we might choose to consider these stories, the fact is that more and more late-term diagnosed twins are vanishing—some within hours of birth. These are not just sonogram-pictured babies, but little ones whose heartbeats and body sizes were physically monitored and accounted for throughout the entire gestational period. The absent twin sometimes disappeared without a trace, and sometimes an empty placenta was born along with the single survivor. The medical community has no explanation to offer mothers demanding answers.

A contemporary theory is that the sudden disappearance of evidence of a twin in an advanced pregnancy is proof that the fetus must have been abducted by aliens (a counterpoint to Elvis's suspicion that he himself was somehow "alien"). Amazingly, there exist toddlers much too young to fancy such things who describe in detail the lives of their other halves as they grow up aboard spaceships.

Caryl Dennis has explored this area for many years. She has interviewed some 130 people involved in multiple births, the missing twin phenomenon, and UFO contacts. Her self-published book, *The Millennium Children,*[7] delves into a broad range of issues that suggest the degree to which today's youngsters are changing in behavior, ability, and temperament. Although Dennis's research protocol leaves much to be desired, what she discovered is well worth considering; her conclusions are similar to my own about kids who had near-death episodes.

In her book Dennis presents case histories of twins who have vanished early in the mother's pregnancy as well as just before birth, and she describes the empty feeling of the woman after the disappearance of a pregnancy. Of special relevance, though, is what happens to the surviving twin. Most go on to actively dialogue with their "other" (whether that twin is in spirit form or believed to be living among aliens), and, according to Dennis, they display unusual talents, faculties, and intelligence enhancements, and become creative thinkers.

Just as near-death children (and often the separation from and loss of a twin is part of a near-death scenario), single twins deal with aftereffects that can confuse, disorient, or frighten them. Even in the most tolerant of families, the idea of an ongoing relationship between the dead and the living can create schisms that result in the surviving twin's being institutionalized as mentally ill.

Dennis points out that some therapists are now specializing in this field, and that there is a magazine called *Twins World* for twins in general and a newsletter called *Twinless Twins* for singles who are attempting to deal with the grief of losing their twin and the driving need they feel to find him or her so they can be whole again.[8]

I have found that missing twins occasionally befriend or function as spirit guides for relatives besides their surviving singles. One of the participants in my research experienced an incredible healing when the dead twin of her son returned in spirit form to help her. Robin H. Johnson of Plymouth, New Hampshire, is the mother. She had three near-death episodes—the first at age two from drowning, then one during a health crisis at age twenty-three, and the third during surgery at age thirty. Of the three, the childhood incident had the greatest impact on her and set the stage for how she would face the challenge of growing up.

Recalling the event, Robin winced. "I didn't talk about the pain of almost drowning, because I was too excited about having just seen Jesus. But when I began to tell my mother about seeing the movie of my life go by, she froze like a statue. Then she said, 'That must have been some movie, Robin, as young as you are.' I think she thought I was trying to get out of having been bad. I shouldn't have been near the drop-off, the part of the river that abruptly became deep. I had made a mistake, but I wasn't a liar.

"I suddenly felt so alone," Robin continued. "I could not communicate to her. She didn't believe me. She actually seemed embarrassed that someone would hear me, like I really had lost my mind. I felt abandoned. For the second time that day, I felt terror. Who was I? Where was I? Her sternness was a warning to me that I had better drop the idea of ever sharing that I thought I had seen life from a different perspective."

Robin was assailed with guilt and fear after this experience and fell into a habit of denial that would result in self-betrayal, the total distrust of her own inner knowing. "My journey out of denial and into my full awareness of my connection with the Divine came after a spiritual awakening when I was thirty." And that awakening was her third near-death episode, preceded by the "appearance" of her son's deceased twin, Sarah.

"It wasn't until I met my nonphysical daughter, Sarah, that I learned that her purpose for being in my life was to teach me to have unequivocal trust in my intuition, my knowing." In this case, it was not the surviving twin who formed a relationship with his deceased sister, it was the mother. By communicating with Sarah, Robin was able to reclaim what she had lost at the age of two and heal herself.

EXPRESSING "SELF" IN MULTIPLES

What happened to Robin Johnson is an unusual twist to the missing twin phenomenon. Here's another one. Frank Henniker, also of New Hampshire, has to this day a vivid prebirth memory involving his twin that led to "both of them" being hit by a car and experiencing a near-death scenario when four years old.

According to Frank: "Life for my sister Cynthia and I, though quite unconfirmable, began as two eggs, not one. The outside world's vibrations made my sister want to abort before we were recognized as existing. Our parents did not get along and the water we lived in was constantly invaded with negative energy. I was told that I could not leave, by a voice known to me as Eros Thor. Eros and I had been together before. Not having the option my sister wanted, I pulled her inside me. We literally became twins in one egg. At six months in the water, we were hit by our daddy. This was confirmed before our mother died years later."

Frank's memory is of being born as two beings in one body: he and his twin sister, Cynthia (a name he has always called her). To please a violent and demanding father, the two created subpersonalities—twenty of them by the age of four. They were unsuccessful in their attempt to win their father's approval by appearing to be "other people," and their mother at last intervened for them and kicked the man out. Even though only one body existed, the twin duo of visible and invisible siblings referred to themselves as "we" until that fateful day around the time of their parents' last fight.

"It was a bright, sunny March day when Cynthia found an opportunity to end what she perceived as her own life. She took the body into the street, where a car ran over us with its rear tire, spinning us like a top. Witnesses said we went the height of a telephone pole and landed on our back. The body remembers the pain that came from landing spread-eagle, the bones shattering, and the skull bursting on the pavement."

Frank described a lengthy near-death scenario that included a struggle between the two siblings. Cynthia remained long enough to help him revive in "the body shell" and then disappeared. Cynthia was not a "created personality" in the sense of the subpersonalities they *together* created, a psychological phenomenon known as dissociative identity disorder (DID), formerly called multiple personality disorder (MPD). From the beginning, the two existed as two and interacted in a manner now recognized as typical for twins. They knew each other, even as cells were dividing in the womb to form the body they would eventually cohabit. *And they took part in the cell division process consciously, actively, and from the awareness level of developed minds.*

This is congruent with the cases of near-death survivors who had full knowledge and full memory of having chosen the life they were about to have before conception—their parents, their genetics and characteristics, their actual birth, and the basic tendencies of the personality self—and were participants in the act of their own creation. These experiencers knew, absolutely knew, that the self they really were was the "higher self," and that they as a soul were eternal and motivated to take on life in the world of matter to learn certain lessons, experience contrast and change, and fulfill a mission of greater import—to help make the world a better place. Almost in chorus, they claimed that the biggest mistake people make during their sojourn on the earthplane is to think that they could ever exist separately from the Source of All Being. "Aloneness," they said, "is a joke our Soul plays on us so we will fine-tune the gift of free will."

Frank Henniker's case adds a new dimension to our understanding of twinning and the complexities of missing twins, not to mention the dynamics of birth and the miracle of cocreation. It also introduces the topic of multiple personalities and how the mind can defend itself through the process of dissociation. A research bulletin from the Institute of Noetic Sciences featuring the article "Multiple Personality—Mirrors of a New Model of Mind?"[9] offers the intriguing idea that what has previously been treated as a disorder could possibly be the emergence of new order. Rather than splitting off, the mind is becoming more adept at manipulating consciousness; it has learned how to switch into different gears.

To be fair, DID child experiencers confront serious challenges, such as the conflict between the love they find on the Other Side versus the absence of love in their lives on this side, compounded by questions of trust and truth telling. (Like experiencers of any age, they tend to lose basic self-defense cautions until such time as they are able to reassess their life and its purpose.) Positives usually outweigh negatives, however, as in the case of P. Ann Baillie, a DID from Michigan.

Baillie had two bouts with death before her first birthday and experienced a near-death scenario each time. Even though being sent back to her mess of a family felt like a betrayal to her, she has this surprising commentary to offer:

"I believe that the near-death experiences had a profound effect on the multiplicity. The level of fragmentation that I developed may have been a result of being unable to let go of my 'core self' and let her sleep [while another personality took over] the way many in my situation have done. I was unable to give up, even in times when surrender may have been a good idea. I also think that the near-death experiences have made conventional therapy largely ineffective for me. While I have an enormous capacity for anger, I have little for hatred and tend to pity those who abused me, much to the confusion of people around me. I have little ability or desire to relive the past, often a prerequisite with therapists who treat DID. It feels like enough for me to acknowledge and honor it, but I don't seem to abreact [release psychic tension by acting out] the way many multiples do."

Baillie speaks tenderly about the universal love she encountered during her near-death episode and how the memory of it has helped her break through the barriers she had to erect in order to survive her youth. What was once a nightmare has given way to a sense of unity and inner strength, with a steady decrease in her personality fragmentation.

TAKING A SECOND LOOK

Can science tell us anything that might shed some light on prenatal awareness?

Well, we know that the recognition of language begins in the womb, not in the nursery, since sounds and voices register early on, and continuously, for the fetus. Geoffrey Cowley wrote about this research in his article "The Language Explosion." He noted, "Babies just four days old can distinguish one language from another.[10] *The Secret Life of the Unborn Child* details the pioneering work done by Thomas Verny, M.D., that led, in the early eighties, to the breakthrough revelation that the fetus makes decisions that require conscious thought, sucks its thumb, hiccups, and responds appropriately to any given stimuli, especially the emotional state of the mother.[11]

Add to this research the remarkable work of psychologist David Chamberlain, Ph.D., author *of Babies Remember Birth,* who clinically hypnotized young children and discovered that they possessed pre- and perinatal awareness as newborns and were fully cognizant of their inherent selfhood at birth despite the lack of anatomical maturity—which refutes the notion that birth memories are fabrications or guesswork.[12] David B. Cheek, M.D., a retired obstetrician and past president of the American Society for Clinical Hypnosis, continued the quest to determine at what age a baby is aware, and he found evidence to suggest that by the time a woman realizes she is pregnant, the embryo is already aware of her and her surroundings—indicating that awareness may begin at conception.[13]

Concerning reincarnation, the most notable authority on the subject is Ian Stevenson, M.D. His meticulous research on this topic is the world's best; his books *Twenty Cases Suggestive of Reincarnation*[14] and *Where Reincarnation and Biology Intersect* are unparalleled as objective examinations of the phenomenon—and what he has uncovered is stunning. Written from a skeptical reporter's view of Dr. Stevenson's work is the remarkable book by Tom Shroder entitled, *Old Souls: The Scientific Evidence for Past Lives.*[15] Many since Stevenson have also come forward with credible material underscoring the phenomenon's validity. Of the newest offerings, the one most relevant to our discussion is Carol Bowman's book *Children's Past Lives: How Past Life Memories Affect Your Child.*[16]

Because there is such a high rate of pregnancies that have been diagnosed as twins but resulted in only one birth, most doctors dismiss the vanished "other" as having been claimed by nature's efficient "waste disposal system." The thinking is that fetuses that may have been damaged, malformed, or incomplete are either absorbed by the healthy twin or reabsorbed by the mother. All of the obstetricians I interviewed about this felt that the exceptional incidence of twin loss was "no big deal." The mothers who suffered such a loss disagreed—many were distraught.

Two major national debates have brought the issue of missing twins to the forefront. These are the abortion conflict and a growing concern, even among the mainstream populace and credible researchers, about alien abductions. The question I must ask differs from those addressed by either debate: In cases where there is a verifiable death of one twin, why do so many surviving twins report having an ongoing relationship via spirit with their other half? This question deserves clinical study.

The fact that people can remember their births, have awareness in the womb, see the unborn and the missing, remember past lives, alter destinies, and interact with the living or dead has inspired new fields of research besides the near-death experience. They are:

NDA Nearing-Death Awareness[17]
ADC After-Death Communications[18]
PBE   Prebirth Experience[19]

As research continues to become more sophisticated, the idea of a life continuum is no longer relegated to the dustbin of sloppy interviews or dismissed as wish fulfillment. We are coming of age as we advance further into the third millennium, and we are seeing ourselves through a broader and more exacting lens. What we are discovering is what we've previously overlooked—that other dimensions of life, other realities, have always existed. We just didn't have the right tools before to properly identify them.

NINE

Ⓖ

Alien Existences

*Architects of the future are being brought onto your planet
from their home civilizations. They asked to come, and
come they will. They each have a mission.*

—TAURI, OF THE OGATTA GROUP

BESIDES THE PHENOMENON of missing twins, we have the enigma of
missing fetuses. This mystery occurs when women find themselves pregnant without having had sexual contact with a man and then suddenly are
not pregnant weeks or months later. This is termed the "missing fetus syndrome."[1] Seldom is there verification of these reports—a fact that does
nothing to quell tales of "space nappings," of aliens swooping down to
reclaim "half human/half alien" babies that will finish developing and be
raised aboard their spaceships (note the similarity to claims about some
missing twins). The purpose of these "hybrids," a few women have been
told via mental telepathy, is to seed a new race of beings.

Investigations into these strange pregnancies, as well as of extraterrestrial contacts and UFO abductions, involve millions of people worldwide. Gone is the day when the subject of alien existences could be
tossed off as fodder for bad dreams or creepy fiction. Currently, enough
evidence exists to put the subject on the table for legitimate discussion.
Since human genetics, fertility, and children are now considered central

to the entire alien issue, and because so many kids report varied types of contacts with such beings, we are obliged to talk about it too.

I first began tracking otherworldly contacts in the sixties. Then as now, I noticed that experiences involving aliens often ran in families. It was the five children of nurse-turned-psychic Pamela Williams of Mason, Michigan, for instance, who caused her to think twice about the reality of extraterrestrial visitors, particularly when her son Leonard was four. "I got up in the night to check on the boys in their upstairs room," remembered Pamela, "and to my surprise Len was sitting on the floor looking out the window. I asked what he was doing out of bed. 'I've been talking to the star people.' He then pointed out the window and I saw a bright light in the night sky. 'What are they saying to you?' I asked. 'They're telling me that is my home.' [When he got] a little older he began seeing UFOs almost daily, and being a typical boy, thought it was fun to upset his father by pointing them out." David, her youngest son, was even more emphatic. "Before he was eighteen months old, he would greet and talk to beings I could not see. He had dramatic dreams very young, science-fiction dreams of other planets, other races, spaceships, etc. He was always waking me up in the night to tell me about them."

A successful psychotherapist (who prefers to remain nameless) confided to me similar memories from her own childhood: "I was said to have walked and talked very early, but to have been adultlike and solemn. At four or five I remember standing in our backyard looking at the southern sky, and thinking 'That is my home. My real mother and father left me here and when I've suffered enough they'll come back and get me.' Throughout the years I had waves of what I called homesicknesses: an overwhelming longing that came and went periodically no matter where I was and had nothing to do with my earth family or where we lived."

While researching the near-death phenomenon, I routinely encountered child experiencers who would say things like, "I feel like an alien" or "a misfit" or "a foreigner." And they'd admit to being *homesick* for what they had to leave behind in order to come to earth. As compelling as these stories are, and there are many of them, I question whether the claims made by kids really signify extraterrestrial origination, or if, maybe, something else is involved.

Numbers from my research reveal:

Adult Near-Death Experiencers (based on 3,000 interviews)
Identified with being from another planet   20%

Claimed to have been abducted by a UFO	9%

Child Near-Death Experiencers (based on 277 interviews)

Identified with being from another planet	9%
Identified with being from another dimension	39%
Claimed to have been abducted by a UFO	14%

Not as many adult experiencers said they had been abducted by a UFO as did child experiencers, although a few of them noted that they occasionally dreamed of seeing spaceships. The most surprising difference I found between adults and children concerned "place of origin." Adult near-death survivors who remembered either during or right after their episodes that they had come to this planet from another one numbered 20 percent, a figure dwarfed by the percentage of youngsters who recalled not so much other planets as multidimensional realms. No adult I interviewed ever expressed his or her origin in terms of multidimensionality; only kids did this.

Before we explore this unusual variance, it would be helpful to first gain a sense of how child experiencers express themselves on the subject of alien existences.

Larrick Stapleton, Wynnewood, Pennsylvania. NDE at age four, tonsillectomy. "I was raised in a traditional southern Midwest, WASP household, was confirmed as a Presbyterian in a somewhat fundamentalist church, and did extremely well in school and with all matters academic. I saw colors and lights as a small child and have always heard 'music,' and was the subject (victim) of some form of abduction experience when I was just an infant. Like most matters out of the ordinary, none of this was ever discussed and it was in fact denied."

Robin H. Johnson, Plymouth, New Hampshire. NDE at age two, drowning. "The same spiritual being who I envisioned when I drowned later appeared before me and two other women, this time in a prearranged conscious state. After both encounters with this being, I was visited by extraterrestrials. Unlike other abductees, I love my abductors and miss them when they leave."

P. Bradley Carey, Burlington, Washington. NDE at age thirteen, choked by another child. "My first alien encounter was at the age of ten. My father realized that he had left his wallet at the lake, but he didn't want to go back alone, so I went along. We were about three-quarters of the way there, in a very isolated area, when the lone streetlight went out, and the lights and car engine suddenly stopped. My father shifted the car into park and was about to turn the key, when we both saw a strange glowing ball in the sky above and to the front of us. We watched this ball until it disappeared between the hills. [In] what seemed only moments later, the streetlight was suddenly on, as were the car lights and engine. Never once did my father touch the key, so there is no way he could have restarted the car. Without saying anything to each other, we continued on our way, found the wallet, and headed back home. Once we arrived, we discovered that the entire trip took nearly three hours longer than it should have."

Diego Leon Valencia Lopez, Bogotá, Colombia. NDE at birth, during emergency surgery; several more NDEs in adulthood. His wife, Dina, is the translator. "When Diego was five years old, a member of his family died. He walked to a cornfield on the family ranch while waiting for the adults who had gathered. There he saw a kind of robotic figure surrounded by a luminous brilliance. Telepathically the figure called to Diego. It seemed to him that the being picked up something, then the light disappeared, and Diego remembers having floated.

Stylized creation made by Diego Lopez to depict his emotional response to the actual visitations he says he has witnessed.

Portrait of Diego sketched by his wife, Dina, while he was meditating.

"When [Diego] had chicken pox, his room in a very big old house was in the corridor and had no windows. Suddenly, there was a yellow glow in the middle of the room that made him immensely happy. His brother also saw the light before it disappeared.

"At the age of seven, [Diego] went with his brother to the farm and saw a bright light. They both lost four hours and don't remember what happened.

"At nine, he left school at 11:00 A.M. with a friend. Diego sat on the footwalk and gazed below at lots of fruit and vegetable trees. Among very high weeds he saw two beings with casks. One of them inclined toward the other and had a kind of strainer. Diego could see them clearly, yet suddenly and instantaneously, he found himself in a very different place without having walked there, and was very tired. When he finally made it to his friend's house for lunch, he discovered that he was two and a half hours late and his friend had already left for school.

"Again that same year, he was hiding in thick bushes with his brother. Unexpectedly, he saw a splendorous light from which a voice spoke to him. His brother fell asleep in the grass, and Diego was lifted up. He flew to a faraway place. He remembers saying good-bye, and then [he] returned to find his brother still sleeping. This splendorous light being appeared many times after that, with a special murmur [Diego] learned to distinguish."

Francis Piekarski, New Martinsville, West Virginia. NDE at age five, drowning; at twelve from high fever and bone infection. "I feel called to warn the world of impending danger. Chernobyl was an example come true. Shortly, I feel that the world will be in turmoil. UFOs will play a big part in the transition. The Blessed Mother (Marian devotions) will play an equally large part. I personally feel I must help after the disasters to start a new lifestyle. We have formed a group here to investigate psychic revelations and alien contacts."

Joe Ann Van Gelder, Newport, Vermont. Nine NDEs as a child, varied causes. "I had a past-life regression to inquire into a recurring dream I'd had over the years. In this regression, the dream was experienced as a partial memory of a time when I'd come from Venus to help those on Mu [a 'lost continent' in the Pacific]. When the [regression] facilitator told me to 'Go home to Venus,' my reply was, 'I'll go to Venus, but it's not home.' She then instructed me to 'Go home,' and my consciousness 'flew.' I left this galaxy far behind. When the sense of movement stopped, my consciousness was suspended far out in the Universe in what I described as 'the plasma between the planets and the stars.' When the facilitator asked me for a description, I 'saw' that I was one of a small group of Sparks of Light. When she asked me what I was doing, my consciousness merged with the Spark that was me, and I experienced it consciously. I told her, 'I'm not doing anything; I'm being . . . waiting to be sent out again.'"

Renditions of alien existences from child experiencers rarely match adult accounts. Children, for the most part, are seldom impressed with the idea of extraterrestrials or spinning spheres. For them, coming from Venus, Mars, Sirius, or the sun is not so much an indicator of "home," as Joe Ann Van Gelder made clear, as it is recognition of a way station. Most regard the special lights they see as guides who accompany them through stages of learning as their soul progresses along God's Eternal Spiral of Remembrance. It is teen and adult experiencers who are excited by the proposition that they are the aliens and that they came to earth from another world, or that they were abducted and taken aboard a spaceship and that they now have an ongoing relationship with aliens—even though little ones ages three to five actually report more of this than do experiencers who are older.

Children, especially the very young, strongly relate to something else entirely . . . *life in other dimensions of existence.* Two distinctive expressions of this awareness were evident to me back in the sixties; this same pattern emerged again in my near-death research, and I have encountered it regardless of country or culture throughout the millennial generation. Because this pattern of multidimensionality is so pervasive, it behooves us to take a deeper look.

There are two distinctive expressions of multidimensionality.

Orientation To The Life Continuum. People with this orientation are concerned with life embodiments and the progression of souls. Their memories embrace prebirth and after-death realms as exit and entrance points to a single lifestream or life continuum inhabited by the type of spirit they once were and will be again their true home. (The majority—about three-quarters of the total—recall this.)

Orientation To The Cosmos. People with this orientation are concerned with the universe's inner workings and the progression of Creation. They identify with formlessness: gases, attractors, particle sparks, waves, energy pulses, plasma, and so forth, as if the substance of their being and their place of residence were one and the same—part of the mechanism and structure that hold together and maintain Creation itself. (Fewer respondents—about one-quarter—claim this orientation.)

In the following sections I interpret these two types of multidimensional awarenesses, based on the research I have conducted.

ORIENTATION TO THE LIFE CONTINUUM

The first three paragraphs of *The Famished Road,* by Ben Okri, are the best example I can offer of what this orientation seems to be like for youngsters and how they tend to reminisce from this perspective:

> In the beginning there was a river. The river became a road and the road branched out to the whole world. And because the road was once a river it was always hungry.
>
> In that land of beginnings spirits mingled with the unborn. We could assume numerous forms. Many of us were birds. We knew no boundaries. There was much feasting, playing, and sorrowing. We feasted much because of the beautiful terrors of eternity. We played much because we were free. And we sorrowed much because there were always those amongst us who had just returned from the world

of the Living. They had returned inconsolable for all the love they had left behind, all the suffering they hadn't redeemed, all that they hadn't understood, and for all that they had barely begun to learn before they were drawn back to the land of origins.

There was not one amongst us who looked forward to being born. We disliked the rigours of existence, the unfulfilled longings, the enshrined injustices of the world, the labyrinths of love, the ignorance of parents, the fact of dying, and the amazing indifference of the Living in the midst of the simple beauties of the universe. We feared the heartlessness of human beings, all of whom are born blind, few of whom ever learn to see.[2]

A multidimensional child oriented to the life continuum is similar to other child experiencers, except that he or she has a unique focus or sense of self as spirit and as a resident of the realms of spirit. These children know from their earliest years that their existence on earth is temporary and for the purpose of fulfilling the progression of the soul, their own and others'. Because "Home" is the luminous lifestream they came from and will return to, many of them speak objectively about past lives and incarnations in life-forms one might consider alien. A higher level of spirituality and truth is more important to them than parental preferences. As a result, they are open to and highly tolerant of diverse viewpoints. Attempts to make them fit society's mold are usually a waste of time. Service occupations and philanthropic endeavors interest them.

ORIENTATION TO THE COSMOS

Youngsters who identify themselves this abstractly seem to be possessed of almost pure intellect. They spout advanced concepts about things like waveforms, energy sources, and power grids in the same manner in which the average child might quote football scores. And they are explicit about their origins: "Not here, not there—elsewhere." Just because these children occasionally mention other planets does not mean they consider themselves to be from them. To make such an assumption completely misses the scope of their panoramic worldview. "Home," for them, is the universe at large.

Multidimensional/cosmos children are unlike those who remember going back and forth through the life continuum, although most are knowledgeable about soul progression. These kids act as if they have never been on this or any other planet before, and, frankly, they consider the human body a useless, clumsy appendage. They seem utterly unconcerned with family issues or personal relationships. What matters to them is saving the earth and making repairs, which means they are drawn to vocations in fields such as ecological sustainability (the "green" movement), alternative power sources, leading-edge science, large-scale economic and medical reforms, and photonics.

These children present us with an entirely new slant on the way "life" is defined. For them, each aspect of Creation has its own aliveness and consciousness; for instance, they insist that the very gases we breathe are living intelligences. Often they refer to themselves as stewards, guardians, or "keepers" of that which enables cells and molecules to exist, rather than as evolving spirits. Although their memories could be interpreted as awareness in the womb (plasma, waves), these youngsters are insistent on being here for "the changes," and insistent that the universe they refer to is the larger one, the cosmos. Most state they were "called" here by a signal the earth sent out for help, not by their parents' desires.

I have observed that multidimensional/cosmos children in general:

Live in their own head to the extent that it's almost as if nothing else exists from their neck down. As a result, they tend to have body-coordination problems. Exercise and massage can alleviate this and help them connect with their bodies. Tai chi, aikido, and mind-stretching games generally appeal more to them than sports like football or wrestling.

Are either unusually slow or fast to speak, walk, and learn basic tasks. They do not respond to injury, pain, or illness as other children do, since they dissociate easily. It often may seem as if they're "not all there," when in fact they are actively engaged. These children readily "see" the soul level of a person; hence, they tend to know the truth of a given situation before those around them, and are not easily fooled.

Are not social by nature, nor are they distracted by sexuality, except to ponder why distinct genders exist. Large crowds bother them.

Are ultrasensitive to pollution emissions, heavy ozone levels, loud sounds/music, intense sunlight, temperature and pressure variations, unpleasant vibrations and odors.

Do not understand death, nor the fact that they could lose their body if they don't take care of it. Often they don't even relate to primary survival needs. Role-playing games help them identify with human selfhood and show them how to thrive and enjoy life on the earthplane.

Experiential hands-on projects enable them to appreciate the solidity of matter and its purposefulness.

Are very loving but emotionally "removed." Caring for pets, creating gardens, and doing volunteer work are the kinds of activities that allow these children to experience the give-and-take of relationships while learning about emotions and the myriad ways to express them.

The key to successfully raising multidimensional/cosmos children, at least so far as I have seen, is to arrange opportunities whereby they can relate one object to another, one feeling to the next, each action to its consequence. Once they catch on to the basic maneuvering of physical matter and human behavior—and it may take them longer than the average child to figure this out—they more than make up for lost time in their rapid-fire manner of absorbing information.

Two examples of this unusual type of child are the Cabobianco brothers, Flavio and Marcos, of Buenos Aires, Argentina. Underpinning their story is what their parents, Alba and Nestor, both Freudian psychologists, went through in trying to understand them. Raising their unusual sons opened up vast spiritual realities unexplainable using Freud's limited analytical techniques. So, Alba and Nestor switched to the field of transpersonal psychology and were instrumental in introducing this new field to psychology professionals in Argentina at a time when the totalitarian government there still squelched independent thought. That they were successful is amazing in itself.

Alba had a near-death experience as an adult after succumbing to toxic gases. She feels that her episode prepared her for the sons she would have, by opening her consciousness to otherworldly realms and greater truths. Through correspondence translated by Alejandra Warden, a close friend of the Cabobianco family, Alba revealed that she kept a journal of her sons' prescient disclosures, and noted the age at which each boy provided another glimpse into their multidimensional/cosmos world. While still quite young, Flavio began to write and called himself a "cosmic messenger," here to speak about spiritual things. "Now that this world is starting to be less physical, other children like me are going to come," he presaged. "Human beings are different now. They are going to be more open. I am here to calm people who are frightened by the changing energy of Earth. But I am also here to help the guardian souls, the nonphysical beings, who are involved in the changes." According to Flavio, the guardian souls keep the systems of creation going. They maintain the different levels of universal integrity. He feels that his job as a communicator is to be a bridge that reaches in both directions—to humans about the truth of spiritual worlds, and to the guardian souls about how people on earth are adjusting to planetary change.

At eight years of age, Flavio Cabobianco met Ama, a woman interested in the notes his mother took, in his drawings, and in the little books he made. She edited the material and was instrumental in writing out his explanations of the diagrams he and his brother, Marcos, made of the universe. As a book took shape, Ama suggested the order of the chapters and that family comments be included. Before Flavio was a teenager, *Vengo del Sol (I Come from the Sun)* was published in Argentina and became a best-seller.[3] "When I wrote *I Come from the Sun,* I was very young and I knew few words," Flavio admitted. "I want to make clear that it isn't the physical sun I'm talking about, but the spiritual sun."

Vengo del Sol is the most astonishing book written by a child that I have ever seen. The drawings, and Marcos's and Flavio's explanations of them, bespeak a consciousness far wiser than that of most adults; the tower diagram, which shows how all of creation evolves and was done when Flavio was seven (Marcos helped), is nothing short of spectacular.

When I met the brothers (thanks to Alejandra Warden we were able to engage in spirited dialogue), I was struck by what I had recognized decades before: there seems to be a class of people who incarnate on earth and have detailed memories of having existed as bits and pieces of Creation before hearing a call for help and agreeing to take on density of form so the call could be answered. It's almost as if *the universe is capable of using parts of itself to save itself.*

I know this idea is far-fetched, but consider a paper published in 1998 in *Frontier Perspectives,* a publication of the Institute for Frontier Perspectives then located at Temple University in Philadelphia, Pennsylvania. In "Is Dead Matter Aware of Its Environment?"[4] the author, Peter Graneau, dissects physics and comes to the conclusion that either an outside agency controls universal gravitation, or particles of matter have knowledge of each other. Children have been telling me for decades what Graneau arrives at through physics: *the universe is alive!*

There have been "bridges between worlds" such as Marcos and Flavio Cabobianco throughout history; but now there are more of them. Their bodies seem to have a different density than those of "regular" people; they are extraordinarily sensitive, especially to touch and to food; and many find it imperative to wear nonallergenic clothing. Living around others or being in a crowd can be difficult for them, as they have no "armor" from previous incarnations to help them handle negativity.

Certainly there are child experiencers of near-death states who report interactions with extraterrestrials and speak of worlds and races unlike those associated with earth. Spaceships fascinate them and the abduction drama becomes an almost routine part of their daily lives. These youngsters, however, are in the minority.

Intriguing to our discussion of alien existences, though, is the book *The Omega Project: Near-Death Experiences, UFO Encounters, and Mind at Large,* by Kenneth Ring.[5] A retired psychology professor who has spent nearly thirty years (a few more than me) researching near-death states, he has come to recognize similarities between people who experience abduction incidents and those who have near-death episodes.

Ring posits the existence of an "encounter-prone personality" found in people who have distinctive, spiritually sensitive, and visionary psyches that may, collectively, represent the next stage in human evolution. He found that many of the people who report extraordinary encounters had childhoods marked by various patterns of trauma, stress, and/or child abuse. "They're more likely to dissociate from ordinary reality and then tune in to other realities where they can feel safe," he explained. And these other realities, or "imaginal realms," as Ring calls them, are not to be confused with fantasy worlds. "Imaginal realities have a matrix or structure to them, and you can tune in to them if you have the right faculty of perception. If you are already sensitized to these imaginal realms, then your imagination, acting like an organ of perception in its own right, can simply detect these realities. When you talk to people who have had NDEs, they say things that imply that this is a hyperreality. Things like, 'This experience was more real to me than life itself is real.' Here's an analogy: We cannot see the stars when the sun shines, but when sunlight is absent the starry heavens are revealed. But, obviously, the stars have been there all along." Ring continues: "I think these people may possibly be—one word I could use is *edglings*. They may be closer to a higher development of human potential than most of us. What happened to them is exactly the same thing that happens to a person being trained to be a shaman in a tribal society . . . [they] develop a kind of spiritual sensitivity and a sense of the sacredness of Earth."

Ring's work relies heavily on child abuse issues to underscore his theory of encounter-prone personalities. I did not find this same degree of cause/effect relationship in my own research, even though some of my cases do fit his model. His ideas about the existence of imaginal realms and the sensitivity that can be achieved to access them does correspond with what I have seen. Having a near-death experience, regardless of how it is caused, is sufficient to sensitize an individual to multiple dimensions of reality. The link is not child abuse, but a brain shift/spirit shift. Many children are now born this way. It is a characteristic of what may be a new race emerging in our midst.

Unlike in previous years, recent newspaper headlines have forever changed how we regard the notion of life in outer space. One scientific finding after another has heralded: "Mars was once warm and moist, and may have supported life." "Discovery boosts odds for life on Jupiter moon." "Black holes, neutron stars make space swirl like water." "Hubble telescope snaps picture of undetected giant in Milky Way." "Massive pillars in Eagle nebula harbor a stellar nursery." "Evidence of anti-gravity force found." "Particle found to have mass." "Extra-solar system planet photographed."

The arrogance of thinking we are the only life form in our universe is weakened not only by science, but by some of our astronauts, who are breaking their code of silence about UFO-type craft accompanying their space flights. Some of their revelations were printed in the newsletter *Woodrew Update*.

Greta Woodrew, LL.D., and her husband, Dick Smolowe, LL.D., for seventeen years published the *Woodrew Update,* a newsletter devoted to the exploration of alien contacts, health issues, and ecological responsibility.[6] Both are businesspeople with sterling credentials whose lives were turned upside-down when Greta was first contacted by Tauri, an extraterrestrial who said she was from the "Ogatta Group." In *Woodrew Update* volume 17, number 3, Greta and Dick quoted statements made by American astronauts, among them Gordon Cooper: "For many years I have lived with a secret, in a secrecy imposed on all specialists in astronautics. I can now reveal that every day, in the U.S.A., our radar instruments capture objects of form and composition unknown to us. And there are thousands of witness reports and documents to prove this, but nobody wants to make them public." And from Scott Carpenter: "At no time, when the astronauts were in space, were they alone: there was a constant surveillance by UFOs."

I have no doubt that extraterrestrials exist in some form and that they are capable of making contact with human beings. Physical evidence is too great, sightings too numerous and confirmed by too many people, to be tossed aside as group hypnosis or self-deception. But neither am I convinced of the extent to which this phenomenon is organically composed. Imaginal worlds, as defined by Kenneth Ring, are much more powerful in their effects on experiencers who visit them and in their utter realness than most of us can appreciate. And imaginal worlds are multidimensional in appearance and are associated with the life continuum in the sense of being like layers of luminous fabric enfolded throughout coherent worlds of structured form. People can be taught how to access these realms; some have a natural talent to do so, or accidentally find themselves there because of a sudden occurrence like a near-death state or a shamanistic vision quest. (Shamanistic-type consciousness is often initiated by some sort of near-death-like ritual or mind-altering drug, which is not to say that such states can be sustained for any period without considerable training.)

Once an individual's perception is opened to the "bright worlds," that individual is never quite the same again.

When traveling "behind the veil" we may find ourselves on an alien planet, or in the life continuum, or as part of the plasma that fills the so-called vacuum of outer space, depending upon which layer or matrix we have accessed. During our visit, we may experience our selfhood in ways that would be considered extraordinary in human terms. Tom Repasky of Portland, Oregon, describes such a trip, labeling himself a "walk-in."

Tom fell off a cliff ledge when he was fourteen years old, and bounced for twelve feet after striking rocks. Although he does not remember a near-death episode, he does display the full range of aftereffects, including an extremely high IQ. He is employed today as an expert in the computer industry, is married, and has a daughter. According to Tom: "About twelve days after the accident, I (the current occupant) found myself wandering about space. I was aware of my awareness and was able to examine my history. This history was many years long (thirty-five thousand years). During that time I had been only an observer of life and the planet earth. I felt a strong desire to experience life as a human and began my journey into a human form. The result of this journey was my entering the form I now animate, [which] is called Tom. I began life within a fourteen-year-old body without any personal body memories. My first action was to cause the form to move and in doing so, I surprised the hospital staff, who said I had been in a coma. Of course, these words were just noise to me, and it was not until several weeks later that I began to understand and imitate human speech."

Ruth Montgomery, in her book *Strangers Among Us*,[7] coined the term "walk-in" to accommodate situations in which one soul could exchange places in a given body with another one; in other words, the resident or birth soul could "walk out" or leave for whatever reason, and a new one could "walk-in." Ostensibly, this exchange would take place during periods of unconsciousness or as a result of a near-death experience. In Montgomery's view, the two souls must agree to the exchange or it couldn't occur, and the incoming soul was obligated to fulfill the duties of the birth soul before new goals could be initiated. Today, the term "walk-in" has become in some circles a generic catchall to explain away the aftereffects of a brain shift/spirit shift as evidenced by a transformation of consciousness. Curiously, all of the various indicators of a "soul exchange" that are generally cited by proponents of the walk in theory *exactly* correspond to aspects of a typical near-death scenario and the aftereffects that follow. So far, the brain shift/spirit shift model has held up to rigorous scrutiny; the walk-in theory hasn't.

Tom Repasky's experience matches the criteria for a walk-in as currently espoused by an organization called Walk-ins for Evolution (WE) International,[8] with one important distinction. Tom remembers being without form during a 35,000-year history as an aware intelligence. As he tells it, "There wasn't one [soul] to replace another." Tom's description of his former existence echoes the multidimensional/cosmos child's explanation of the formlessness with which he or she identifies. Could brain damage account for his inability to embrace selfhood in a personal manner? Perhaps, but this ready explanation does not address why his superior intelligence and cascade of aftereffects can be traced directly to his accident. I suspect that Tom is brain shifted, not brain damaged, and multidimensionally oriented to the cosmos rather than a "walk-in."

Tom, like ever so many of the child experiencers quoted in this book, bears all the marks of a new vanguard of children who have been entering the earthplane in large numbers since the sixties, and especially since 1982. These children regard themselves and the lives they lead quite differently than have their elders, and in terms that bespeak a more quixotic viewpoint. They are tolerant of ambiguity, capable of parallel-thought processing, unusually creative, and at home with a complexity of lifestyles that would seem foreign to the generations before them. And with each decade that passes, their creative and intuitive intelligence soars. They are tomorrow's children, today.

TEN

❀

A New Race Aborning

Evolutionary quantum leaps occur when a species is faced with possible extinction. Now, at such a threshold, we are discovering the neurological methods that medicine people and visionaries have mastered so elegantly and have used to make quantum leaps into the future. These capabilities of our brains, once awakened, allow us to enter a transtemporal reality where we can hear the voices of the ancient ones in the wind, heal our planet, and summon our destiny.

—ALBERTO VILLOLDO

THE SIGNS ARE EVIDENT, all of them, that a new race is emerging in the midst of us *right now!*

Child experiencers of near-death states present us with the best possible model we can use to recognize this birthing. And the Millennial Generation, children born from 1982 to about 2001–2003, as named by William Strauss and Neil Howe in their seminal achievement *Generations*,[1] are "marked" in the sense that already many of them are displaying characteristics typical of the psychological and physiological changes that are indicative of the brain shift/spirit shift engendered by the near-death phenomenon.

Youngsters are being flung into this shift quite literally by the millions worldwide, and a whole generation is being born this way, as if they were

167

somehow preprogrammed. One does not have to be a scientist or a psychic to know that something astonishingly spectacular is rising from the "knife's edge" of birth and death . . . a new force awakens.

Linda Silverman, Ph.D., one of the leading authorities on giftedness,[2] contacted me after reading the original edition of the book and said "Your work supports mine and my work supports yours." She went on to say that a remarkable number of exceptionally and profoundly gifted children (160–262 IQ) were the products of excessively long labors, precipitous births (being born too quickly), overdoses of a drug called pitocin, or other birth traumas that might have caused near-death experiences in their birthing. "They demonstrate characteristics that are very similar to those of child experiencers of near-death states." Her research does not address the near-death experience per se—therefore there is no data on anyone in her study reporting such an episode as an infant. However, much of the children's poetry and many of their drawings suggest that such an incident could have occurred. (This is reasonable to me, as I found in my research of child experiencers, that they are six times more likely than adults to forget, block, or repress their experience. It is possible that her gifted kids could have reacted to any episode they might have had in a similar manner.) The Gifted Development Center has assessed eight hundred exceptionally gifted children in the last twenty-four years, with IQ scores above 160. Nearly all of them exhibit "whole brain development" (left and right brain hemispheres operating as if an integrated whole). They are abstract conceptual learners, mature beyond their years, with strong moral sensitivity, compassion, and intensity. Some are passionate about their mission in life, and their mission has to do with spirituality and projects dealing with human rights issues and protecting the environment.

Money does not motivate most of them and schools cannot handle them. More and more are dropping out and are being homeschooled or are teaching themselves via the internet. "Even more remarkable," said Silverman, "I've come across children who are so far evolved beyond anything I've seen in my four-decade career in this field that neither heredity nor environment can explain their achievement. The only explanation is evolution."

All cultures that have ever existed (and that can be traced) have had legends and stories that describe major evolutionary leaps in consciousness and in genetic structure that have occurred and will yet occur in the human family (comparable to the spread of change across population groups that Dr. Silverman and I have been finding). The purpose of these leaps, it is said, is to quicken and refine our species in a vast process of growth that will advance humankind from hardly more than a probability at the dawn of time (or, some say, as mere drones engineered for slave labor by an elitist class bent on mining the earth's gold for their home planet),[3] to the highest and best achievement level and frequency of vibration possible for us to attain in a quest to become more intelligent and godlike. And each such advancement, we are further instructed to know, is visibly marked—the people differ afterward and their differences show.

Since these ancient legends and stories exactly portray our current situation, a synopsis of their message is in order. Visionary truth is just as important as scientific findings. We need both to give us perspective.

Various traditions of esoteric knowledge (loosely referred to as "mystery school teachings") mention the altering of the lifestream whereby new "waves" or "rays" or "worlds" can arise. Earlier in this century, the famous seer Edgar Cayce[4] called these time frames "the coming forth of root races." He did not mean "race" in the context of genetic subgroups, but used the term "root races" to indicate species-wide, evolutionary mutations. He targeted 1998 to 2010 as the years when the next "advancement" would be recognized.

Other, older teachings predicted that a total of seven root races would appear, each one fulfilling its potential, before the human species reached ascendancy. The first four races were essentially described as soul, amorphous thought forms, physical thought forms, and human beings. What was presaged for our current period is the emergence of the fifth root race,[5] those who have quickened in spiritual awareness and genetic makeup. This collection of visionary knowledge holds that two more root races will emerge before the development of "Hu-man" ("God-man") is over. The Christian Bible has in essence the same message—that we are gods in the making and that we are ever growing in spirit. An example of this message is Psalm 82:6: "I have said, ye are gods; and all of you are children of the most high."

By using the colors of the rainbow to depict the energy levels of vibrational frequencies, it is possible to combine esoteric teachings, be they from psychics, mystics, prophets, or visionaries, into one comprehensive chart. This chart focuses on the soul's evolution through human form via the stages of a mind awakening to its greater potential.

ESOTERIC TEACHINGS OF SOUL EVOLUTION THROUGH THE AWAKENING OF THE HUMAN MIND

Levels of Energy	States of Awareness	Types of Consciousness
Red	Physical	Physical: the earthplane; survival issues and individual power
Orange	Astral	Astral: invisible "blueprints"; inner guidance and heightened sensitivity
Yellow	Mental Concrete	Mental: the intellect; decision making and personal will
Green	Mental Abstract	Buddhic: awakening to spirit; initial enlightenment and enlarged worldview
Blue	Higher Intuition	Atmic: self as individual; enlightened knowing and wisdom
Indigo	Inspiration	Monadic: fully individuated; the indivisible whole
Violet	Spiritual	Divine: aligned with soul power; surrender to God's will

If we take the concept of root races (for example, soul, amorphous thought forms, physical thought forms, human beings, and those quickened in spiritual awareness and genetic makeup, as well as two more higher forms of embodiment yet to come), and insert each type into the chart beginning at the top, we arrive at a broad picture of what may indeed be the evolutionary destiny of humankind—a growth progression referred to in esoteric traditions transculturally. According to the diagram, the fifth root race, which is aborning now, comes under the purview of the blue vibration.

And the "blue race" has specifically been mentioned in some prophesies as the quantum leap that would evolve from within the midst of the human family during the final years of the Piscean age. Supposedly, this "fifth race" would be as unlike its predecessors as crystal is unlike clay. Zodiacal cycles, or ages, are approximately 2,160 years long. We are now living in the third millennium. It has been predicted by many that by the year 2020, or soon after, we will enter the long-awaited age of Aquarius, presumably a time when the rigors of science will join with the wisdom of inner knowing to produce societies dedicated to the economics of shared projects and international achievement, rather than to the wanton violence and enslavement of dictatorships.

The current, or more "transcendent," representatives of the blue race, as the architects of the Aquarian age, are said to be exceptionally aware, highly developed both intuitively and intellectually, and comfortable with ambiguity and complex challenges, thus made to order for the demands of the twenty-first century. Visionary traditions also refer to differences in their biological structure—unusual digestive systems and allergies, differences in eyesight, heightened faculties, a noticeable sensitivity to foods, light, sound, and energy fields, plus an amazing ability to function with the least amount of stress during difficult situations.

Descriptions of the blue race are resonant with the typical aftereffect characteristics of the average child experiencer of near-death states, as well as with what pediatricians worldwide are reporting about the newest crop of infants.

A contemporary voice on the subject of a new race aborning in our time is Gordon-Michael Scallion. He is known as an intuitive futurist and modern-day prophet, and is probably most famous for his "future maps" of North America, as well as his predictions of global earth changes. It was he who several years ago affirmed that the fifth root race is the blue race and linked it with the then soon-to-appear blue star, which he later identified as the comet HaleBopp. He associated the manifestation of both of these developments with Christian beliefs about the Second Coming of Christ, and also with the Native American prophecy of the White Buffalo and the portentous 1994 birth, in Janesville, Wisconsin, of an all-white female buffalo calf, since identified by tribal elders and medicine men as the fulfillment of their prophecy and the signal that the New Age has begun.[6]

In his book *Notes from the Cosmos: A Futurist's Insights into the World of Dream Prophecy and Intuition,*[7] Scallion discusses the blue star at length, saying: "All children born after '98 shall be telepathic at birth and many born prior shall exhibit such abilities. The physical body shall change to reflect the vibrational changes of Earth. . . . All races of people shall have a bluish tint to the skin as a result." Scallion also predicts changes in the makeup of the human eye and the way the new race will see, and claims that communication will be possible between these new humans and the animal and spiritual worlds.

By the age of two, Scallion says, many will have mastered multiple languages; by three or four, they'll be aware of their most recent past life. Blue race humans will also have a much longer lifespan, upward of about two hundred years, according to Scallion, and they will put service to others above personal gratification.

If Gordon-Michael Scallion's predictions have any bearing, then blue race people will be more spiritually inclined than their mothers and fathers. One such person of bluish skin has already made an impact in her native land of India and in other countries where she has traveled. As word of her existence and her powerful spiritual teachings spread, her influence is fast becoming global. Her name is Mata Amritanandamayi, and her story is both a tear-jerker, because of the abuse she received as a child, and an inspiration, because she turned her own nightmare into a miracle, enabling her to help transform the lives of thousands.

Mata Amritanandamayi: A Biography, written by one of her devotees, Swami Amritasvarupananda,[8] tells of a poverty-stricken mother who had a wonderful dream about giving birth to Lord Krishna (one of the most popular of the Hindu deities). The next morning, without a single clue that she might be about to deliver a real baby, she intuitively realized she must prepare to do just that. With hardly enough time to spread out a mat and lie down, she gave birth to a daughter. But this was no ordinary daughter. Not only were the entire pregnancy and birth pain free, but the infant was born smiling and without a cry; she lay in the lotus posture of hatha yoga, her fingers in the position symbolizing oneness of the individual self with the Supreme—and she had dark blue skin! The parents were panic-stricken and feared that the baby's strange complexion might be a symptom of disease, the peculiar posture she assumed at birth perhaps a sign of abnormal bone structure. Medical exams detected no abnormalities, nor was there anything in the family's genetic line to account for this. The baby they named Sudhamani was an anomaly.

As stated by Swami: "Eventually, over the course of time, this dark-blue changed into black. Yet, when the little girl's desire to behold the vision of Lord Krishna intensified, her skin colour once again assumed its blue hue. Even today, especially during the Divine Moods of Krishna and Devi, one can observe this dark blue skin tone. Ironically, it was due to this blue-black hue that in the future, Damayanthi [Sudhamani's mother] and other family members would look upon the child with great disdain. This aversion for the dark child would eventually become the cause of her becoming the downtrodden servant of the family and relatives.

"From the moment of the tiny girl's birth, the family began noticing unusual signs which would only be understood years later. . . . One day, after turning six months old, the little girl suddenly stood up and straightaway walked across the verandah. Soon after this, she started running which filled everyone's heart with wonder and joy. Unlike most other children her age, Sudhamani started speaking her mother tongue Malayalam when she was barely six months old. Her passion to sing the Divine Names manifested as soon as she began to speak fairly well. At the tender age of two, without instruction from anybody, she began saying prayers and singing short songs in praise of Sri Krishna."

As a toddler, Sudhamani established a daily habit of melodiously chanting the Divine Names aloud, a practice that continues to this day, and she would sing with devotional fervor compositions she created to honor Lord Krishna. By the time she was five, her spiritual activities had become extraordinary. In school she evidenced a brilliant intellect and memory that so threatened her parents that they pulled her out of her classes, assigning to her instead an ever-increasing load of chores. This only served to intensify her ecstatic devotional moods. Yet the more spiritual she became, the more determined her family was in heaping hard work and physical abuse upon her, convincing themselves that she must be insane. That Sudhamani survived her childhood is a miracle in itself. She forgave all her tormentors, noting that they had committed their crimes in ignorance. All later became her students once she was recognized as a teacher and servant of God. Today she is referred to as the Mother of Immortal Bliss.

Although having blue skin is not necessarily a condition of blue race "membership," Mata Amritanandamayi has exhibited all the traits of a brain shift/spirit shift since her birth in 1953. Her exceptional devotion to God and knowledge of a higher, more spiritual order of life mark her as one of those "blue ones" of the fifth root race.

The human race is adapting, mutating, altering, transforming. We are becoming something else.

As *Homo habilis* we were hardly more than fossils.
As *Homo erectus* we were active, social, and inventive.
As *Homo sapiens* we were highly organized thinkers and clever builders.
As *Homo sapiens sapiens* we went to the moon and computerized society.

John White, who has written extensively in the fields of consciousness research and human development,[9] classified our fifth species advancement as *Homo noeticus*. This advancement will have the ability to access the higher mind. Declares White: "There will never be a better world until there are better people in it, and our potential for growth to higher consciousness is what enables us to 'build better people,' beginning with ourselves."

I would be exaggerating here if I claimed that all those born into the Millennial Generation are fifth root race types. What percentage will actually represent evolution's quantum leap, or, perhaps, signal a devolution into children incapable of caring or compassion, no one really knows. Today's headlines are crammed with ample stories of both extremes. Still, it is possible to project ahead to surmise about what I am certain will be the majority of our new citizens—the fourteenth generation of the United States. Few are better qualified for such a task than historical demographers William Strauss and Neil Howe and the respected astrological researcher E. Alan Meece.

Strauss and Howe remark that, even now, the larger number of these youngsters are proving to be unusually civic minded, optimistic, collegial, competent, possessed of a powerful type of energy, and collective in purpose, expecting praise and rewards while generously passing on the same to others. And they save more money than they spend on conveniences. "The Millennials show every sign of being a generation of trend—toward improved education and health care, strengthening families, more adult affection and protection, and a rising sense that youths need a national mission."[10]

E. Alan Meece, in his tour de force of astrological patterns in history *Horoscope for the New Millennium*,[11] further delineates what might be expected from the Millennials by dividing them into four categories according to year of birth. The early wave, born from 1982 to 1983, he calls an exuberant yet mellow group, like children of the seventies, often lacking in discipline and focus, yet definitely explorers who like to live on the edge. Those born from 1984 to 1988 he terms "benevolent entrepreneurs" who, unlike the first group, are ambitious and disciplined, rather conservative, but with a sense of great duty to society and humankind. He notes that a very precocious bunch with outstanding potential checked in between 1988 and 1995. But he warns that while they possess great talents and leadership skills, they could also be cold, calculating, and one-sided in their assessment of how the world should be changed. The final group, born from 1996 to about 2001–2003, he claims will be "flame throwers" with exceptionally outgoing, irrepressible, freedom-loving, rebellious natures—reformers quick to challenge authority.

Make no mistake, youngsters born before and during the millennium's turn are already and will continue to be as demanding as they are curious, and they are powerfully obsessed with a need to change things. Although many of them come across as all heart, at least initially, that seeming compassion can readily devolve into senseless acts—as already evidenced by kids who have killed other kids in Littleton, Colorado; Pearl, Mississippi; Jonesboro, Arkansas; Edinboro, Pennsylvania; and Springfield, Oregon. As Strauss and Howe pointed out, the Millennial Generation *must have a national mission,* clear goals to aim for, and teachers unafraid of their unusual abilities—or the awesome promise they carry within them could be misdirected or squandered.

One woman keenly aware of the Millennials' collective drive and how to direct it is Linda Redford of Santa Monica, California. An adult experiencer of a dramatic near-death episode, she was given instructions while "dead" on how to create a learning program for today's children that would enable them to address their personal concerns, while disciplining their minds and restoring a sense of honor and value to their world. Named The Adawee Teachings (*Adawee* is Cherokee for "guardians of wisdom"), the learning program has already been tested in a number of schools. One teacher said, "I have never experienced such unity in a classroom [as I have] since this pilot project ended." The program, written in collaboration with Redford's daughter Anne Vorburger, consists of course studies, a self-discovery book, and a T-shirt each student receives that says, "*I am important to the world. The world is important to me.*"[12]

"My vision, instead of healing the damage from childhood, is to stop the damage from happening in the first place," Redford explained. Just tallying up the faxes and messages on her Web site from children participating in The Adawee Teachings, and from teachers clamoring for more information on how to continue the program, proves that her guidance to do this was right on. With Redford's permission, I offer you the honor code from The Adawee Teachings.

THE HONOR CODE

Principles for Planetary Citizenship. For each principle, the adult version is presented first, followed by the child's perspective.

Humility

I am aware that I can learn from all that was created.
I can learn from the sky, a clock, a tree, my friends, and my mom and dad.

Responsibility

I am aware that my words and actions are powerful and have a positive or negative impact on my life, as well as on others and the environment.
When someone is sad I can sit quietly and talk with them until their sadness leaves, or I can tease them and make them sadder.

Respect
I am aware that all that was created has purpose and value.
I'm learning that even a tree has a living spirit that I need to honor.

Honesty
I am aware that being truthful takes courage and is easier when I am open to my feelings.
When I'm truthful with others they learn to trust me.

Generosity
I am aware that sharing my abundance creates harmony and balance.
When I share with others, I feel good inside.

Forgiveness
I am aware that mistakes can be opportunities for growth and understanding.
When I say I'm sorry I understand that I have hurt you, and when I hurt you I hurt myself.

Wisdom
I am aware that there is an intuitive knowing within me that can guide me to make wise choices.
I am learning that inside me I have a wise part that knows what's best.

All children crave knowledge and hunger to learn. All children know that each thing is alive and can communicate. All children often flow into mind states that heighten knowing. All children are as much aware of spirit realms as of the earthplane. All children like to test their perceptions for usefulness. All children are emissaries of divine love and forgiveness.

A child's reality is the basis of a child's truth. Deny the reality, and you deny the child.

ELEVEN

The Promise

The true doctrine of omnipresence is that God reappears with all his parts in every moss and cobweb. The value of the universe contrives to throw itself into every point. If the good is there, so is the evil; if the affinity, so the repulsion; if the force, so the limitation. Thus is the universe alive.

—Ralph Waldo Emerson

MAINSTREAM SOCIETY tends to marginalize creative intuitives.

Individuals interested in consciousness transformations, those who have been through one (such as experiencers of near-death states), along with others of like mind, have for years been busily networking with each other to counteract mainstream bias and create a subculture of their own within society. Their preferences as a group include:

Community-based economies and regional trade;
Revitalized main streets, amateur theater, and open workspaces;
Small-scale, sustainable developments with Internet sales capacity;
Appreciating the uniqueness of place and history, the importance of neighborhoods;
Individual knowingness and intuition in health and healing;
Handmade objects over mechanical or plastic ones;

Homes that fit into natural landscapes, herbal gardens;

Recycling, remodeling, and restoration;

Pilgrimages to sacred and holy places, respect for the feminine;

Commitment to lifelong growth and learning and the exchange of ideas;

Loving, committed relationships, a sense of global as well as national citizenship;

Public service, volunteerism, civic responsibility;

Spiritual development, the personal experience of awakening to spirit realms and communicating with Source.

Thanks to early prototypes of the fifth root race, the steady groundswell toward a definable subculture that is more holistic in attitude has exceeded expectations and is now recognized as a force to be reckoned with by opinion pollsters.

Sociologist Paul H. Ray, vice president of the San Francisco–based market research firm American Lives, Inc., labels this growing faction as "cultural creatives." In his book *The Cultural Creatives: How Fifty Million People Are Changing the World*[1] he estimates that one in four Americans fit this category. He considers them to be a kind of integral culture that merges modernism with traditionalism, East with West, to create a Renaissance mindset. Ray warns that cultural creatives are almost angry in their demand for authenticity, an observation underscored by Charlene Spretnak in her book *The Resurgence of the Real: Body, Nature, and Place in a Hypermodern World.*[2]

At the current rate at which cultural creatives are becoming politically active, and to the degree to which fifth root race newcomers continue to identify with them and support their agendas, a tipping point, or change threshold, may soon be reached. Tipping points are endemic to history, always unpredictable as to exact timing, but ever fateful in collapsing that which has grown inefficient, top-heavy, or "out of touch" with the citizenry (e.g., the dismantling of the Berlin Wall, and the fall of every dictatorship that has ever existed). There comes a time when sheer numbers are enough to trigger a massive shift in the prevailing order. (Sometimes other tyrannies arise, but the original one does not and cannot last.)

Societies everywhere are now in this position, vulnerable to a tipping point. Computerization has made it possible for any individual to coparticipate in dissolving borders and outmaneuvering governments. A sense that moral integrity and social justice should matter more than global power relations and religious fundamentalism is gaining majority strength.

Nothing less than the evolution of society itself is at hand; the subculture is poised to become the dominant culture.

The twenty-first century will bear witness to the driving force of this "third wave," which is neither left nor right, liberal nor conservative, traditionalist nor modernist, but an integrated stream of consciousness that is intolerant of business as usual; it is more reformist than revolutionary. And, as this third wave moves deeper into the third millennium, "third-way" principles will emerge as the way to live and do business.[3]

I devoted an entire chapter in both *Future Memory* and *Solstice Shift: Magical Blend's Synergistic Guide to the Coming Age*[4] to a discussion of third-way principles. Here is a summary of what I have discovered about the Third Way:

> I have noticed that when faced with life issues, we tend to react in one of three ways: (1) we play ostrich and pretend the situation away; (2) we label it an enemy or a devil and attack; or (3) we confront the situation squarely and honestly, search for the truth behind the appearance, and take decisive steps to initiate a constructive solution. The first way creates victims, the second victors (conquerors), and the third responsive and responsible participants in life, committed to growth and learning.

This third way of dealing with life issues is the way we transcend duality, get beyond victors and victims, good and evil, darkness and light. The Third Way requires mediation and diplomacy skills, mindful attention, and a willingness to consider what is appropriate as a greater priority than self-centered interests. It takes time to learn and patience to initiate, and it necessitates cooperation and compromise, but it is the only modality that holds any promise for a worthwhile future. The Third Way upholds dignity and authenticity and wholeness, and wholeness is spirituality made manifest.

When we live in accordance with the Third Way, we decrease tension. While a certain amount of tension is necessary for existence, too much tension depletes initiative and restricts growth. The fulcrum of Third Way balance is *forgiveness,* as forgiveness releases tension and promotes patience. When we resist forgiveness, the resulting tension keeps us from transcending. We need to let go to grow. We need to forgive.

Another individual who has written extensively on third-way principles is Walter Starcke, a former Hollywood luminary who underwent a spiritual transformation many years ago and has since become a devoted student of the Christian Bible and a mystic. In his new book, *It's All God,*[5] he reveals that the Third Way (ascension consciousness) is *reconciliation.*

But he cautions: "As long as we believe that we must constantly and only think beautiful, subjectively satisfying thoughts, we are creating the very duality we claim to deny. What I am saying is, we can reconcile the objective level [materiality] without denying its subjective nature [spirituality] only if we simultaneously see both its infinite oneness and its limited form. By doing this, we close the gap and experience the only true absolute: All inclusiveness."

Reconciliation and inclusiveness are the keys to understanding what fuels millennial generation attitudes and the cultural creatives as a subculture. For them, elitist thinking has lost the fashionable appeal it once had.

The "age of globality" arrived in 1998. With it came the realities of photonics (enhanced fiber optics for the information superhighway); interspecies communication (apes trained via sign language to converse with humans); biochemistry "marking" (medication engineered to meet the needs of each person as an individual); natural-systems agriculture (high-yielding perennial grains grown together to cut waste and weeds); weather pattern study (links between weather effects and sex repression, warfare, and social violence),[6] cloning issues (life-science companies dominating seed and DNA sequence patents).[7] The third millennium is quickly becoming a science-fiction world made fact.

Curiously, the vast majority of children rescued from death's finality by advanced technology have near-death experiences that prepare them for . . . advanced technology.

These kids aren't coming back as the dutiful fulfillments of their parents' dreams so much as, in their own unique way, the mountain movers of the twenty-first century. And don't breathe a sigh of relief that at last we have a generation of children who are courteous and civic minded. *These youngsters are instilled with a sense of mission, and they are powerfully obsessed with a need to change things. This is their promise and their destiny.* And they will insist upon the spirit-led worship and uncommon lifestyles that arise from having a personal relationship with God.

They are "imagineers," creative problem solvers rewired and reconfigured to make significant contributions to a society desperately in need of fresh new ideas. But it will take innovative and courageous adults to point the way.

The exceptional legacy of retired teacher Muriel Freifeld of Potomac,

Maryland, gives us such a model. She experienced a near-death episode while stuck in the birth canal that infused her with a lifelong mission to educate children in ways that would empower them. She suffered frequent parental and sibling abuse as a youngster, but what hurt her the most was her inability to communicate her visions and her inner knowing. She was branded "stupid" and became suicidal. Her extremely high IQ wasn't recognized in time to prevent her rebelliousness, low grades, and school truancy. She "knew" her subjects but fumbled over the technicalities of how to format what she knew (the same situation faced by Bill of Atlanta, in chapter 3).

Once Muriel was an adult, she began the college track, did well in math, showed an unusual sensitivity to music, won many prizes in art, and excelled in the double major of psychology and early childhood development. Her career as an innovative teacher and later as founder of New Visions for Child Care, Inc.,[8] a project endorsed by the governor of Maryland, is exemplary. And, of her three children, two have become pioneering physicians in new surgical techniques and treatment of infectious diseases, and the other is a well-known southern artist. Muriel's life is an example of what can happen when the potential enhanced by a brain shift/spirit shift is unleashed, to the benefit of the many.

According to my research statistics, child experiencers of near-death states, like Muriel Freifeld, are showing us how to have long-lasting, healthy relationships and marriages; how to excel in work and succeed in spite of the stress from downsizing and layoffs; how to live simply, yet more enjoyably; how to have a meaningful, satisfying, and active life. Those who seemed socially retarded during their earliest years have established that the learning reversals and faculty and intelligence enhancements that may have seemed burdensome when they were children and young adults can indeed be integrated, and in ways bordering on the miraculous. Some of the participants in my study, for example, are now doing advanced DNA research, working on new healing tools for surgeons, producing significant patents and inventions, establishing compassionate birthing and dying centers, and creating new measures to recycle waste materials, protect the environment, and build better homes for less cost. Not all are college graduates. They don't have to be. Even as amateur scientists and social visionaries, their achievements already have astounded and amazed us, and will continue to do so.

It is true that child experiencers do not process brain shifts/spirit shifts in the same manner as do adult experiencers, and their episodes are likely to impact them in more powerful ways—as the cases discussed in this book illustrate. Aftereffects tend to overwhelm, because the context in which they must be integrated has yet to be established in the lives of the children who must grapple with them. A simple chart puts this situation in perspective.

EFFECTS OF A TRANSFORMATION OF CONSCIOUSNESS (BRAIN SHIFT/SPIRIT SHIFT)

Adults	renewal	new life	a growth event—"course correction"
Children	rebirth	new race	an evolutionary event—"species advancement"

To transform the world, people must transform . . . and they are.

Those who were thrust into this transformational shift via the near-death phenomenon may be so changed that even before-and-after photographs may bear little resemblance to each other, to say nothing of attitudes, personalities, and body functions; their lives are often turned upside down. But even those who have been touched by the Holy Spirit during church services, people who have gone on shamanic vision quests, or those who have devoted themselves to lives of service and prayer may exhibit the same aftereffects, the same shift.

While near-death states might be Creation's way of selecting helpers who might not otherwise volunteer, transformations by choice enable one to be more in control of any trauma or confusion the aftereffects may foster. In other words, 'tis better to go willingly than to be shoved, for the spiritual will not forever be denied.

The brain shift/spirit shift that happens in such large numbers to today's youngsters offers the most compelling evidence yet that mind itself, that collective "reservoir" of intelligence, is also evolving. It is possible, for instance, to take the four types of near-death experiences discussed in chapter 3 and reconsider them in this manner.

- *Initial Experience:* an introduction for the individual to other ways of perceiving reality; stimulus.
- *Unpleasant or Hell-like Experience:* a confrontation with distortions in one's own attitudes and beliefs; healing.
- *Pleasant or Heavenlike Experience:* a realization of how important life is and how every effort that one makes counts; validation.

- *Transcendent Experience:* an encounter with oneness and the collective whole of humankind; enlightenment.

Rather than looking at these as four types of near-death experience, we might more appropriately recognize in them four stages of awakening consciousness. These stages of awakening begin with the first stirring of something greater, an initial awareness; then move to confrontation with the bias of perception, followed by opportunities to cleanse and start anew; then to the bliss and the ecstasy of self-validation and the discovery of life's worth; until, at last, the moment comes when unlimited realms of truth and wisdom are unveiled.

Since consciousness appears to have the capacity to grow, change, and evolve, individually *and en masse,* one implication is the existence of thought fields that all of us must be capable of drawing from and adding to automatically or at will. This idea has been postulated scientifically and is currently being tested at the urging of Rupert Sheldrake, best known for his breakthrough theory of "morphic resonance" (the existence of universal thought fields), detailed in his book *A New Science of Life: The Hypothesis of Formative Causation.*[9]

The fact that so many children experience near-death episodes indicates to me that the mechanism for stimulating a brain shift/spirit shift may be part of our "equipment" as human beings—our birthright—nature's assurance that, as individuals and as a species, we will continuously readjust as evolution readies itself for major advancements.

After decades of research and sessions with thousands of people, I am convinced that once we understand the import of *brain shifts* (which are visible and can be clinically tested and measured), and *spirit shifts* (which are invisible and signify the movement of spirit forces and the development of true faith) . . . we will solve the secret of how the human family and mind itself evolve and for what purpose.

I can make this extravagant statement because my work has shown me that *brain shifts/spirit shifts are the engine that drives evolution and thus the destiny of humankind.*

Experiencers of this dual shift have described the "light" that they encountered in terms that suggest there may be three very different types of light that exist beyond those we are consciously aware of and beyond the light known in the realms of earth life.

THE THREE TYPES OF SUBJECTIVE LIGHT

Type	Color	Function
Primary Light	Colorless	A pulsating presence or luminosity usually perceived as frighteningly awesome, a piercing power, raw essence; the Origin of all origins.
Dark Light	Pure black yet often with velvety tinges of dark purple	A shimmering peaceful depth usually perceived as "The Darkness That Knows," a source of strength and knowing, healing sanctuary; the womb of Creation.
Bright Light	The range of yellow-gold-white	A brilliant radiance usually perceived as an almost blinding glow that emanates unconditional love, a warm inviting intelligence, union; the activity of Truth.

These three lights are consistently referred to, irrespective of person, age, or background, as more real than the manifest light on earth and more powerful than any source humankind could harness—including the sun's rays and "zero-point" energy (the "stuff" of the universe, untapped electromagnetic energy).

These lights seem to reveal aspects of Creation in a manner that implies that they may represent the outworking of Divine Order. There is no human connotation given to their function by most experiencers (such as black as negative/evil, or white as positive/good), but, rather, an identification is made with the handiwork of God.

The main effects I have observed in the people who claimed to have experienced them were: from Primary Light, deep mystical knowings and more radical changes in a sense of reality and life's purpose; from Dark Light, gentle reassurances of being nurtured, healed, and supported while linked to larger evolutionary processes; from Bright Light, displays of a broad range of visibly heightened abilities and sensitivities as if the physical body was transmuting.

It is my belief from what I have seen that the "light" and light imagery of near-death and other transformative and enlightening states are but the reflection of a power surge as it registers upon or imprints the consciousness of the one who experiences it. What is perceived as light may well be a "power punch," varying by degrees of charge. To dub transformative episodes as mere "light experiences" misses the rich complexity of their true nature.

Individuals who return to earthplane awareness after such an event almost immediately gain a sense of future. Irrespective of the other aftereffects and whether that sense of future can signal higher brain development and the emergence of the higher mind, the futuristic revelations that pour forth from experiencers are often literal. With child experiencers, however, their futuristic visions differ somewhat from those of adults.

Kids seem only moderately interested in any kind of dire scenario numerous prognosticators and prophets targeted for the years between 1998 and 2007. But, jump ahead to a time when they could be parents or even grandparents, and their composure abruptly changes. "That's what I came back for," they say, "to help the earth and prepare the people. I am here for *the changes*."

This message of theirs sounds similar to that of adults, until the math is calculated as to how old each child would have to be to match the description they give of themselves during that cryptic time. Regardless of the child's age when interviewed, the same period emerges—between 2013 and 2029.

This same time span was highlighted by Strauss and Howe in their study of repetitious cycles in American history. To understand the significance of this period, Strauss and Howe ask that we recall the parallel eras of the Glorious Revolution, the American Revolution, the Civil War, the Great Depression, and World War II. "How will this crisis end?" they wonder. They then offer this comment: "Three of the four antecedents ended in triumph, the fourth (the Civil War) in a mixture of moral fatigue, vast human tragedy, and a weak and vengeful sense of victory. We can foresee a full range of possible outcomes, from stirring achievement to apocalyptic tragedy."

Of interest is the fact that on December 21, 2012, the Mayan calendar ends—shortly before the "darkening skies" of the crisis projected by Strauss and Howe. The Mayans believed that time "as it currently is experienced" will end when their calendar does. Strauss and Howe, although hopeful about the future, admit that all indicators do indeed predict this period as one of unusual importance, and in all probability global in its repercussions.

Yet the ending of the Mayan calendar does *not* signify an end to history, just to time as we know it, for their calculations were based on sun cycles of approximately 26,000 years each. What ends in 2012 is the span of the Fourth Sun. The Fifth Sun begins immediately after, with the fifth root race at the ready to handle the possible acceleration of time and energy as the earth passes into a region of highly charged particles called the photon belt. Slated to last for two thousand years, this photon immersion elicits curiosity from scientists who remain unconvinced of its supposed effects, if any, and awe from the more mystical who see in this event a period when the remaining sixth and seventh root races can emerge to complete the ascendancy of human evolution on this planet. We will have to wait either way to see if the photon belt is a fizzle or a true phenomenon. Regardless of how things turn out, the years 2013 to 2029 can't help but be momentous as we enter a new timespan—that of the Fifth Sun.

Right now, however, an extraordinary credo begs for attention—the integration of science and religion, the reconnection of the head with the heart. And this affects near-death research, as well.

Ken Wilber, who almost single-handedly launched the transpersonal revolution in psychology several decades ago with the publication of his first book, *The Spectrum of Consciousness,*[10] granted a rare interview with Mark Matousek that was carried in the July/August 1998 issue of *Utne Reader.*[11] In the article, Wilber confirmed that the relationship between science and religion is the most critical issue facing society, a rift that he believes is tearing the planet apart. "When you take into account that 90 percent of the world's population has a religious outlook based on some kind of mythology—God the Father and so on—and that the standard scientific view gives these myths as much credibility as they give the tooth fairy . . . you see the problem clearly. There's an enormous split between reason and meaning that must be healed."

Wilber builds a compelling case stating that prerational "messages" and "channeling" are all too often little more than New Age silliness when compared to the mystical, esoteric core undergirding all of the world's great religions—a truth based on direct experience that was thoroughly tested before it was offered to adherents as a reproducible experience. States Wilber, "Science has managed to reproduce itself for two to three hundred years, while mystical science has been doing it for at least two to three thousand years. This is not insignificant." In *The Marriage of Sense and Soul,*[12] his newer work, he describes how art, ethics, and science can be integrated without compromising their important differences.

Pierre Teilhard de Chardin[13] has been my inspiration because of how he managed to combine the intellectual with the spiritual. Even in consideration of the numinous power I experienced in death, it has been the quarter century I spent tempering revelation with careful fieldwork and analysis that showed me the real wonder of life's pulse. My discovery was

Teilhard de Chardin's—research *is* the highest form of adoration—for me a marriage of science and spirituality as Wilber described.

THE BIG PICTURE

In *Beyond the Light,* and the chapter called "Revelations," I summarized comments made by thousands of adult experiencers of near-death states regarding "The Big Picture," what they had observed from the Other Side of death about life and the lives we lead. I want to do the same thing with child experiencers.

To a child, though, Truth with a capital "T" covers smaller ground and is simply put. In honor of this, I now offer you a summary of comments made to me by child experiencers of near-death states. Bear in mind that most of these children have a more mature way of viewing reality than their agemates. Imagine as you read the children's version of "The Big Picture" that one of these special youngsters is lecturing you about the real truth of life based on what he or she learned through dying or through coming close to death. These kids do tend to lecture, as they are quite confident about what they know. And they often alternate languaging between childish phrases and more adult terms; this is normal for them. I've tried to convey this in in my summary.

There is no afterlife—just an ongoing lifestream we leave and return to as we take part in different experiences.

God exists. It doesn't matter what God is called, God is still God. And we are each part of God, always. We only think we can be separated from God. Really, we can't.

We each have a purpose in a Larger Plan, and we are important to that Plan. We each have a job to do. Large or small doesn't matter.

It doesn't matter if you know what your job is. If you follow your heart and pray about it, you'll be shown or nudged in the right direction.

Worship is important, so is an altar of some kind in your home or in your bedroom. And whatever is on your altar is holy. Church is important, too, some kind of church or place of worship, inside or outside, forest or big building—because church is God's House.

Church shouldn't put people down. Everyone has the right to ask questions and to want to know more. If a church doesn't let people do this then it isn't God's House anymore.

Prayer is powerful. You can see it and feel it. Prayer power travels in beams and when a prayer beam hits you, you feel warm and good all over.

Food tastes better if you say Grace before you eat, and have candles and flowers on the table. Most foods are okay to eat, but you need to ask the food first if it wants to be in your tummy. Sometimes the food says no. If we would listen better, we would feel better. We should listen more to our body, too. It tells us more than our head does, sometimes.

Animals are our friends. They help us learn to share and to give. Rocks are our friends, too, and so are fish and water and plants and all kinds of things. Everything is alive—that's why we need to respect our world.

We need to respect each other, too, even babies who aren't born yet.

You don't need a body to see, hear, think, feel, touch, smell, and know things. All that stuff is easy to do without a body. The only reason anyone needs a body is to grow. You can't grow if you don't have one. That's what makes a body important, and you need to take care of what you have—or it can't take care of you.

We have the families we have because we need them. Sometimes we choose our family, and sometimes we get what we get because it's our assignment and we get "brownie points" for saying yes. Other times we're just "booted" in because it's our turn.

Mistakes can be corrected. We're never stuck. We just forget how The Plan works until something happens to help us remember. We all know more than we think we do. That's one of those things we need to remember.

Life can get pretty scary. Getting in touch with the love that is inside of us can make the scary things go away. If that doesn't work, get help. None of us ask for help like we should. We think we can do everything by ourselves, but we can't. There are always helpers around us ready to pitch in. Some wear bodies and some don't.

Work is important, so is learning. It's okay to buy things and earn money, but what's really special is helping someone, lending a hand, doing chores, cleaning things, making a home, being a friend, getting ready for tomorrow, expressing love, forgiving people. What we do for others matters more than what we do for ourselves.

You can't laugh enough, and play and create things and sing and write poems and scrunch up your nose so your face tickles. Always be loyal and truthful. Lying hurts you or someone else, sooner or later.

No one ever dies. We just trade one body for another one. Sometimes that's a happy thing to do and sometimes it's not. Whatever we experience becomes God's experience, and God never forgets a thing.

Everything is made of light. Spirit is what holds light together so it can become shapes and forms. Spirit is everywhere, like air, and it breathes, but not like our nose does. That means everything breathes. I do. You do. So does God. God's breath is what keeps the universe alive.

We are stuffed full of love 'cause God is. So's everything else. It's a wonder how many people forget that, and they forget about having a soul. We each have one, that's our perfect part. Our soul makes certain we remember who we are, so we can always make our way back to the lifestream—our homey home—no matter how far away from it we travel.

The findings in this book address the next chapter in the human family's mutual quest for knowledge and understanding. This final story about a child of war illustrates the step we need to take in the desire we all have for wisdom:

A friend of mine and fellow near-death survivor participated in some of the most gruesome and horrific battles of the Vietnam War. He was also part of the army contingent that was the first to arrive after the massacre of Vietnamese civilians by U.S. troops at My Lai in 1968. Picking his way through the carnage, he happened upon a little girl digging a grave to bury her family. The task was hers, since she was the only family member left. My friend spoke with the child and she told him she must now do as her father had once asked of her: *look for the light on the dark side of the mountain.* "I will make a garden over the graves of my family and plant food," she explained, "so people going by will never go hungry."

The "wisdom of angels" is in our children, for they *know* what is true . . . thus is the promise of childhood, now, and always.

APPENDIX ONE

Tips for the Child in All of Us

*It takes a lot of courage to release the familiar and seemingly
secure, to embrace the new. But there is no real security in
what is no longer meaningful. There is more security in the
adventurous and exciting, for in movement there is life,
and in change there is power.*

—ALAN COHEN

DATELINE—MAY 1997, Boca Raton, Florida: Beneath the headline, "Dying
Children Lead Atheist Doc to the Lord," Diane M. Komp, M.D. admits that
children inspired her to turn back to God. Komp, a pediatric cancer specialist
at Yale Hospital, New Haven, Connecticut, tells story after story of what
dying youngsters say, in her book, *A Window to Heaven*—like the child who
saw Jesus driving a school bus and another who described the music of a chorus of angels. Of interest here is the fact that there is little difference between
what she reports from a child's deathbed and what children say who have
experienced a near-death episode.[1]

Books like *A Window to Heaven* that discuss these psychospiritual biological events and our reactions to them are becoming more popular as people feel free to discuss the topic of life after death more openly. Physicians,
such as Komp, no longer fear being ostracized by their peers, since many of
them are doing the same thing—taking a friendlier look at things "paranormal." And they are greatly bolstered in their newfound courage by Dutch cardiologist, Pim van Lommel and Associates, and their clinical, prospective
study of near-death experiences, conducted with heart patients, that was published in *The Lancet* (medical journal), Vol. 358, No. 9298, 12-15-01.

The landmark van Lommel study overturned objections to the validity of
near-death states (such as: it must have been a hallucination, oxygen deprivation, etc.) and established that even people who have flatlined (no brain
waves) can still "tour" environments outside the range of physical perception—as if their faculties were fully functional, nonlocal, and encompassed
360 degrees of simultaneous awareness. My discovery that it takes a mini-

mum of seven years to integrate these experiences was borne out in their work; my first book is referenced in their study.

Scientific research is moving ever closer to establishing that the "paranormal" is not paranormal. Yet, the near-death phenomenon still defies any attempt to fully explain its cause or impact. The biggest challenge we now face is the afteraffects—how people change. Although much has been written about the aftereffects, little notice has been given to providing practical tips and suggestions, especially for child experiencers.

A MOTHER'S PUZZLE

Beth Williamson, the mother of Sophia Carmien who drowned at the age of four, expresses the puzzle she faced in dealing with her very different daughter after the drowning:

"It does seem she is different from a lot of her classmates. She has her own mind (rather than being swayed by peer pressure), and a strong sense of ethics and justice. She is a talented writer and expresses deep emotional understanding in her poems and short stories. Also, Sophia and I have very spiritual talks sometimes and I feel I am talking to someone who understands at an equal level. She has developed her own religion with various principles and beliefs. She *hates* scary, suspenseful, and/or violent movies, and will simply go and read in another room at a friend's house if people are watching such a movie. This was true back when she was six or seven at the YMCA afterschool program as well. Movies that most kids (and counselors) thought were fine, Sophia got very upset by. She doesn't really seem to "fit in" generally with her schoolmates, and she says she wishes she had more friends. She's smart and clever and has a good sense of humor. But, at any rate, she does seem to have a hard time being accepted by many of the other kids."

Beth Williamson's words echo those from the typical parent of a child near-death experiencer. What do you do afterward with youngsters who seem to have "changed," perhaps radically? What measures do you use? How do you help them integrate in a positive way what they experienced?

Appendix 1 addresses the human side to this puzzle—what to do about near-death kids and the "child" in all of us, for we can all benefit from what aids children. It is filled with helpful hints to aid in understanding, coping with, and integrating the aftereffects of near-death states, as transformations of consciousness—no matter how caused. Since the aftereffects of near-death states are the same or similar to those of transformative events (like a vision quest, baptism of the Holy Spirit, rise of kundalini, an incident of enlightenment, or the result of a lifetime of devoted prayer and meditation), what makes a difference for near-death experiencers can indeed apply across the entire field of consciousness studies. Highlighted here, though, are how these episodes tend to affect children, their families, schoolteachers, and the professional community of caregivers. I cannot guarantee the outcome of utilizing any of the services or ideas or people so presented in this section. I simply offer this material as a gesture of sharing some of the best resources I have yet to find in this field. Use them at your own discretion.

TIPS ON INTEGRATION AND COUNSELING

Right off, I want to state that you don't get back the child you "lost" to a near-death experience.

Many parents have contacted me, most of them panic-stricken, as to what they might do to help their suddenly remote or aloof child return to "normal." They already have tried expensive medical tests, counselor after counselor, psychotropic drugs, medical specialists, but to no avail. Their unexplainably different child remained "different."

Parents are not prepared for the fact that child experiencers of near-death states have aftereffects just like adult experiencers. And, aftereffects are not something you "heal" from—you adjust to them. What sets most of the children's cases apart is that the brain shift/spirit shift occurred during critical junctures in brain development. Before they could integrate into this world, most were jerked back to another, only to be returned after suddenly reviving or being resuscitated. Literally, they underwent a "second birth." And, as the second born, they truly are unique.

This can be a tremendous blessing if the family is willing to explore the possible ramifications of what has happened. Such openness provides the perfect atmosphere for the young to chatter away without embarrassment or censure, or maybe act out the memory of their episode via a puppet show, children's theater, or family fun night. Everyone benefits when this occurs, not just the child. New ways of thinking, new modes of family behavior and interactions, a new reverence for life invariably result.

Should the family refuse to admit what happened to their child, or deny or ignore the aftereffects, alienation often follows and can lead to behavior problems with the youngster, both at home and at school.

Yet supportive parents, although important, are not enough. Child experiencers need more than that— they need freedom "with a fence around it" so they can safely test the multiple realities they know exist. (Freedom "with a fence" around it" refers to an open, supportive environment, where kids can explore and experiment without criticism or censure, yet rules are in place— the "fence"—to instill discipline and respect for self and others.

Child experiencers don't have to feel as if they are "outcasts," nor must they face the prospect of losing their childhood. Parents can help kids:

- Own their experience
- Revisit their experience
- Adjust to the aftereffects

Of the child experiencers in my study who had attained adulthood, the majority did not "own" or claim what happened to them until they were in their late thirties—even though they perfectly fit the profile of aftereffects as youngsters. Cherie Sutherland, Ph.D., speaks about this, unfortunate situation, at least with adult experiencers, in her book, *Reborn in the Light: Life after Near-Death Experiences* (Bantam Books, New York City, 1995). By tracing "trajectories," she discovered that these people tend to take one of four routes in dealing with their experience: accelerated growth, steady progress, temporarily arrested, or blocked.

Linda A. Jacquin, who "tucked her experience away," made this statement once she finally faced what had happened to her when she drowned at age four and a half: "After I remembered my childhood NDE, I became more of an adult than I ever was before—stronger, more centered, more confident, more open, more insightful. It's like I grew up overnight."

As children age, full recovery of their episode (be it near-death, near-death-like, or nonexperience types), and the subsequent integration of the many aftereffects into their daily lives, becomes increasingly paramount. The majority turn to God for the assistance they need, or ask their angel friends for guidance. Others initiate rigorous programs of study and self-analysis, while a few practice specific yoga breathing techniques that they claim help them to integrate the dormant aspects of themselves. For those who go to therapists, counselors, psychologists, or psychiatrists, benefits or lack thereof have most to do with the sensitivity and training of the professional.

This is so important, allow me to repeat a few quotes given earlier in the book:

Carol Jean Morres, Long Beach, California; NDE at fourteen, extreme pain in epigastric area. "Professionals are generally trained to see things in ways that do not allow for unusual experiences to be viewed as anything other than anomalous or pathologic. Things are changing, but I have yet to meet any 'therapist' who will even listen when I bring up my nighttime experiences, except to label them as products of anxiety or depression. I tend to put mental health therapists in the same category as car mechanics and other rip-off specialists."

Diana Schmidt, El Cerrito, California; NDE at nine, during undiagnosed seizure. "First analyst said, 'You've had a transcendent experience.' We never discussed it or my psychic abilities, as he felt threatened. Second analyst said, 'I had one of those NDEs.' She treated me like an equal. This nurtured me and I felt very valued by her. Nineteen years after my third near-death experience, my new neurologist in with our HMO asked me for details and wrote my NDEs into the Medical Record. Prior to this, I'd been told I had a mental problem and had had a hallucination."

Tonecia Maxine McMillan, Oxon Hill, Maryland; NDE at eleven, drowning. "I told my therapist about the recurring nightmares. I told her about my episode, but she really was *not* helpful in this area. She really did not have a clue! She wanted to know all about my near-death experience, but I think she was just intrigued with the whole idea."

A rare success story with counseling is that of Beverly A. Brodsky, Philadelphia, Pennsylvania, who "died" when she was seven and a half during a tonsillectomy. "My mother said that I was a happy child before the surgery. Shortly after, I was so depressed I spent most of my time thinking about the Holocaust, war, and suffering. I withdrew from the world. I remember wanting to be a monk and live in silence. I hardly talked to anyone."

As an adult, she sought out the services of a healer/therapist who led her through a visualization exercise. "I had been so terrified of remembering my near-death episode that I had resisted going on, and had to return for a second session. This time, I was sent back to a hall of knowledge I had visited in my experience and saw and felt that same black wave coming to cover the Earth—like in the Dylan song 'A Hard Rain's A Gonna Fall'—the roar of the apocalyptic ocean. Within this wave (which I recognized as created by human thought) were fear, anger, pain, rage, injustice, despair, and all negative things. And I saw the same small white circle inside, like a bubble in the wave, only now I felt it was an escape, like the Yang circle within

Beverly Brodsky's first attempt to revisit her near-death episode that of a black wave coming to cover earth.

Beverly Brodsky's entire near-death experienced changed once she was ready to forgive the negative parts and emphasize the positive.

the Yin darkness. I think what happened after my near-death experience was that I didn't understand there was an alternate route and got 'swallowed up' by the wave, hence the negativity of my teen and early adult years.

"To change the ending, I took my younger self through the bubble and into the realm of beauty, love, and light, where I had been earlier in my episode before the wave came. This is the realm of true power. I then saw the sun move up next to the earth and bathe it in light. Then I saw that both the dark wave and perfect Light exist simultaneously—it's all a matter of what you choose to focus on! So I took the sun and *smashed* through the wave. The healer/therapist said that darkness is a part of our experience in life, with the body's limitations, our apparent separation from spirit, and instinctive behaviors like fear and anger. At the end of the session, I gave myself a symbol to remember this truth."

By reconciling memories of the heaven and hell that had haunted her since the surgery, Brodsky purposefully changed the outcome of her scenario during her second session and created a new symbol of understanding. She found great peace in doing this.

The difficulty both child and adult experiencers have with professionals relates more to prevailing notions of what is culturally accepted than to the judgment factor of whether or not the experiencer is mentally and emotionally stable.

Sometimes an experiencer is lucky enough to find a therapist who is also an experiencer. When this occurs, there is instant rapport, and miracles follow. To the extreme, I've actually seen people involuntarily committed to psychiatric hospitals simply because they displayed the typical aftereffects of the average near-death experiencer, then later released when a new therapist assigned to their case (who happened to have had such an episode) recognized them as a near-death experiencer. Those professionals who usually have the best record working with adult experiencers are the ones trained in **transpersonal psychology.**

Joseph Benedict Geraci, an adult experiencer, who is now an administrator of the New Britain School System in New Britain, Connecticut, did his Ph.D. dissertation at the University of Connecticut on research that addressed "Students' Post Near-Death Experience Attitude and Behavior Toward Education and Learning." Some pertinent comments from his paper: "Transpersonal psychology addresses those human experiences that take consciousness beyond the ordinary ego boundaries of time and space. . . . Emphasis is placed on the concept of consciousness which is a most important variable in human development. In comparison to the behaviorist, psychoanalytic and humanistic forces of traditional psychology, transpersonal psychology describes three levels of consciousness: lower level, incapable of an ego-self and reflective consciousness (infant); personal, having an ego-self (adolescent); transpersonal, ego-self and beyond, and identity with the essence of life through direct experience, not deduction. Experiences include unitive consciousness, cosmic awareness, mystical experiences, and maximum sensory awareness." Transpersonal psychology, as a legitimate field of understanding and exploring varied states of mind, is by its nature geared to experiencers.[2]

Hypnosis can be a positive step in the therapeutic process, but far too many times it's anything but beneficial. If the hypnotist is not careful to choose his or her words with discrimination, the client can be led on, or steered in the direction the professional wants the individual to go, rather than providing opportunities for authentic discovery. As a result, **false memories** can be created or planted in the client's mind, memories that seem so real the individual will swear that's what really happened, when nothing of the sort ever occurred. I've encountered this situation so often when interviewing experiencers, that I've learned to be cautious of any retrieval of an individual's near-death scenario if a hypnotist was involved.[3]

An exciting new development in therapy today is the **philosophical counselor.** Numbers of practitioners are rising steadily to meet the demand of people who want to use the lens philosophy provides, to examine their lives from the broader scope of satisfaction and meaning. This is part of an international movement that began in Germany in the early 1980s—the trend is catching on. An interesting article on this subject appeared in the Jan/Feb 1997 issue of *Utne Reader,* pages 50–51, entitled "Thinking, Not Shrinking." It was written by Laura Wexler, and focused on a session she had with a philosophical counselor by the name of Dr. Kenneth Cust, an assistant professor of philosophy at Central Missouri State University, Warrensburg, Missouri.

Another route is that of a **consciousness coach,** usually an experienced personal growth specialist, who inspires individual clients to identify and then realize their fullest potential. At frequent intervals, they provide the insight one can get from being coached. (Two consciousness coaches I know with a successful track record in working with people who have undergone impactual transformative events, are Diane K. Pike and Arleen Lorrance, both with the Teleos Institute. Query for more details: Teleos Institute, 7119 East Shea Blvd., Suite 109, PMB 418, Scottsdale, AZ 85254-6107; (480) 948-1800; e-mail Teleosinst@aol.com; Web site http://www.consciousnesswork.com.

CHILD EXPERIENCERS

But, what if the experiencer is still a child?

As mentioned earlier, three key factors play a large role in the child integrating their near-death experience into their living reality. When all three factors are present, there exists the greatest likelihood of a healthy integration process. The three factors are:

1. The child is willing and able to talk about his or her experience.
2. The child's parents create a nurturing atmosphere in which the experience is validated and into which it can be integrated.
3. Adult and professional resources such as counselors, therapists, and doctors who are open to the child's experience and able to recognize common characteristic that help them assist the child if needed.

It is rare, however, that all three factors are in place at the same time. Consider the following real-life scenario (for obvious reasons, no names can be used—the psychologist is the narrator).

"The four-year-old was born with a serious heart defect that demanded surgery within the first few weeks of life. He underwent several more surgeries in his short life, was on medication to control the rhythm of his heart, had to be monitored constantly, and was rushed to emergency rooms numerous times. In spite of all the pain and suffering he endured, he was cheerful and uncomplaining.

"I asked him to draw a picture as an 'ice breaker' and as a way to establish rapport. He drew some parallel lines with scratches wobbling between, a circle or two, and a face. When queried about the content, he replied, 'This is a person climbing a ladder to another dimension.' *Please*, a four-year-old? Hardly the language of the usual child, but his mother denied any chance he could have picked up such words from anyone in the family. She was as puzzled as me, and a little spooked.

"Months later she reported that this child, while riding in the car with her, had invited her attention by patting her arm and saying, 'Mom, mom, remember when I died?' 'Oh, no, no, you've never died.' 'Yes I have, you know,' and he proceeded to describe one emergency in a particular hospital emergency room. His mother continued to quote his words, 'When I died the light was so bright, I thought I should have brought my sunglasses! And the angels wanted me to come with them, but I said I couldn't because I had to stay and take care of you and daddy. But I made them promise when I did die, and you died and daddy died, we could all be together in God's house and they said yes.' She noted that he seemed very proud and happy. It was clear, however, that his mother was not pleased with my statement that his report was typical of a genuine near-death experience. The family terminated treatment shortly thereafter."

In this case the psychologist had experienced a near-death episode herself during the first week after her birth and displayed the full range of aftereffects throughout her life. She was well informed about the phenomenon, as well, and was quite literally the perfect candidate to work with this boy. The youngster was ready to talk about his otherworldly journey and willing to make it a part of his everyday life in whatever manner his parents might approve. The parents shut the door to the opportunity.

Most likely, the parents were acting out of a desire to protect their child. Perhaps they were scared (as is quite common) that their child would be considered "crazy." It is only as our society becomes more informed about near-death experiences and their impact on experiencers that we will be able to penetrate ignorance-based fear. In the meantime, the resources I've listed in this appendix should serve to assist those parents who *are* willing to accept the near-death experience in discovering the tools they need to help create a better environment for their child's integration.

Since research about children's near-death states and their unique response to the aftereffects is difficult to find, no psychologist or counselor at this writing has had specific training in how to handle the child experiencer (unless that professional was once a child experiencer). This situation will change eventually; but, until then, a discussion of additional or alternative approaches to counseling is appropriate.

TYPES OF THERAPIES FOR CHILDREN

Other therapies that seem to work the best for experiencers who are still kids are *touch based:* things like creating scenes in sand trays or making shadow boxes (analyzed by professional practitioners); and shaping pottery on a potter's wheel or learning how to finger paint (monitored by art therapists). Actual method or medium doesn't matter, as the idea is to provide a way for the child to use hands or feet to **express and receive feelings.**

Nothing I have yet seen, however, works as well or is as effective for children as the child **creating a book about his or her near-death episode.** Encourage your child to do this, to make a book about what happened. Here's a few suggestions to get things started: Have lots of paper handy, maybe even colored sheets for the cover and back page and for special pages that need special colors.

- Have a hole punch for left side of paper or top (depending on how the child wants to bind it). Ribbon to run through the holes, or secure the pages in a regular binder.
- Sit down with the child, preferably at a table with the supplies spread out, and just chatter awhile, maybe laugh, or daydream together. Set the mood where the child can cut loose whenever he or she is ready (even if that means leaving the supplies spread out for another day).
- Give to the child any newspaper clippings or printed data that mentions in any manner what actually occurred. These items help to establish the realness of the incident, and should be in the book, even if it's just a note from the doctor or nurse.
- Encourage the child to write his or her story, and draw lots of pictures of the event itself. Also include what the child witnessed beyond death's veil, any "visitors" before/during/after, what it was like to return to the body he or she left, any messages given, whether or not he or she was believed or listened to afterward, how was it going back to school and living again in the same family, sleeping in the same bed—all of this and more.
- Invite the child to write about "since then," and what it is like now for him or her. Any differences? Did friendships change? Is school harder or easier? What does the child feel about what happened and is continuing to happen?
- Suggest making room in the book for current and continued drawings, more pictures, poetry, wonderings, questions, comments.

Remind the child to create a title for the book. This book should be private to the child, unless he or she wants to share it and tell others. Some children make their book quickly as a special project, and that's that. Then they tuck it away for a special time in the future. Other children use it as a diary, and add to it on an ongoing basis. Making their book validates the experience in a way the children can respond to and understand. It opens the "magical door" to other worlds and makes it okay to talk about "experiences"—even those that may still be occurring. Children who do this, and are taught the basic steps for revisiting their near-death experience (see visualization techniques on pages 210-211), seldom face the type of challenges that are confusing or upsetting to child experiencers of near-death states.

Never is it too late to make this book. Many child experiencers who are now adults are doing it, and with surprising results. The exercise seems to free them and enable them to rediscover the value of intimacy and of trusting their own truth. It is a very healing and fun thing to do. You'll remember that in chapter 5, I mentioned Aafke H. Holm-Oosterhof and what she did in finally making her book (and she even self-published it—refer to note 7, in chapter 5, for details). I met Aafke when I was in Holland several years ago, and I can personally attest to how happy, relaxed, creative, and spirit-filled she now is, compared with before. She claims her turning point came after she published her book. (Those who know her confirmed the changes.)

Another incredibly clever and innovative approach to therapy and making your own book is an online journal on a personal Web site. Jet van der Heide, a thirty-year-old Dutch mother, wife, and artist is doing this, and with amazing results. She is revisiting her childhood near-death experience and allowing herself to express what she never could before, as she begins to plumb the depths of her own psyche to discover and explore her many "differences." She is doing all of this in an intimate, personal way, an ongoing process of creating her "book." This act of "opening up," of expressing herself in ways she never thought she could, has been immensely freeing for her—as if there had been some unknown obstacle blocking full disclosure. You can check out her evolving story at http://www.preciousenterprise.makes.it; or reach her by email to visit or share commentary at preciousenterprise@planet.nl.

For older child experiencers and those who are now teenagers or adults, and for adult experiencers, too, there exists a new choice in therapies. Designed by near-death experiencer Robert Stefani, as part of earning his master's degree in counseling at California State University, Fresno, California, the **Eclectic Group Intervention** covers a ten-session program. According to Stefani, "Group participants need not be limited exclusively to near-death experiencers. Family members and close friends of experiencers may need support, too, as well as people who are losing (or have lost) a loved one, who have questions about death, or who are themselves dying."

Briefly, the goals of Stefani's intervention program are:

1. Educate the experiencer to understand that the intrapersonal changes that may have taken place in their attitudes and beliefs are not signs of mental instability or psychotic disorder. Redefine normality.
2. Help the NDEr to integrate changes in attitudes, beliefs, values, and interests with expectations of family and friends.

3. Alleviate interpersonal fears of separation and rejection by assisting the experiencer in learning to communicate with significant others who have not shared the experience.

4. Reconcile the new spiritual transformation—based on universality, oneness, and unconditional love—with prior religious beliefs.

5. Overcome the difficulty in maintaining former life rules that no longer seem significant, and reconstruct a purposeful life balanced between the aftereffects and the demands of everyday living.

6. Address the dissolution of major relationships or careers, if the NDEr finds it impossible to reconcile same with the changes he or she has undergone.

7. Accept the limitations of others in human relationships, in spite of one's personal feelings of unconditional love gained through the NDE.

8. Utilize the gifts and insights gained from the NDE to help comfort those who are dying, grieving the loss of a loved one, or learning to accept their own NDE.

For more information about "An Eclectic Group Intervention for Near-Death Experiences," write to: Robert Stefani, 2808 Forist Lane, Merced, CA 95348; or contact California State University, Fresno, directly.

Another helpful approach was developed by G. Scott Sparrow, Ed.D., LPC, a psychotherapist who lives in Virginia Beach, Virginia. **Inner Life Mentoring** is the name he has given to a unique counseling style that recognizes the relationship between therapist and client as being one of **mentor** (teacher) and **initiate** (student). "In order to arrive at the deep realization that one is an initiate," explained Sparrow, "the client must first explore and honor his or her wounds and grievances therapeutically as a part of healing and developing beyond them. The client's **creative response** to life's challenges becomes the single most important criterion of development and fulfillment.

"Both mentor and client seek to create the conditions in the relationship for the descent or intervention of the spirit," he continued. "Dream work, breath work, and brief meditations during the session may be used to enhance this potential. Because the **mentoring process encourages personal empowerment and ongoing spiritual practice**, appointments can potentially be scheduled infrequently, or on as-needed or as-wanted basis." Sparrow offers an Inner Life Mentoring Certificate Program for professionals who want to incorporate the technique into their own practice. He also publishes the newsletter,

"Psychotherapy and the Inner Life." Contact him directly: Dr. G. Scott Sparrow, 1212 Barn Brook Road, Virginia Beach, VA 23454; (757) 496-2501.

An alternative approach is the ancient practice of **soul retrievals.** In the body of knowledge known as shamanism, **it is taught that parts of our soul can split off from us and go to other realms** if we suffer physical, psychological, or spiritual loss of power. Such fragmentation is said to prevent us from living healthy, happy lives. Sandra Ingerman, in her book *Soul Retrieval: Mending the Fragmented Self* (HarperSanFrancisco, San Francisco, CA 1991), says: "Soul is our essence. It's our vitality, our life force. Basically, it's what keeps us alive. What is traumatic for one person may not be traumatic for another person. But if an event or situation is experienced by a person's psyche as traumatic, then soul loss is likely to occur. Soul loss happens so that the body can survive the trauma."

Ingerman practices and teaches **the art of "going into spirit"** to retrieve whatever is missing from a person's soul and reunify the part with the whole. To reach her, or inquire about the soul retrieval process, or other shamanistic trainings, contact: Foundation for Shamanic Studies, P.O. Box 1939, Mill Valley, CA 94942, (415) 380-8282.

William J. Baldwin, D.D.S., Ph.D., has created **Spirit Releasement Therapy,** a technique for professional counselors that is **based on the art of soul retrievals.** Through the Center for Human Relations, he not only practices and teaches spirit releasement, but is well known for his ability to facilitate present-life and past-life recall, birth regression, and the clinical treatment of negative spirit attachments. *Spirit Releasement Therapy: A Technique Manual* is geared for professional therapists and, as such, is the best such rendering I have yet found. To obtain his travel schedule, list of Center activities and conferences, or to procure the manual, contact: Center for Human Relations, P.O. Box 4061, Enterprise, FL 32725, (407) 322-2086, e-mail doctorbill@aol.com.

TIPS ON EDUCATION, MUSIC, AND THE ARTS

Rudolf Steiner—one of the greatest thinkers of the twentieth century, founder of the **Waldorf schools** for children, a clairvoyant, and mystic—had an unusual way of understanding how individual consciousness unfolds during the wonder years of childhood. He taught that, up to the age of seven, little ones operate most from the limbic system of the brain and, through imitation, develop **the will.** From seven to fourteen, they are conscious more of their rhythmical systems, heart, and lungs, and, through the creation of a moral sense, develop **feelings.** From fourteen to twenty-one, Steiner felt that young people center in their brain and nervous system and, through critical questioning, develop **thinking.** Of these three stages, he emphasized the first, saying that the strength of one's will determines the outcome of one's life. (For general information about Steiner's teachings, contact: Sunbridge College, 260 Hungry Hollow Road, Chestnut Ridge, NY 10977, (914) 425-0055.)

Steiner's teachings give us pause as we face the fact that today many children lose their creative edge while still youngsters. Some of the following elements may be contributing factors for this decline:

Social Conditions: Medically, a child born in the 1990s can look forward to reaching the age of 100; socially, the trend is just the opposite. In 1973, the social health index of our nation measured 77.5 out of a possible 100, a high score showing that most kids can grow up healthy and have a good life. As of 1995, however, taking into account child abuse, teenage suicide, drug abuse, and high school dropout rates, the score had fallen to 38. The severity of the social crisis for children has nullified medical advances and reduced life success prospects.

Legal Drugs: In the fall of 1997, it was reported that one out of every twenty kids was legally drugged, usually with Ritalin, for treatment of such conditions as ADD (Attention Deficit Disorder) and ADHD (Attention Deficit Hyper-Activity Disorder)—both virtually unknown in previous decades. The number of children affected has risen significantly since the 1997 accounting. Most of the requests for treatment come from overworked schoolteachers, not from parents or family physicians. Among these drugged, "disordered" children are not only those authentically disturbed, but also many classified as overactive, highly curious, creative, inventive, independent types who disrupt the class by "asking too many questions."[4]

Television Viewing: The average child spends more time watching television than going to school. Aside from deplorable programming, television imagery robs the limbic system in the brain of the emotional values and spatial reasoning it receives from imagination, creativity, intuition, and hands-on experience. The fragmented, inadequate brain patterning that results (along with the "startle" effect that heightens interest), is carried over into adulthood, limiting the individual's ability to make value judgments, respond to committed relationships, and recognize the context of a whole—the "framework" that holds parts of a whole together.[5]

LIFESTYLE ISSUES

Daria Brezinski, Ph.D., author of *Education in the Twenty-first Century: Teaching the Whole Child* (Prima, San Francisco, CA 1998), comments further on the condition of today's youth: "Children's distorted perception of reality is our fault for condoning—either through silence, apathy, or buying into the marketplace—all the unnatural ways we are living. Our children have underdeveloped consciences, lack motivation to do meaningful work in life, and have lost their souls by the very fact that we separate their spirits from everyday living. They flounder because they find no real life purpose. Adults spend their days telling children what to do and how to do it, creating dependent, unmotivated, misdirected youths who have not a clue why they are here on this planet." Brezinski points out that, *"Education, to be wholistic, must face the difference between intelligence and intellect.* One is right brain thinking and the other is left. These two are on a collision course in the traditional schools. Intelligence is of the heart and intellect is of the mind."

Certainly, kids mature younger now than they did several decades ago, and they face serious challenges. Even so, child experiencers of near-death states and those of the new root race must deal with even greater challenges. For instance, since they often appear to be social misfits at the outset, the current social decline can hit them doubly hard. In addition, they are by their very nature overactive, highly curious, creative/inventive/independent types who ask lots of questions and are difficult to manage. This makes them obvious candidates for a misdiagnosis of ADD or ADHD, and could put them on the very drugs they are least able to tolerate and that may threaten the development of their unusual minds. Seldom, though, do they slow down long enough for television's imagery to substitute for their own. This can frustrate parents who value the "baby-sitting" aspect of television over the type of personal attention their "strange" offspring demand.

Regardless of how high their IQs, the majority of these special children are capable of focusing in multiple directions simultaneously and of parallel thought processing. They are gifted creative problem solvers. Unfortunately, the public school system is not set up to handle them, much less teach them how to best use their abilities. Because of this, it might be helpful for us to take a look at what could work in the field of education.

The ancient Greeks used the concept of "education" as a reference to the art of recollecting knowledge the soul forgot at the moment of birth into a physical body. Transmigration of the soul was integral to their worldview. **"Education," as we use the word today, actually means "to draw from that** which was already known" (an extension of the soul memories idea). Child experiencers resonate to this older concept. They often translate the idea into a hunger for knowledge about human history as if they were exploring what they might have done or been before the life they have now. Their interest is not in dry intellectual renderings of historical data, but, rather, in the excitement of history's human drama——the intuitive, visceral, imaginative realness of what occurred.

G. Howard Hunter, chairman of the History/Social Studies Department of Metairie Park Country Day School in Louisiana, wrote an essay about this type of history entitled, "Did You Hear the One about Plato? Students Need Stories of the Past to Experience the Present."[6] In his essay, he reminded us that if we are ever to be a part of the collective human race, we must know history's story, for it is our story—who we were, where we went, what we did, and who we now are—exactly what child experiencers want to learn.[7]

Very few grade schools in the nation offer philosophy as a subject of study, and that is a mistake as almost all children would benefit from such a course. A program entitled "Philosophy in the Third Grade" has been tried. It involved an instructor at Piedmont College in Charlottesville, Virginia, traveling on a regular basis to schools in the central part of the state, teaching this class. The program was geared to help kids tackle unanswerable questions in a format that encouraged critical thinking and respect for opinions other than their own. It was highly successful, but was canceled due to budget cuts.

Many child experiencers, once grown, reach back to help the young in powerful ways. Mary Cosgrove of San Francisco, California, is one such individual. She "died" at the age of thirteen from severe meningitis. "I am now actively helping to create the vision of a community-based education center for middle and high school students, and assisting in community-wide education in ecological fields and the arts."

Even adult experiencers are inspired, like Linda Redford of Santa Monica, California (refer to chapter 10), to reach back and help others. The Adawee Teachings that she and her daughter designed enable children to address their personal concerns, while at the same time disciplining their minds and restoring a sense of honor and value to their world. The program consists of course studies, a self-discovery journal, plus students receive a special T-shirt that says, *"I am important to the world. The world is important to me."*

Here is the pledge school children take when enrolled in the course:

Honor Pledge

"I honor myself; I live by principles that benefit future generations; I communicate in a peaceful manner; I respect all cultures and honor their differences; I acknowledge that females and males are equal in their importance; I understand what I believe about myself and others creates my world; I feel in my heart that I am connected with all creation."

The Adawee Teachings are produced as part of "The Honor Series of Entertainment/Educational Tools." For more information, contact: Linda Redford, 1034 9th Street, Apt. 9, Santa Monica, CA 90403, (310) 392-1200 or (310) 927-3623. Web site www.honorkids.com.

THE HEALING EFFECTS OF MUSIC

Evidence is growing that there is a **direct connection between music and intelligence.** Studies over the last several decades show that listening to classical music or learning how to play a musical instrument makes kids smarter. Example: students with a background in music outperformed others on the Scholastic Assessment Test. According to the College Entrance Examination Board, 1997 test results have shown that students who studied music for at least four years scored 59 points higher than others on the verbal and 44 points higher on the math portion. Even short periods of exposure to music created by composers such as Mozart had such a beneficial effect on intelligence that the phenomenon has been dubbed **"The Mozart Effect."** In the years since this report, it has been found that other types of music can be helpful, as well—the link, though, between music and intelligence still holds.

Music truly is a language that speaks directly to the subconscious. It's tonal poetry operates on the bodymind even deeper through the medium of suggestion. Robert Haig Coxon, a popular Canadian musician, has found a way to **"massage" the soul with "the sounds of light."** The result is perfect for relaxing into higher states of consciousness. Check out his album "The Silent Path" and his three-tape Cristal Silence Series of "The Silence Within," "Beyond Dreaming," and "The Inner Voyage." His tapes/compact discs are available through Audio Alternatives, 300 Quaker Road, Chappaqua, NY 10514; 1-800-283-4655.

Near-death experiencer Ruth Rousseau, during her near-death episode, experienced the rapture of Creation embracing her in **a swirl of sound that took the form of an angelic presence.** As she stood in the midst of the sound's resonance, she was able to see everything unified within Creation itself. "This was truly a gateway opening from Source," she said. "When I returned to life, I asked how I could share this with the world. Within a short period, the inspiration came to sing (me, a person with no prior training or musical inclination). Once I did this, the mist of energy again emerged and the magic of Creation put forth *"The Keys of Sound."* From this outpouring, Ruth Rousseau produced four individual cassettes (or a 72-minute compact disc) of the unique music she believes creates a pathway for anyone to connect with inner wisdom. Her **"Keys of Internal Wisdom"** manual is a self-teaching, home-study course in awakening, co-creation, empowerment, and unity. To inquire about her work, contact: Angel Touch Productions, P.O. Box 1894, Casper, WY 82602; (307) 235-2577.

Life without creativity is devoid of meaning and excitement. The very existence of inner conflict is, at its core, a sign of repressed creativity. With children this is especially true, for **art is how the young touch their soul.** Emotions and ideas fairly leap from their words, drawings, dances, sculptures, songs, or from a thousand other ways they might choose to express the essence of who they are. If children are to develop the potential of their mind and their spirit, be whole, healthy, and intelligent, they must have ready and continual access to the arts, as well as open-ended and unstructured time for cultivating the wellspring of imagination that colors their life and ensures their growth.

Excellent resources and classroom opportunities are now available on any aspect of the arts no matter where you live. Among "what's out there" are **two books that are so exceptional,** they should be incorporated into the curriculum of school systems everywhere. Both volumes were written by Julia Cameron: *The Artist's Way: A Spiritual Path to Higher Creativity* (J. P. Tarcher, Los Angeles, CA 1992), and *The Vein of Gold: A Journey to Your Creative Heart* (Putnam, New York City, 1996).

TIPS ON BEING IN SPIRIT

The world as experienced by the young is fresh and new and exciting and awesome and horrible and wonder-filled. Kids are clear-eyed and possess a true instinct for vision that supersedes the limitation of "can't," "shouldn't," and "shame on you." Although their reality balances on a "razor's edge" of joy and pain, magic and terror, **kids really do see angels and fairies.**

It is commonplace, even necessary, that little ones engage with many-faceted beings in the "invisible" worlds, as doing so creates a context for this world and the cultural expectations inherent in the maturation process. With older children, this engagement is a form of reassurance and validation of their worth and readiness to assume their life role.

What adults seem to have forgotten or refuse to admit, is that a child's mind interacts and co-creates with **spirit energies** that are absolutely and positively real to the child's perception. Telling any young person at any age, "Oh, it's just your imagination," is the equivalent of lying to him or her. The child knows better. And the child is right, for all things first begin as an idea or image within the mind. When we teach kids to discern for themselves the difference between what is helpful and what is not, we accomplish far more than denying the natural progression of brain development and hormonal fluctuations. Does identifying these perceptions as related to physiological growth invalidate the invisible creatures and critters that a child "pretends with" or the spirit manifestations they witness? Not at all!

Imagined realms are quite real and consistent cross-culturally. Shamanism, for instance, is based on the actuality of multiple worlds and the ability of the shaman to transmigrate between them. Any form of creativity, mysticism, and spirituality ceases to exist if we are not accepting of the reality of the nonphysical, the intangible.

There have been numerous studies done on the inner life of children, and all have revealed surprisingly active interactions between the kids, the realms of spirit beings, and the life continuum. Frankly, the average youngster is much more spiritually inclined and psychic than either parents or the professional community are willing to recognize. Several books that detail such findings are:

Visions of Innocence: Spiritual and Inspirational Experiences of Childhood, Edward Hoffman, Ph.D. (Shambhala, Boston, MA 1992). Hoffman compiled accounts from around the world of people who, when young, were so deeply impacted by being "touched" by spirit that they never forgot what had occurred. The incidents he relates are not the kind of imaginative fantasies one might associate with kids, but, rather, moments of great clarity, depth, and maturity.

The Wisdom of Fairy Tales, Rudolf Meyer (Anthroposophic Press, Hudson, NY 1988). Meyer gives compelling evidence that the wild and nonsensical imaginings that kids love to engage in may well be picture-remnants of the soul faculty of clairvoyance. He demonstrates how fairy tales as "teaching tools" help youngsters become more humane, handle relationships, overcome the lure of darkness and fear, gain respect for animals and nature, and adopt the refinements of good behavior. In other words, he found that make-believe is important.

Robert Coles, in his book, *The Spiritual Life of Children* (Houghton Mifflin, New York City, 1990), quotes a nine-year-old who explained: "When you're put here, it's for a reason. The Lord wants you to do something. If you don't know what, then you've got to try hard to find out what. It may take time. You may make mistakes. But if you pray, He'll lead you to your direction. He won't hand you a piece of paper with a map on it, no sir. He'll whisper something, and at first you may not even hear, but if you have trust in Him and you keep turning to Him, it will be all right."

Having freedom to explore their creative nature, to question and invent, to manifest an idea and then experiment to see if it works, builds a solid basis for a child's self-confidence and respect for others while emphasizing honesty. **Youngsters cannot grow up believing in themselves if they are denied the right to communicate their own observations.**

Learning to test the truth of their experience, rather than negate it, enables the young to retain their creative genius into adulthood. Thus, the "trust factor" remains in tact, empowering them to feel good about their own perception. We learn most by what we **feel**. And that feeling of what happens to us is the trigger we can use for memory recall. This is important to know, for it means **anyone can revisit his or her near-death experience.**

Wherever we have once been in consciousness, we can return to . . . at any age, at any time.

To revisit a near-death experience, we first need to re-create the feeling response of that time in our life. We do that by giving ourselves permission to, then: relax, affirm, visualize, sense, allow, and offer thanks. Consciousness easily slips in between our thoughts if we render the moment to Source.

Basic Steps for Revisiting a Near-Death Experience

- Find a quiet place where you can be alone for a while without interruption. Relax.
- Gently state your goal, affirm God's protection. Close your eyes.
- Visualize being there. Embrace all aspects of your experience—see, feel,

hear, sense, smell. Experience every detail, every emotion, fully and completely. Involve all your sensory faculties and your imagination. Surrender. Allow. Be there.

- Do not set limits, only direction.
- Adopt an attitude of gratitude. Be thankful for the opportunity to revisit your near-death experience. Recall it clearly, knowing that it is all right for you to do so.
- Relax again as you affirm that you are now back to full consciousness in your body at present time. You are alert and awake, healed and whole.
- Open your eyes and stretch your limbs. Drink some water. Breathe in some fresh air.

Again, wherever you have once been in consciousness, you can return to. You can revisit your near-death experience at will, go back there, regardless of how young or old you are or how long ago the episode occurred. Do be honest about your intentions, though, in doing this. "Going back" shouldn't become an excuse to escape your present life condition, but, rather, an opportunity to uplift and enrich it.

Some people prefer to play special music as an aid to attaining the degree of relaxation necessary for journeying into inner landscapes. Modern renditions of **hoomi singing** are made-to-order for achieving higher or more awakened states of consciousness. Hoomi singing comes from ancient Mongolia, and it is a way to use vocal chords plus various other parts of the body to refract sound and create overtones. This music is performed by David Hykes and the Harmonic Choir; two of their albums are *Hearing Solar Winds* and *Harmonic Meeting*. There are many cases of **trancelike, ambient sounds** to be found in popular Western music as well. A good example of this might be the song "Echoes" from the 1973 album *Meddle* by Pink Floyd. The composition is twenty-eight minutes long, and consists of very distinct segments that correspond to being in spirit and journeying to spirit worlds. Any musical outlet or metaphysical bookstore should be able to obtain any of these audiocassettes for you.

Three books that address the subject of **capturing the essence of near-death states and journeys out of the body** are: *Anyone Can See the Light: The Seven Keys to a Guided Out-of-Body Experience,* Dianne Morrissey, Ph.D. (Stillpoint Publishing, Walpole, NH 1996); *Out-of-Body Experiences: How to Have Them and What to Expect,* Bob Peterson (Hampton Roads,

Charlottesville, VA 1997); and *Adventures Beyond the Body,* William Buhlman (HarperCollins, New York City, 1996).

The organization internationally known for training people in how to safely alter their consciousness and have out-of-body experiences is Monroe Institute, R#1, Box 175, Faber, VA 22938; (434) 361-1252. Feel free to inquire about their programs and classes.

Other ways to alter consciousness for the "inner journey" are **flow states** and **meditation.** Flow states are an important part of childhood, especially for child experiencers who seem to "trade in" their nap time for states of free-flowing consciousness. Mihaly Csikszentmihaly, a psychologist at the University of Chicago, and author of *Flow: The Psychology of Optimal Experience* (Harper and Row, New York City, 1990), defines an internal flow state as the state of being so absorbed in what you're doing that time and space cease and a euphoric feeling of complete clarity and sense of purpose takes over. Being in this state of mind he refers to as **"going with the flow."** People lose a sense of self in this state. One becomes both actor and observer, irrelevant stimuli are shut out, time and space distort, and there comes a knowing.

Meditation is a lot like a flow state, only it is deeper. Children can be taught to meditate by learning how to slow their breathing, relax, visualize their favorite place in nature, experience peace and thankfulness in that place, and return to waking consciousness feeling refreshed and happy. Although meditative sessions with kids need to be brief, the ability to meditate can become a valued skill—helpful to use if the child is ever hurt (pain relief) or in need of additional guidance (clarity).

Next Steps for Dealing with Spirit

Child experiencers become creative intuitives. Kenny Loggins, the musician, once said: "Feeling is God's mirror; intuition is God's telephone." Nothing could be truer for children as their point of awareness expands. For instance, everything is alive to them. Many can even "see" energy, humidity, pressure, sound, temperature. Stimuli come in multiples (synesthesia); spirit realms become as real as a fork and spoon. To help parents appreciate this, I recommend a sampler of different books: *Subtle Energy: Awakening to the Unseen Forces in Our Lives,* William Collinge, Ph.D. (Warner Books, New York City, 1997); *Hands of Light: A Guide to Healing Through the Human Energy Field,* Barbara Ann Brennan (Bantam Books, New York City, 1988); *A Change of Heart,* Claire Sylvia with William Novak (Little Brown, New York City, 1997); *Practical Intuition,* Laura Day (Villard Press, New York City, 1996); *Divine*

Revelation, Susan G. Shumsky (Fireside, New York City, 1996); and *The Element Illustrated Encyclopedia of Mind, Body, Spirit & Earth: A Unique Exploration of Our Place in the Universe,* Joanna Crosse (Element Books, Rockport, MA 1998)—this book is geared to ages nine through fourteen.

It is impossible to deny **the non-ordinary states youngsters know are true,** nor can they be kept from **experimenting with psychic abilities and divinatory skills.** All kids flock to things "paranormal" because such mindplay is one of the major ways they have to test the value of perception and sensation. Rather than admonish with fear tactics ("it's the work of the devil"), it is better to approach the topic as an opportunity to develop inner wisdom and truth-sense ("gifts of the spirit"). Rumi, the great Sufi poet, put this in perspective when he said: "Do not be content with the stories of others, unfold your own myth." Here are some positive and immensely rewarding ways to **validate** the wonder-filled world of spirit for yourself:

Storytelling: Communicating your near-death event to others through story-telling is a profound experience. To learn more about the art of story-telling, contact: The National Storytelling Association, Box 309, Jonesborough, TN 37659; (423) 753-2171. Also refer to: *The Healing Art of Storytelling,* Richard Stone (Hyperion, New York City, 1996); and *The Three Learning Stories* (boxed set) and *The Walking People* (an oral history put to words)—both written in the Native American tradition of storytelling by Paula Underwood and available from A Tribe of Two Press, P.O. Box 216, San Anselmo, CA 94979; 1-800-995-3320.

Dreams: Over 40 percent of the Christian Bible is based on dreams, visions, and revelations. Likewise, child experiencers also have an active dream life, with vivid imagery of almost photographic fidelity. Tips: record dreams daily in a dream journal; write down the theme and explore emotional content in conjunction with theme; learn to recognize symbolism that applies to you and the current happenings in your life; actively solicit guidance.

For a historical overview of the study of dreams and different approaches to the dreaming process, refer to: *Our Dreaming Mind,* Robert L. Van de Castle, Ph.D. (Ballantine Books, New York City, 1994).

For individual pointers in dream recall, check out *The Secret Language of Signs*, Denise Linn (Ballantine Books, New York City, 1996); *The Dream Dictionary,* JoJean Geubtner (Pilgrim Books, New York City, 1983); and *Where People Fly and Water Runs Uphill: Using Dreams to Tap the Wisdom of the Unconscious,* Jeremy Taylor (Warner Books, New York City, 1992).

Life As a Waking Dream is not only the title of a book by Diane Kennedy Pike (Berkley Publishing Group, New York City, 1997), but it is also the name of a workshop in **The Theatre of Life Experiential Program** for people who want to transform their consciousness while deepening their experience of the spiritual. Contact: Teleos Institute, 7119 East Shea Blvd., Suite 109, PMB 418, Scottsdale, AZ 85154-6107; (480) 948-1800. Web site: http://www.consciousnesswork.com. Also refer to: *There Are No Accidents: Synchronicity and the Stories of Our Lives,* Robert H. Hopcke (Riverhead Books, New York City, 1997).

Divination: After my third near-death experience, I was privileged to "happen" upon a set of true casting runes that trace back to glyphs used over twelve thousand years ago near the Black Sea, around what is now the Ukraine. At the suggestion of another, I named them **Goddess Runes** because of their connection to the ancient goddess cultures of Old Europe, and because they work together as a single unit (in relationship) for use in free-form casting. Easy and fun to use, they comprise the most dynamic divinatory system I have come across that fosters **"whole-brained" development, not just right-brain.** My original book, *Goddess Runes* (Avon Books, New York City, 1996), and now out of print is being republished and in a better format by A. Merklinger Publishing, P.O. Box 4548, Santa Fe, NM 87502; Web site: http://www.mysteriesofthemind.com. Announcements about this new edition, a brief instruction booklet, and audio cassette/CD are on my home page at http://www.cinemind.com/atwater.

Another divinatory system that deserves special mention is **Inner Child Cards,** created by Isha Lerner and Mark Lerner (Bear & Company, Santa Fe, NM 1992). These seventy-eight cards, adapted from a traditional tarot deck, concern themselves with fairy tales, myth, and nature. Using the cards helps to reawaken our **"inner child"** via the universal symbols of otherworld journeys. Kids enjoy them as much as adults. Also to be considered is *Angel Blessings: Cards of Sacred Guidance & Inspiration,* created by Kimberly Marooney (Merrill-West Publishers, Carmel, CA 1995). These forty-four cards are actually reproductions of paintings by the Masters. Each is inscribed with an angel's name and mission. The Guidebook illustrates nine different ways you can use the cards to connect with angel wisdom.

Gardening: I cannot speak highly enough of the spiritual aspects of gardening, whether it be a fairy garden complete with gazing balls and bird baths, an herb garden, or a vegetable garden. While tending to soil and plant, you can merge into the essence of each and commune with their **"deva"** or **"spirit-light"** (angelic presence). Organizations that have pioneered ways of communicating with **"the intelligence of nature,"** are: The Findhorn Foundation, The Park, Findhorn Bay, Forres IV36 OTZ, Scotland; phone 44-1309-673655; and Perelandra, P.O. Box 3603, Warrenton, VA 20188; 1-800-960-8806 and (540) 937-2153, fax (540) 937-3360. Query both for list of publications and services. For other viewpoints: *Listening to the Garden Grow: Finding Miracles in Daily Life,* Betty Sue Eaton (Stillpoint Publishing, Walpole, NH 1996); and *Bringing a Garden to Life,* Carol Williams (Bantam Books, New York City, 1998).

Labyrinths: Labyrinths are tools for journeying to the center of your being, cleansing the inner self, and then raising your consciousness to the next highest level possible for you to reach at that moment. **Where a maze is meant to confuse, a labyrinth is designed to bring you to that point of stillness and wisdom where healing can occur.** The most famous of all labyrinths is on the sanctuary floor of Chartres Cathedral in France. An exact replica can be found at Grace Cathedral in San Francisco, California. An individual dedicated to reviving the sacred use of labyrinths is Rev. Dr. Lauren Artress. Her book is *Walking a Sacred Path: Rediscovering the Labyrinth As a Spiritual Tool* (Riverhead Books, New York City, 1995). She uses a canvas version in her travels giving labyrinth workshops, as part of **The World-Wide Labyrinth Project.** To obtain the project newsletter and keep abreast of numerous personal growth opportunities that are offered, contact: Veriditas, 1100 California Street, San Francisco, CA 94108; (415) 749-6356; fax (415) 749-6357. To build your own labyrinth, obtain the video *Building Labyrinths on the Earth* with Marty Cain, VHS 60-minutes. Order from: The American Society of Dowsers Bookstore, 101 Railroad Street, St. Johnsbury, VT 05819; (802) 748-8565 or 1-800-711-9497. Another good book on labyrinths is *Exploring the Labyrinth: A Guide for Healing and Spiritual Growth,* Melissa Gayle (Broadway Books, New York City, 2000). *Future Memory:*

How Those Who "See the Future" Shed New Light on the Workings of the Human Mind (hardcover—Birch Lane Press, New York City, 1996; softcover—Hampton Roads, Charlottesville, VA 1999) is a book I wrote that was mathematically patterned on the format of a labyrinth. This was done so the reader could **feel** what I was writing about, not just read it. The book covers the inner workings of creation and consciousness in a manner that "enfolds on itself" (which is how a labyrinth works). Read straight through for the labyrinth effect (no skipping around or you'll miss it).

TIPS ON COPING WITH SPIRIT

The "double whammy" that child experiencers contend with after their episode necessitates that they quickly learn to tell the difference between "real" and "unreal." Take the puzzle of **ghosts and invisible spirit beings,** for instance.

A typical child is attuned to realms beyond that of earth and to realities of existence beyond what most adults can readily access or appreciate. **Brain shifts such as those that occur during a near-death state or other spiritual awakening intensify what is natural to childhood; they expand, enlarge, and accelerate whatever potentialities were already present.** This overall effect seems to be consistent irrespective of the experiencer's age.

What follows are three stories, from Donna DeSoto, Gordon Overbo, and a book by a man named Fynn. These stories illustrate a child's reality and demonstrate the kinds of effects a child's special awareness can manifest.

In 1997, when Donna DeSoto appeared as a guest with John Bradshaw on his nationally televised *The Bradshaw Show,* her adopted son Ben, then six years old, rushed from his seat in the audience to the other side of the studio during the break and begged his mom to tell Mr. Bradshaw about the angels who had touched him while he was in bed. Bradshaw was so impressed with Ben's story that he did his next program segment about the boy. Not long after, mother and son were taking a drive when, with great excitement, Ben shouted: "Mom, Mom, look, there are angels all around our car. Look quickly in your rearview mirror. They're holding hands."

As Donna DeSoto was telling me this, she recalled that once on a family vacation when they had stopped for refreshments, Ben headed for the souvenir shop and bought a license plate that said, **"God Is My Co-Pilot."** It currently hangs on his bedroom wall, a treasured reminder to him of the Truth behind all truth.

Ben's relationship with angels has supported him in becoming a healthy, well-adjusted youngster. Surprisingly, not only has this situation convinced his parents that they made the right choice in bringing him into their lives, but it gave them the "signal" they needed to proceed with a special project. Ben, a Hispanic-Indian, was abandoned at birth by his natural mother and tossed aside in a paper bag. His parents (of European ancestry), the DeSotos, adopted him as their second son; their first, Robert, had been adopted via regular adoption proceedings. An adult near-death experiencer, Donna had been told during her episode that if she wanted a second chance on earth she must do something to help save God's children. She agreed. After what happened with Ben, she discovered the **"discarded baby phenomenon."** This experience, underscored by Ben's close connection to God, fueled her desire to help other people do what she and her husband had done. With her husband's encouragement, Donna DeSoto founded **"SAV-BABY,"** a nonprofit alternative to baby abandonment. Through "SAV-BABY" she has been able to locate loving homes for many such infants.

You can reach the office of "SAV-BABY" by calling (210) 270-4600 or (210) 710-6929, or by writing SAV-BABY of Texas, 301 S. Frio, Suite 480, San Antonio, TX 78207. She has an excellent track record for rescuing such infants and finding them good homes. The story of DeSoto's near-death experience is on pages 89–91 of the 1996 publication *When Ego Dies: A Compilation of Near-Death & Mystical Conversion Experiences*. This book was a group project of experiencers who attended the Houston, Texas, chapter of IANDS (International Association for Near-Death Studies). If your favorite bookstore cannot find this book for you, order direct: Emerald Ink Publishing, 7141 Office City Drive, Suite 220, Houston, TX 77087; (713) 643-9945; fax (713) 643-1986.

Not all children are as fortunate as Ben DeSoto. Gordon Overbo of Santa Barbara, California, was supersensitive as a child. He regularly "flew" to the stars, merged into nature, "lived" what he read in books, and hounded his schoolteachers with questions like: "What's light? Where is God? Why do you make me stay in this room?" Says Overbo: "I was raised on a farm that had a large house, and at times I would find myself alone while other family members went to visit neighbors or go to town. I was okay until dark. Then all hell broke loose. I could feel the presence of spirit beings around me, although I only remember seeing one. I would try and hide, but would eventually run out of the house. On one occasion, I was so scared I climbed the windmill that was next to our large barn, jumped from it to the barn roof, and sat there alone in the dark until someone came home. I was told that there is no such thing as ghosts, it's my imagination, but that's not true."

By the age of thirteen, Overbo turned to alcohol. "There was no one I could talk to, not even God. I was all alone in the dark, all alone in the terror of knowing something was after me. I feel fortunate that I did not go insane and now understand why I started to drink so young. **Drinking made me unconscious of the spirits that would haunt me.** It freed me to express the love and joy and happiness I felt deep inside. People would say, 'Oh, Gordy was just a little drunk.' As far as I was concerned, that was a lot better than saying, 'Gordy is crazy.' **For forty-seven years I have been trying to remember the first major lie that I came to believe. Being told, 'There's no such thing as ghosts,' is it.** The second lie was, 'People will think you're crazy if you talk about ghosts and spiritual experiences.' Believing these two lies, from the standpoint of the child I once was, started me on a life-long journey of denying my own truth. I can think of no greater offense than to tell a child something that creates such pain and suffering."

Fynn (that's the only name he uses) was a strapping six-foot-two-inch, 225-pound Welshman when an abused and abandoned waif by the name of Anna came into his life. He described himself at that time as a "myopic materialist" whose only interest was his next meal and how much money jangled in his pocket. Although Anna did not live long, she invited Fynn to share in the reality of her inner world during the time she continued to survive. In doing this, Fynn discovered the brilliance of the child who could see through any falsehood, forgive any aggressor, figure out the answer to any puzzle, dispense advanced concepts of higher mathematics (which always proved correct), explain the principles of spiritual truth, and serve, in general, as a messenger of God's love to all she met. **After her death, a very transformed Fynn wrote a book about Anna as a way to celebrate her life and the genius inherent in every child.** His book, a perennial masterpiece, is entitled *Mister God, This Is Anna* (Ballantine Books, New York City, 1974—in continuous printings).

The connecting thread weaving together the stories of DeSoto, Overbo, and Fynn is the validity of a child's inner world and how that can impact the child and anyone else so touched.

Listen to children as they chatter. Hear their songs. Read their poetry.

Watch their facial and body expressions. Study their drawings. All children "speak" from their feeling center in a language as unfettered as they are.

We now know, thanks to scientific research, that tiny ones can hear and remember words, that the first year of life is when language patterns are established, and that **any experience that overwhelms**, especially if repeated, **changes the child's brain structure.** Refer to the outstanding issue of *Newsweek* magazine, dated Spring/Summer 1997, on "Your Child, from Birth to Three," and specifically to the article, "How to Build a Baby's Brain," by Sharon Begley, pages 28–32. The PET scan maps of an institutionalized child versus one raised by parents are shocking to see in what they reveal about temporal lobe damage—the effects of extreme touch deprivation and a lack of personal attention in infancy.

Our long and culturally revered custom of trouncing children who report seeing and hearing spirit beings and spirit realms can lead to detrimental effects in other areas of their life, as with the case of Gordon Overbo. The brain literally cannot distinguish "real" from "imagined." That's why admonitions of "right" or "wrong" applied to a child's reality confuse instead of clarify.

An example of this occurred while I was investigating altered states of consciousness and spiritual transformations back in the sixties. I was impressed then, and still am, with how consistently children responded to certain **"invisible beings."** I remember one such being in particular . . . **the red man.**" From Germany to deepest Africa, to Brazil, to the state of Kansas, it didn't seem to matter where, a child who "saw" the red man always acted in the same manner—he or she would start crying. It was never a red woman they saw, always a man and always red, and **always "he" was a harbinger of fever.** His coming meant the youngster was about to get sick, real sick, with a high temperature. Not once did any child of any age in any culture interpret the red man as being anything other than the manifestation of illness, specifically fever.

Another type of "invisible being" most children see is **demons,** and of every possible shape and color. **These ominous "shadows" present themselves whenever youngsters are overly sensitive, fearful, or timid.** One possible interpretation of these entities is that they serve to teach the young how to deal with situations or people that overpower them. Solving the problem of pesky or threatening demons empowers the child to stand up for him- or herself with courage and confidence. One young boy, harassed by a ghoul, told me: "I had to pass the hall closet every time I went to the bathroom. The devil, or something like him, would pop open the closet doors and jump at me and scare me. On the third night, I took my baseball bat with me and I was going to hit him.

That was the last time I ever saw that devil." Needless to say, the youngster benefited tremendously from confronting his tormentor.

Whether "the red man" or "the demon" could be thought of as an apparition (a counterfeit or phantom image), or an accommodation (a particular image that lasts only as long as it takes to relax or alert the experiencer), there may be yet another explanation. Such manifestations may actually be the "out-picturing" or "outworking" (from spirit into human consciousness) of universal archetypes (symbolic energy patterns common to the human family). It would seem that besides the "blueprints" of shape and form stored in our temporal lobes, there must exist some type of "etheric library" or "subconscious storehouse" of symbols and signs the lobes help us to tap into and draw from as need or desire arises.

Caution: When seeing a ghost or spirit being, always affirm God's protection and know, positively know, you are safe. Most such beings are benign and will vanish if you assert your right to your own space without any intrusion from them. Earlier, I had spoken of the little boy who decided to face the demon who had been scaring him. The minute he grabbed that baseball bat and stood his ground, the demon disappeared. **Confident, enthusiastic people, child or adult, rarely have any problem with the manifestation of spirit beings.**

Even so, it is still wise to have some way to **discriminate** between those beings who are basically helpful and supportive (like a Guide or Guardian Angel), and those who seek to confuse or possess (like a mixed-up or angry disincarnate). Hesitation is healthy, especially if "channeling" is involved (where voices or thoughts other than your own seek attention or try to express themselves through you). "Gifts of the spirit" are not always what they seem, neither are they necessarily positive. The chart on page 221 highlights **the real source of power behind spirit manifestations,** and gives you comparisons to use as an aid in cross-checking motive.

An understanding of magic also enables you to cross-check yourself and your own attitudes. That's because, regardless of conflicting views on the subject, the word "magic" simply means "receptive." It comes from the Babylonian and Persian word for receptive, which was "magno" ("magnet," "magnetic," and "magi" derive from the same term). These ancient peoples knew that when someone was receptive, or displayed receptivity (a willingness to receive), that person could then draw to him or her all manner of unique or desirable happenings with little or no effort, almost as if "charmed" (possessed of magic). **In modern parlance, the word "magic" is an indicator of "influential powers"** recognizable by the "color" of how they're used:

White Magic: *Spirit based,* for the purpose of healing one's self and others; emphasizes growth and guardianship; enhances, charms, protects.

Black Magic: *Ego based,* for the purpose of adding to one's self-importance; emphasizes possessions and status; indulges, exploits, enslaves.

Gray Magic: *Belief based,* for the purpose of acquiring attention or imposing a point of view; emphasizes wishful thinking and cultural fixations; entices, coerces, programs.

Real Magic (transparent): *Feeling based,* for the purpose of establishing an open and accepting mood; emphasizes receptivity and sensitivity; enables, readies, resonates.

Soul Magic (luminous): *Source based,* for the purpose of learning through experience so the soul can evolve; emphasizes self-empowerment and personal responsibility; uplifts, frees, brings together in wholeness.

SUBJECTIVE VOICES, SUBJECTIVE VISITORS— DISCERNING THEIR TRUE SOURCE

Lesser Mind	Greater Mind
The Voice of Ego	*The Voice of Spirit*
Personality Level	*Soul Level*
flatters	informs
commands	suggests
demands	guides
tests	nudges
chooses for you	leaves choice to you
imprisons	empowers
promotes dependency	promotes independence
intrudes	respects
pushes	supports
excludes	includes
is status oriented	is free and open
insists on obedience	encourages growth and development
often claims ultimate authority	recognizes a greater power, or God
offers shortcuts	offers integration
seeks personal gratification	affirms Divine Order along with the good of the whole

As you can see from this chart, which highlights the real power behind spirit manifestations, and from our brief examination of magic, **the degree of vulnerability we feel is what determines how successful or unsuccessful we are in coping with spirit.** In other words, there's no substitute for the strength faith imparts or for the confidence that can be gained from reasoned thought.

Right brain/left brain, intuition/logic . . . we need them both to be **whole.** It is important that child experiencers realize this (my child's colorbook entitled *The Frost Diamond* illustrates this concept of wholeness and is available on my Web site).

Ingmar Bergman, the famous Swedish movie director and producer, defines the subject in this way: "I throw a spear into the dark—that is intuition. Then I have to send an expedition into the jungle to find the way of the spear—that is logic."

Intuition, psychic ability, the wonderful world of spirit, are only valuable to us if we remember to ask questions and reserve the right to challenge answers. **"Surrendering to God does not require blind obedience."**

Although the subsequent study seems unrelated to near-death experiencers, be they child or adult, it does make a crucial statement about intuition. Nursing educators Richard W. Paul, Ph.D., and Penelope Heaslip, RN, BScN, MEd, in writing for *Journal of Advanced Nursing,* 1995, 22, 40–47, show that critical thinking actually enhances intuition in how it helps us discard the erroneous. "It's not what you don't know that hurts you," they argue, "but what you think you know that's not so!" They claim that an expert intuitive functions in harmony with his or her other well-developed faculties.

The secret of success in coping with spirit, then, is being whole-brained . . . where intuition is the equal of intellect, and "the only way out is **in.**"

Children need extra help, as discernment skills take years for them to develop. Many child experiencers, too many to my way of thinking, contend with tremendous amounts of confusion, not to mention repressed guilt. That they often withdraw or act out, signals the extent to which they are unable to process their emotions. Depression and loneliness can become an issue.

RITUALS AND ROLE PLAYING

Rituals and role-playing games offer a solution because they bring people together in mutually supportive ways. And that's exactly what child experiencers need—social activities that promote creativity, experimentation, and commitment . . . **the commitment to use one's gifts for the highest good of all**

concerned. (If you don't have a sense of what your mission in life is, using your gifts will eventually lead you there.)

Rituals uplift, empower, and excite. They embrace non-ordinary states of reality and altered states of consciousness in a manner that fosters trust, bonding, release, reconciliation, and renewal. And they enable parents and kids to reconnect with the earth, their community, and their sense of value and purpose as individuals and as souls. Many families and religious communities practice their own time-honored rituals, unique to holidays and certain **"rites of passage."** Yet anyone can create personal times of celebration and not just for entertainment, but to instill a sense of respect and dignity and sacredness. Refer to: *Rituals for Our Times: Celebrating Healing, and Changing Our Lives and Relationships,* Evan Imber-Black and Janine Roberts (HarperCollins, New York City, 1992); and *Ritual: Power, Healing and Community,* Malidoma Patrice Some, Ph.D. (Penguin Books, New York City, 1997).

Role playing or ritual games are equally dynamic, loads of fun to play, and unique in the way they can empower players. They are therapeutic without resorting to "preachiness" or self-righteous rules of behavior. **"The Bone Game"** is one of them. Developed by Michael H. Brown, Ed.S., and based on a Native American ritual, this weekend retreat teaches players how to relax deeply, clarify values, listen with respect to others, communicate authentically, make decisions on the basis of consensus, and enjoy an amazingly magical sense of community consciousness. Contact Brown directly at 4889A Finlay Street, Richmond, VA 23231; (804) 222-0483. Although he works with people of all ages, Brown is especially good with teenagers, and is willing to travel to other locations to hold the retreat.

"The Journey" is a self-discovery program especially for teenagers that was created by David Oldfield, director of the Midway Center. This program combines the appeal of fantasy role-playing games with shared group therapy to help today's teens find positive solutions to "the necessary crises of adolescence." Ask for program schedules: Midway Center for Creative Imaginaton, 2112 F Street NW, #404, Washington, DC 20037; (202) 296-4466.

Also named **"The Journey" is a weekend retreat for spiritual self-discovery** put together by staff member John Keathley as part of an outreach program for teenagers through the Association for Research and Enlightenment (ARE). The ARE is based on the psychic readings of the late Edgar Cayce, and is one of the most active and respected organizations of its kind in the world. A holistic, spiritual approach is their strength, along with an emphasis on "testing the spirits" through extensive research programs and member services. They also offer summer camps for kids and a large selection in their bookstore for children and their parents. Inquire about book catalogue, activities, and services: ARE, 67th and Atlanta Avenue, Virginia Beach, VA 23451; (757) 428-3588 or 800-333-4499.

"Adventure Camp," a challenge for teenagers, is run by the highly respected Rowe Camp and Conference Center. Their yearly activities schedule is built around the very concerns, opportunities, and joys that would interest near-death experiencers of any age and anyone else preferring a more creative, intuitive, and holistic lifestyle. I mention them here because of the unique programming they offer for children, as well as teens, with "Junior High Camp," "Young People's Camp," and "New Camp." Contact: Rowe Conference Center, Kings Highway Road, Box 273, Rowe, MA 01367; (413) 339-4216; fax (413) 339-5728; e-mail RoweCenter@aol.com.

As an aside, here are a couple of books for a more positive approach to anger and fear: *Make Anger Your Ally: Harnessing Our Most Baffling Emotion,* Neil C. Warren (Doubleday, Garden City, NY 1983); and *The Gift of Fear: Survival Signals That Protect Us from Violence,* Gavin de Becker (Little Brown, New York City, 1997).

For **younger** near-death experiencers, here is a book just for them: *Mountains, Meadows, and Moonbeams: A Child's Spiritual Reader,* Mary Summer Rain (Hampton Roads, Charlottesville, VA 1984).

TIPS ON SOULMAKING

"Being all that you can be" means reconnecting with your soul.

The soul evolves in the sense that, as we learn to be aware of our spiritual nature, that font of guidance within us opens wide and becomes ever more available. We are **"soulmaking"** when we develop and refine our sensitivity to this divine guidance. Soulmaking can be tricky, though. That's because, as we become more sensitive to and reconnected with higher realms of spirit, we also become more vulnerable to the power of our own ego and the wants and desires of the lesser mind. The result, invariably, is an exaggerated and overblown sense of self-importance that erodes the very reconnection we thought we had achieved.

Since this is a major issue for near-death experiencers **of all ages,** and for anyone else who has undergone a transformation of consciousness no matter how, a few cautions are in order. **Fresh new visions of the spiritual are always needed, but when they're based on "power over" instead of "power to," gullibility reigns—blinding both the visionary and those affected by the visionary.**

Let me tell you about one such case. By 1837, Hung Hsiu-ch'uan, a peasant farmer's teenage son, had failed for the third time to pass the official state examination in Canton, China. He fell into a prolonged delirium, his body wasting away as he lay near death for forty days. He revived after having a miraculous "vision" that portrayed him and an "elder brother" searching out and slaying legions of evil demons in accordance with God's will (scenarios involving "judgment/punishment" themes are reported with some frequency in Asia). Six years later, Hsiu-ch'uan came across a Christian missionary pamphlet. He used what he read in the pamphlet to "substantiate" his conviction that his "vision" was real, and that he, as the younger brother of Jesus Christ and God's Divine Representative, was ready and willing to overthrow the forces of evil that he saw as the Manchus and Confucianism. With the help of converts to his cause he established the God Worshipers Society, a puritanical and absolutist group that quickly swelled to the ranks of a revolutionary army. Numerous power struggles later, Hsiu-ch'uan declared war against the Manchus as part of the Taiping Rebellion and **helped launch a civil uprising— the bloodiest in all history—that lasted fourteen years and cost 20 million lives.**

Hsiu-ch'uan, who changed his name to T'ien Wang, the Heavenly King, was transfigured and transformed by his near-death experience, and became zealous in his desire to "wake up" the deluded of his day. He felt the **Real Truth** had been revealed to him and to him alone, and thus it was his duty to "save" the populace. Wholesale carnage followed, ripping asunder the very fabric of China. The Heavenly Dynasty was established soon after. The movie *The Last Emperor* is about T'ien Wang's grandson.

Just as some of the most enlightened figures in history have been near-death experiencers, so, too, have been some of the most twisted. Among the many lessons we can learn from T'en Wang's case is this one: **anyone who claims to be the only source of a spiritual revelation is either a fool or a fake.**

Such a claim always creates a "false god."

According to Rev. William T. Curtiss, a well-respected minister: "A false god is something that we have to support; the real God is something that supports us. A false god has no power other than the power we give it; the real God is all power, and it empowers us. Fear is a false god. It is not an entity, it has no power, it makes no choices. When we withdraw our support, it simply disintegrates. How do we do this? Simply by refocusing our attention upon the real God within us, and allowing God to support and empower us."

Elaine Pagels, in her book *The Origin of Satan* (Random House, New York City, 1995), posits **how the concept of the devil began.** From a little-used term in the Old Testament that had several meanings, "devil" evolved into a full-blown conspiracy theory in the New Testament that served to "pass on the blame" as to why Jesus was rejected, abandoned, and executed by his own people.

Whether you agree with Pagels's theory or not, **the term "devil" is still used today as an allegation of blame that overrides or avoids facts.** For instance, near-death experiencers of all ages are routinely accused of operating as "agents of the devil" or being "possessed of the devil," the Light they see, that of "Lucifer," when people are frightened of them or do not take the time to investigate near-death research.

One nine-year-old boy, a near-death experiencer I had a session with, was visited weekly over a period of several months by his family's minister, who told him and his mother that the boy would be damned to rot in hell if he did not publicly recant what he claimed to have seen when he "died." Needless to say, the mother was terrified by this, and her son, confused.

Sadly, some churches have gone to exceptional lengths to stem the migration away from their fold, even to the point of making **false accusations.** For example, a fellow researcher called my attention to one Web site entitled "The Vine" which carried this announcement under the heading, **"Counterfeit Angels"** (dated November 1996, Vol. 1, Issue 4, http://members.aol.com/polmin/html/vnov96). The complete text:

> Not all angels are of God. Jesus told his disciples that Satan has his angels, also, and God has prepared a place of punishment for them, (Matthew 25:41). Paul tells us that the devil himself often appears as an angel of light deceiving those not grounded in God's Word, (II Corinthians 11:12–15). There is a mighty battle between good and evil, between God and Satan, for the souls of mankind. Scriptures tell of battles fought by warring angels, where satanic angels fight to keep God's work from being performed. We must be able to discern good from evil, right from wrong, satanic spirits from God's spirit. God's angels will never say, do or suggest anything contrary to God's Word. Examples of counterfeit angels are those formerly called "spiritual guides" by the New Age movement, and "angels" described in accounts

of people who have undergone near-death experiences. On the other hand, we can be assured that God sends his angels to protect us, and even if we never physically encounter an angel in our lifetime, it is certain that God, as the loving Father of those who believe in God's Son Jesus Christ, has dispatched angels to assist us in our journey through this life.

As a footnote to the subject of **"counterfeit angels,"** certainly, accommodations can and do occur in near-death imagery. Yet, accommodations are *not* counterfeit in the sense of being false; they're like a temporary overlay to relax the individual until he or she is able to acclimate to new surroundings. (Refer back to chapter 8 and the case of Jimmy John and his "little" brother, a sibling who appeared in the boy's near-death episode—yet he had been aborted by his mother many years before—an abortion the mother had told no one about. The appearance of a "little" brother was obviously an accommodation: the brother was real, his size and looks as younger than Jimmy John were not.)

The irony to what was carried on "The Vine" Web site is that two months later the *London Observer* released a "hot" news bulletin by John Hooper that read, "Dialogue with the dead is feasible, Vatican spokesman says." Datelined from Rome, the news clip quoted the Reverend Gino Concetti, **chief theological commentator for the Vatican newspaper, in essence saying that dead relatives can and do communicate with the living and that an afterlife is real.**

It is necessary that any religious standard or spiritual tradition teach its adherents to become more discerning and responsible, but it's unfortunate when "the faithful" resort to superstition to bolster their claims. The body of near-death research, especially that concerning child experiencers, provides ample evidence that the average near-death scenario is hardly "counterfeit."

In his book, *The Meeting of Science and Spirit* (Paragon House, St. Paul, MN, 1990, pages 218–219), **John White eloquently expresses why so many spiritually transformed individuals feel compelled to follow a more personal path than that offered by formal religion.** White, by the way, drowned at fourteen and experienced a near-death episode that transformed his life.

There is no way to enter the Kingdom except to ascend in consciousness to the Father, to that unconditional love for all creation which Jesus demonstrated. This is what the Christian (and, indeed, every true religion) is all about: a system of teachings, both theory and practice, about growth to higher consciousness. But each of us is required to take personal responsibility for following Jesus on that way. That is the key to the Kingdom.

Self-transcendence requires honesty, commitment and spiritual practice to cultivate awareness. The result of such discipline is personal, validating experience of the fact that alteration of consciousness can lead to a radical transformation of consciousness, traditionally called enlightenment. But this, by and large, has been lost to the understanding of contemporary Christendom. Instead, Jesus and the Bible are idolized, and heaven is said to be located somewhere in outer space. Awareness of inner space—of consciousness and the need to cultivate it—is sadly lacking. *Exoteric* Judeo-Christianity must reawaken to the truth preserved in its *esoteric* tradition.

One such forgotten truth described by White is

> . . . the original form of baptism, whole-body immersion, was limited to adults. It apparently was an initiatory practice in which the person, a convert who would have been an adult prepared through study of disciplines, was held under water to the point of nearly drowning. This near-death experience was likely to produce an out-of-body projection such as many near-death experiencers report today. The baptized person would thereby directly experience resurrection—the transcendence of death, the reality of metaphysical worlds and the supremacy of Spirit. He would receive a dramatic and unmistakable demonstration of the reality of the spiritual body or celestial body of which St. Paul speaks in I Corinthians 15:40–44 (apparently referring to his own personal experience with out-of-body projection).

For the sake of child and adult experiencers alike, I want to share some thoughts, using Christianity as a model, to help clarify the issues we've been discussing—**the religious schism that can develop and what can be done to heal it.** The following thoughts are quoted from Walter Starcke's "Quarterly Letter," Summer 1997. Starcke, a former Hollywood luminary, underwent a spiritual transformation many years ago and has since become a devoted student of the Bible:

> All of us have at times been confused in our personal relationships because at one time or another, we have firmly believed that someone we were talking to was disagreeing with us, when in fact they were saying the same thing we were, but, from a different angle or viewpoint. In analyzing a situation, one of us was judging the situation from a left brain or masculine perspective, which approaches things in a logical or objective fashion, while the

other was coming from the right brain which is the more feminine, feeling, intuitive or subjective perspective. Though we would swear it wasn't so, both of us were in complete agreement, but because each of us was talking from a different level of awareness, we thought we were being contradicted and opposed. The same has happened down through history in what I call "the two Christianities."

To clarify what took place, I'll oversimplify and call those early Christians who ended up organizing and institutionalizing the Church and whose approach to the Christian message was more in terms of the historical and objective foundation, "fundamentalist" or "traditionalist"—and those whose more impersonal approach was internal and subjective rather than objective and organizational, I'll refer to as the "mystics" or Gnostics.

The paradox is that both the extreme fundamentalists and the extreme mystics or metaphysicians ended up in the same place. Both ended up denying the importance of the individual. The fundamentalists did it by subordinating the individual to the organization and by denouncing those who looked within themselves for God. The Gnostics denied human existence by advocating the transcendence of one's humanity through a kind of spiritual self-centeredness that didn't take others into account and by ignoring the fact that there were other people with needs.

Although the Gnostic approach has reappeared and then been put down a number of times over the last 1,800 years, nothing in consciousness can ever be lost. It has reappeared in the last hundred or so years with both its virtues and its faults in what is loosely called the metaphysical movement.

For almost 2,000 years, Pauline Christianity has dominated the scene. If it had not been for Paul, his humanity, and his objective approach as a bridge, Christianity might have been only a footnote in the annals of Jewish sectarianism. But, mainly due to the great lights in the metaphysical movement who have relit Jesus' mysticism, we at last are ready to merge the virtues of the two Christianities and experience THE THIRD REALITY—Ascension Consciousness.

Starcke goes on to explain that **the third reality** (Ascension Consciousness) **is reconciliation.**

We can't achieve reconciliation and end contradiction until another paradox is resolved: the apparent incongruity of "double thinking." As long as we believe that we must constantly and only think beautiful subjectively satisfying thoughts, we are creating the very duality we claim to deny. Unless we have the strength to include the objective level [physicality] by looking right at it—recognizing evil for what it is—reconcile the objective level without denying its subjective nature [spirituality] only if we simultaneously see both its infinite oneness and its limited form. By doing this, we close the gap and experience the only true absolute: All inclusiveness.

Walter Starcke's many tapes and books, including his latest, *It's All God*, are available from Guadalupe Press, P.O. Box 877, Boerne, TX 78006; (830) 537-4837; e-mail wstarcke@walterstarcke.com.

Reconciliation is the underlying theme most near-death experiencers give to the effect their episode has had on their lives, and to why other people respond as they do when an experiencer shares his or her story.

Reconciliation is the motive behind the growing movement in the Roman Catholic Church to have the Pope proclaim Mary the Mother of Christ as Co-Redeemer. The male/female, objective/subjective split in Christianity will heal if this occurs. Because of the plethora of Marian sightings in recent years, many feel that the third millennium we are now in should be called **"The Age of Mary."** Refer to: "Hail, Mary," an article by Kenneth L. Woodward that appeared in the August 25, 1997, issue of *Newsweek* magazine, pages 49–55.

Reconciliation is the overall message that emerges from the book *Anatomy of the Spirit,* by Caroline Myss, Ph.D. (Harmony Books, New York City, 1996). By connecting the seven sacraments of Christianity with the seven chakras of Hinduism, and Judaism's Tree of Life, Myss has distilled the seven sacred truths of the spiritual path: (1) all is one, (2) honor one another, (3) honor oneself, (4) love is divine power, (5) surrender personal will to divine will, (6) seek only the truth, and (7) live in the present moment.

Doesn't what Myss uncovered in her research seem like a description of a typical message from a near-death experience as relayed by the average experiencer?

It is as if the entire genre of consciousness transformations (of which near-death states are a part) was **God's Global Grassroots Movement.** Children catch on to this notion automatically, and support it fully.

What appeals the most to a child experiencer as a way to participate in this "Movement" is **prayer and meditation.** Since we've already discussed meditation, let's look again at **the power of prayer,** only this time from several different vantage points. A six-tape audio program by Ron Roth, entitled *"Prayer and the Five Stages of Healing,"* examines how to heal with prayer, ways to transform consciousness, how to awaken the spirit within, as well as other aspects of prayer's power. Available from Hay House, P.O. Box 5100, Carlsbad, CA 92018; 1-800-654-5126.

The centuries-old tradition of **trance dancing or "sweating your prayers"** is said to burn off negativity as it purifies body and soul. Used the world over for self-healing, trance dancing is also a passionate offering to the Divine—whether done in a gym, sauna, or sweatlodge. Refer to *Sweat Your Prayers: Movement as Spiritual Practice*, Grabrielle Roth (Tarcher/Putnam, New York City 1997).

Most child experiencers are modest and humble, and desirous of making the world a better place. They gravitate to whatever is authentic, and to **teachers who practice what they preach.** Florence Shovel Shinn was such a person, and she taught **"the game of life and how to play it,"** along with the power of the spoken word, and the secret of success. Her long, productive life proves that you don't have to be a nun or a monk and withdraw from the world to align with spirituality. Her four books, as applicable today as when they were written, have been condensed into one volume, *The Wisdom of Florence Shovel Shinn* (Simon & Schuster, New York City, 1989—another classic that is still in print).

If given a chance, a child will always embrace **a more holistic way of living.** George Leonard and Michael Murphy have developed a program along those lines and talk about it in their book, *The Life We Are Given: A Daily Program for Realizing the Potential for Body, Mind, Heart, and Soul* (Putnam, New York City, 1995). Their program is "integral" in how it deals with the body (diet, exercise, yoga), mind (reading and learning), heart (group process, community activities), and soul (meditation and imaging).

Let me say, though, that **there is a tremendous difference between visualization and visioning.** Rev. Dr. Michael Beckwith explains:

> *Visualization* involves having an idea of what we want to accomplish or how we want to live our life, then imaging that goal as already achieved and establishing the necessary mental and emotional vibrations to bring it forth and manifest it. When we do *visioning,* on the other hand, we align in consciousness with our divine purpose, which is to love and to express a greater degree of life. Then we open ourselves to catch a sense of how that expression is supposed to occur through us. (Condensed from an article entitled "Visioning" by Kathy Juline, and appearing in the December 1996 issue of Science of Mind Magazine, pages 37–49)

I regard **visioning** as the next step beyond prayer. As we vision, we realign in the center of our heart of hearts and surrender fully to The One True Source. There is no need for begging or supplication in this transcendent state of awareness, and no goals of "spiritual materialism" (imaging ourselves rich and wealthy). There is only the Will of God and our willingness to allow A Greater Plan to have expression through us. Miracles follow because, in the embrace of God's Love, only miracles exist.

As we think in our heart, so are we.

Children know this.

They understand that before we can be whole, we must traverse the eighteen inches from our head to our heart. The perfect measurement from which to judge all things, the spiritual equivalent of the mathematical Golden Mean, is love.

Give our new children and those child experiencers of transformational otherworldly journeys, half a chance and they **will** change the world.

Dee Braker, a loving grandmother from Okemos, Michigan, sent me a most interesting letter. She gave me permission to share it with you:

"When my grandson, Josh, was three years old, he was told by his mother that he was going to have a new cousin soon. Josh asked, 'Where is he now?' His mother replied, 'He is still in your Aunt Joanie's tummy.' Josh said, 'I remember when I was in your tummy.' 'Oh, really, what was it like?' Margie asked. Josh said, 'It was dark and I was like this.' (He demonstrated the fetal position.) 'I couldn't stand up.' 'So,' Margie continued, 'what did you do?' 'I just sucked my thumb and waited to get out,' he replied."

Adults ask, "Where will I go after I die?"

Children ask, "Where was I before I was born?"

Perhaps we can answer both by saying: Before birth, after death, unending life.

Research Methodology

*Science, by definition, cannot explain subjective experience,
so it can neither refute nor confirm the possibility that these
subjective accounts do indeed suggest that some form of personal experience may continue during the unconsciousness
of brain catastrophe or even after brain death.*
　　　　　　—PETER FENWICK, M.D., F.R.C.PSYCH.

IN TRUTH, no one can validate a near-death experience except the one who
experienced it. The thrust of near-death research, then, is to identify elements
and patterns of occurrence, aftereffects and implications, in an attempt to
understand how and why the phenomenon happens and what can be learned
from it—especially as concerns an examination of existence and the prospect
of life after death.

Research on the phenomenon goes back over a century, but didn't take
root as a scientific discipline of its own standing until after Raymond A.
Moody Jr., M.D. coined the term *"near-death experience"* and published his
first book, *Life After Life,* in 1975. Kenneth Ring, Ph.D., by verifying
Moody's work scientifically in 1980 with the book, *Life at Death,* opened the
floodgates of inquiry for serious professionals.

I entered the picture in November 1978, after having visited with
Elisabeth Kübler-Ross, M.D., and learning from her that what I had experienced the year before had an official name and description. She never mentioned Raymond Moody or his book, nor did I hear of either until several
years later when Kenneth Ring bought my self-published rendering, *I Died
Three Times in 1977,* and located me via telephone. (This self-published
book has since been "resurrected" and is available over my Web site at
http://www.cinemind.com/atwater.)

After an overnight stay, Ring was excited to discover that I had independently been researching the near-death experience and its aftereffects and had
amassed a great deal of material. A few months later, at his invitation, I became
a columnist for *Vital Signs Magazine,* a publication of the International
Association for Near-Death Studies, and began to share some of the observations
I had made—observations that later became the book *Coming Back to Life.*

To understand my approach to research, you need to realize that my "agenda" is a little different from most others in the field. My job, as I was shown during my third near-death experience, was to bring clarity and perspective to the phenomenon and to "test" the validity of its revelation. Never has it been my interest or intent to verify or challenge anyone else's work. As "the fates" would have it, though, my findings have indeed become a challenge to the generally accepted "classical" model.

I am a field-worker whose primary specialty is interviews *and* observation analysis; my protocol is police investigative techniques (I'm a cop's kid and I was raised in a police station). I cross-check everything I do at least five times with different experiencers in different parts of the country, and whenever possible with their significant others, as a way of ensuring that any bias I may have as a near-death experiencer will not "cloud" my perception. Questionnaires for me are auxiliary, used only to further examine certain aspects of near-death states. All of my work is original and first-hand. This effort has been a full-time profession for me since 1978, in addition to employment that "paid for groceries." My husband's pet name for me is "the monk in the monastery," as a reference to my behavior when analyzing research; others simply throw up their hands and snicker, "She's obsessed." To date, I have had sessions with over 3,000 adult experiencers and 277 child experiencers, not counting significant others. This number doubles if you consider the research I conducted between 1966 and 1976 in an attempt to understand altered states of consciousness, and mystical and spiritual transformational experiences.

Why all this research for so many decades?

I'm curious. In addition, since my earliest memory, I have had a need to discover the difference between what is true and what seems to be true.

My interview style is straightforward. I ask open-ended questions, such as "What happened to you?" If I want to know more, I signal that intent with forward body movement, a tilt of my head, a smile, and the incredibly magical word "and." Know that I was trained to ask questions by my police officer father. He was quite explicit about this, saying, "In a car accident, you cannot use the word 'car' until the witness does." Hence, when interviewing near-death experiencers, I would never say "light" or "dark" or anything else unless they first used the term. *The experiencer determined how I used language by the way he or she responded to my questions.* To obtain greater detail, I learned to avoid telling anyone I was a researcher, and to rely more on nonverbal facial expressions and body postures than on words. Never did I just listen—I *"watched,"* while keenly aware of feelings and sensations. The "dance" we humans engage in as we relate one to another is quite revealing.

My research, then, is *not* anecdotal-based, but, rather, an amalgam of interviews/observations/questionnaires—empirical in the sense that I maintained a strict code of objectivity. I wanted to examine the near-death phenomenon from 360 degrees, positive and negative—to see what was really there. Anything less, to my way of thinking, would run the risk of self-deception.

All research monies were out-of-pocket. The intuitive readings I gave over the years raised enough extra funds to keep me going. Many of my research subjects were attendees at talks I gave. Others heard about what I was doing and called or wrote and asked to take part. A number responded to ads or announcements I had placed in national newspapers and magazines. But the bulk of those I researched simply "appeared." It was almost magical the way that happened. To get a sense of this, one of the jobs I held required constant travel, and that meant I was exposed to all kinds of people in all manner of situations daily . . . taxi cab drivers, seatmates on airplanes, travelers at airports, customers, truck drivers at way stops, folks in elevators. The majority of people I met turned out to be fellow experiencers. Either they'd say something or I would. That's all it took. It's as if these people were "waiting" for someone like me to appear so they could "unload," share their episodes, and ask their questions in an environment that was safe.

I did alter my style somewhat with children, though, and in this manner:

- No parents were allowed when I was with the kids.
- Same eye-level contact was maintained throughout interview session.
- Changing body postures were used to elicit response.
- Replaced note-taking with a gentle sincerity and steady focus.
- Encouraged them to share their *feelings* as well as their memories.
- Opened myself to sense the "wave" of consciousness they "ride" so I could see through their eyes.

Parents were interviewed, too, as I wanted to know their point of view and whether or not they might have applied any pressure on their child by "making a big deal of it." This is important, as children are capable of slanting their stories to fit the *emotional expectations of their parents*. If I suspected such a compromise had been made, I would retire the account to the "dust bin." I rejected about 15 percent of the interview opportunities I had with children for this reason. Fascination with "out-of-the-mouths-of-babes" reports can mislead more readily than enlighten.

Here is an example of why I make such a statement: after telling me about a long and involved interaction between herself and angels and Jesus and God, the little girl I was having a session with went on to proudly state that everything she experienced during her near-death episode was *exactly* what the nun had taught her in the Catholic school she attended, and wasn't it wonderful that she was able to prove that the nun was right. Her parents then uttered "Amen," and marched her away. This session was a "wake-up call" for me, and I promptly changed how I worked with kids because of it.

For my study of child experiencers, I sought out individuals who remembered having had a near-death episode between birth and the age of fifteen. Of the 277 who qualified, about half were children and the other half were of teen or adult age at the time we met. The older child experiencers enabled me to track the aftereffects throughout the various life stages. My overall racial mix was: 12 percent Blacks (American and Canadian), 23 percent Latinos (Hispanics, Argentines, and Colombians), 5 percent Asians (Malaysian and Chinese), and 60 percent Whites (American, Canadian, French, English, and Ukrainian).

Of the older child experiencers, fifty-two agreed to fill out a lengthy and intense questionnaire: forty-four of them had experienced a near-death state by their fifteenth birthday (the majority before the age of seven), four had an unusually dramatic death dream, the remaining four met the profile of a child near-death experiencer but could not recall ever undergoing any such event. As is typical for me, the questionnaire was supplemental, enabling me to use a different "lens" for re-examining my initial findings.

The most frequent cause of death in my overall study was drowning, followed by suffocation, surgery (even minor surgery like tonsillectomies), accidents and high fevers. However, 42 percent of my cases can be traced to some form of parental *or* sibling abuse. The most common of the four types of near-death states experienced by those who participated overall was the Initial Experience (76 percent), which consists of only a few basic elements. Yet, irrespective of brevity, the full spread of aftereffects ensued. This suggests to me that *complexity is no determinant* of the intensity or impact of a near-death state. In fact, *intensity* alone seems to be the major factor, rather than imagery or length of scenario.

In my previous books, I had stated that small children never experienced the extreme range of scenario types as do adults. This project proved me wrong: 3 percent were Unpleasant and/or Hellish (the youngest only nine days old); but of the 2 percent Transcendent, each had reached puberty before they "died."

The youngest to experience an Unpleasant and/or Hellish near-death episode involved the case of Judith Werner, Bronx, New York. She "died" nine days after birth during surgery to remove an abscess from a severe staph infection. Still vivid in her mind, even as a grown woman, she offers us the drawing of the event on the facing page.

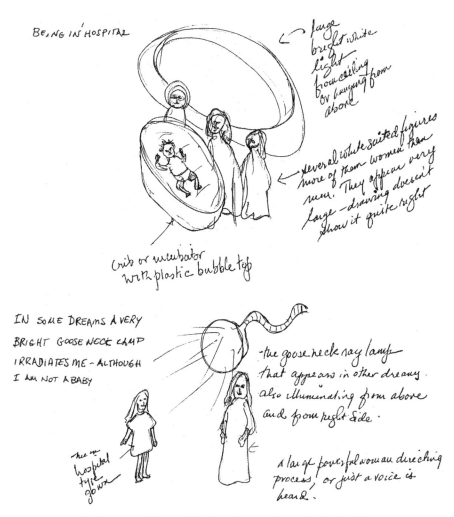

BEING IN HOSPITAL

large bright white light from ceiling or hanging from above

several white suited figures more of them women than men. They appear very large — drawing doesn't show it quite right

crib or incubator with plastic bubble top

IN SOME DREAMS A VERY BRIGHT GOOSE NECK LAMP IRRADIATES ME – ALTHOUGH I AM NOT A BABY

the goose-neck ray lamp that appears in other dreams. also illuminating from above and from right side.

the hospital type gown

a large powerful woman directing process, or just a voice is heard.

Judith Werner depicts her death nine days after being born.

Werner's drawing depicts: crib or incubator with plastic bubble top where she lay, an overhanging large bright light fixture, and huge white-suited figures (most of them women). The images in the lower half are from recurring dreams that haunted her afterward: this time showing the light as a "goose-neck ray lamp," her as a young girl being irradiated by the ray lamp, and a large powerful woman directing the process (sometimes just a voice). She did indeed continue to receive radiation-type treatments until she was older (about school age, although the number of treatments she received is not known).

At first glance one could conclude that her drawing simply shows how a typical surgical room, operating staff and equipment, and the kind of ongoing treatment one might expect, would look to a child so small. But there is more to tell. First, though, a question that begs for an answer is: *How could a nine-day-old infant register so precisely such a scene and remember it lifelong?* Any attempt to answer this question will necessitate a reconsideration of what we think we know about the brain, intelligence, and memory, *and* what newborns seem to already know or can readily "pick up" and respond to.

Werner recalls being terrified of the surgery and threatened by the "light beings" who stood nearby and did nothing as a male-like voice, called "Inner Stranger," demanded that she either do his work or die. She agreed to cooperate out of fear but later repressed the whole episode after being ignored or chastised every time she tried to talk about what had happened. Because of this, Werner's growing years were a confusing struggle until, at the age of twenty-eight, she had a near-death-like experience that closely duplicated the imagery of her original scenario. This time she fully embraced "Inner Stranger," an act that improved her life in a positive way. At thirty-two she became a professional psychic dedicated to helping others help themselves. She has always exhibited the entire profile of near-death aftereffects.

Judith Werner's case is a sobering reminder that not all near-death scenarios are friendly and bathed in unconditional love. They can be judgmental, some with an element of cruelty to them, especially those that come from Asia and various indigenous cultures (refer to the research of Todd Murphy). What I have found with childhood cases, however, is the unmistakable presence of a "critical or caring" parent-type image . . . one that instructs, demands, informs, threatens, predicts, encourages and, in general, focuses on the dos and don'ts the child must respect in order to fulfill his or her destiny. While adult experiencers face their "misdeeds" during the life-review segment of their episode and make "course corrections" later on because of what they were shown or relived, the young are sometimes lectured "for their own good" by a "being" who "gives orders or imparts guidance."

A surprise to me was the importance of "dark light" experiences with little ones under three, and more specifically from fifteen months and under. Of these tiny tots who snuggled into "The Darkness That Knows," the majority wound up more likely to develop genius than those whose episode was filled with bright light. In the questionnaire results, *96 percent of the total of those who had "dark light" scenarios reached genius level of intelligence without genetic markers to account for it, whereas only 40 percent of those who experienced "bright light" episodes did.* After the age of three this disparity ceased. I believe this finding necessitates that we re-examine how we interpret the meaning and power of "darkness and light," as well as the effect a near-death state has on a baby's brain. Note in chapter 3 that IQ enhancements in math and science, along with those of spatial abilities, were the *same* for both sexes in both questionnaire tallies and overall.

Of special interest here is the issue of spatial abilities. Most child experiencers became spatial/nonverbal/sensory-dynamic thinkers after their episode—whether male or female. Nonverbal intelligence includes skills such as running mazes, assembling puzzles, finding new ways to solve a problem—all characteristics of "the spatial child."

John Philo Dixon, Ph.D., in his book *The Spatial Child,* explains:

> Spatial ability is not a simple matter. It is not just a picture-like memory for objects, places, and people. This kind of memory might be helpful in carrying out spatial tasks, but it is not at the core of what is meant by spatial ability. Spatial-mechanical thinking involves the capacity to put the world together inside one's head such that all things relate to all others in precisely understood ways. The distance and directional positioning between a whole host of things is so well understood that all become part of an interconnected whole.[1]

There is a link between spatial reasoning and mathematics and music, in that all three are necessary to arrange schemes that encompass the many-sidedness or wholeness of a given design. For instance, music imparts harmony, how things resonate or fit together; mathematics supplies measurement, the specifics of physical manifestation. Yet it is spatial reasoning that, through creating an overall design, gives meaning and purpose to the task or item at hand, while ensuring that all parts fit the whole.

In the questionnaire, *85 percent of those who displayed math enhancements to the point of genius also showed an unusual interest in and sensitivity to music.* The centers for math and music are located next to each other in the brain. Implied here is that the "charge" of a near-death state tends to jumpstart both areas *as if they were the same unit.* (Even though 48 percent tested genius on IQ tests afterward, if the experience occurred *before the age of six* the percentage was a staggering 81 percent . . . suggesting that the younger the child, the greater the incidence of genius *that cannot be explained via genetic markers.*)

The spatial qualities child experiencers of near-death states exhibit are often shared by quite a different group—those who have autism.

In her book, *Thinking in Pictures, and Other Reports from My Life with*

Autism (Doubleday, New York City, 1995), Temple Grandin, Ph.D., describes her vivid three-dimensional picture-thoughts, which she is able to fast forward and rewind at will as if they were on tape. Unable to appreciate the aesthetic joy of a beautiful sunset, she keenly feels the anguish of suffering animals. Grandin suspects that since the brains of autistic people often reveal immature neural development in the limbic system, there must be damage to that area of the brain that connects emotion to reason.

While there is no known connection between near-death states and autism, there is an observation I can make that is worth considering: where abstract thought processing occurs in the autistic child because of a damaged limbic system, I have consistently noticed *among near-death experiencers that this same phenomenon occurs because of an enhanced and expanded limbic system.* (The limbic system seems to be at the core of near-death states, not as the causal, but as the directive agent once the experience is underway.)

Both autistic and near-death states can produce similar abstractions in thinking modes; but, *whereas autism disconnects normal emotional responses, near-death episodes strengthen and heighten them.* Once again, the "lynchpin" is the limbic. When we can better identify and understand the limbic system's role in transformations of consciousness, particularly near-death states, I believe we will have a handle on how it may serve as the mediator between manifestation and spirit in our species.

The majority of child experiencers overall could remember their birth; one-third had prebirth memories. Yet, *children were six times more likely than adult experiencers to block or "tuck away" their near-death episode.*

Spontaneous recall later in life was common; for most of them that began *after* the age of thirty, usually because of nightmares or in dreams, some because of hypnotic regression, others from reading books about the phenomenon that triggered memory. A youngster having multiple experiences is fairly common. Nearly a third of the overall number I had sessions with went on to describe additional near-death states in adulthood. Almost 80 percent of this larger group were able to watch their death from a viewpoint outside their body, either from above or to one side. What they saw and heard, for the most part, could not have been known by them in advance. If the near-death event occurred during surgery and the child spoke of it after being revived, doctors would routinely tell the kid to "shut up" or "forget what you saw." The medical community should address this, as infants, even newborns, can witness surgery performed on them as if they were observers to the fact, and they can remember what they saw throughout their lives.

Certainly, adult and child experiencers deal with similar challenges, but their response patterns can be exactly the opposite. Examples: children tend to close down after their episode—adults open up; kids are more apt to start attending church as soon as possible—adults leave in droves. On the topic of religion, it is notable that adults generally return to some type of church environment within seven to ten years of their episode. Yet youngsters, if ever alienated, almost never revisit a religious setting again. Evidence of a life continuum is present in children's scenarios; some not only recall life before birth, but *life before earth*!

A sense of judgment is present in many cases of near-death states. With teenagers and adults, it is more likely to be found during the life review; not with some heavenly "Saint Peter" assigning judgment, but, rather, through a review or a reliving of the life. Faults and weaknesses are recognized along with any "error" committed, as are wrongdoings in which others or self were put at needless risk or hurt unnecessarily. (This recognition is usually made by "Self" or soul judging "self"or ego; although sometimes "authority" figures hold court or give verdicts.) With the young, especially in Asian and Native societies, their near-death imagery can and on occasion does include a "parental" authority who demands or insists that certain behaviors be followed, others eliminated, so that the child can grow up in a certain manner (sometimes an "animal" acts as a judge). "One's fate" tends to dominate these scenarios as if it were the "theme" of experience.

THE QUESTIONNAIRE I USED FOR CHILD EXPERIENCERS (WHEN OLDER)

Should you choose to utilize the questionnaire I designed for this project in your own studies, forewarn your participants that the process of filling it out could cause them some discomfort or grief. The questionnaire is supposed to be a tool for probing what might lie *behind* memory. For instance, in the section where I ask about "work, money matters, and ownership," comments can be cross-compared with earlier questions about current employment/home ownership versus how the individual interpreted his or her scenario. Doing this enabled me to confirm a previous observation—that child experiencers tend to have an unusual attachment to "home," not to possessions or money, but *HOME* in the sense of holding to themselves an earthly representation of what they "lost" in their otherworld journey. Their physical home, then, becomes a type of assurance that they can someday progress from the lesser home to the greater. (I have noticed over the years that while adult experiencers can hardly wait to "toss" home mortgages, child experiencers can hardly wait to have one. And once they do, they tend to hold that mortgage, even if bare-bones budgets preclude much in the way of furnishings, so mortgage payments can always be met.)

Technically, the questionnaire functioned well and did its job, as you can readily see. But maybe it functioned too well. Those who filled it out took an inordinate length of time to do so. Why? More than 90 percent found the questionnaire so upsetting that they were plagued with one disaster after another as if they themselves, on some level of awareness, were trying to sabotage the thing. Computers broke down; light bulbs popped; an accident confined some to bed; or just looking at the questionnaire angered others. One man was so disturbed that he threw the questionnaire away and tried to forget ever having received it. Several months later he "died" of food poisoning. Then, after reviving, he was partially paralyzed for a week before he could begin to regain his health. During the crisis, he had another near-death experience *that focused entirely on the circumstances in his childhood that he had steadfastly refused to face—which was precisely what the questionnaire covered.* Nearly a year passed before he could bring himself to tell me this. (No, he never did fill the darn thing out.)

Most of those who "survived" the questionnaire, said that completing it was as life changing as their near-death experience had been. I suspect the reason for all this trauma is that child experiencers never "connect the dots" between what happened to them and what typically occurs after a near-death state. In growing up, they accommodate, compromise, adjust to, and repress, as any child does with what cannot be understood or changed, never realizing that their sense of being an "outsider," of "not fitting in," is *perfectly normal* considering the age when they had their experience. The amount of needless guilt a child experiencer can tuck away because of this confusion is disquieting.

I apologize to anyone who was upset by the questionnaire. Yet, I am sincerely grateful to those who said they received a healing from completing it. Apparently, the questionnaire "worked" on levels above and beyond its original design.

The questionnaire follows. I've included the introduction sans mailing instructions and cover letter. Add plenty of space for answers; mine spread across ten pages.

CHILDREN'S NEAR-DEATH EXPERIENCES QUESTIONNAIRE

This questionnaire is the next step in _____'s project to revisit _____original observations about the near-death experiences of children. The purpose is to recheck those findings, with an emphasis on aftereffects. As a participant in this study, you have already undergone initial screening. It is now time for the questionnaire, an aid for remembering more details. Do not hesitate to contact significant others should you need assistance in memory retrieval.

Please fill out all sections of this questionnaire to the best of your ability, even if some of the subjects were already covered in your initial screening. Do not be constrained by the amount of space available for answers; simply use the backs of pages or add additional sheets. Include *a black and white drawing* of your episode or of any particular scene in it—on a separate page. (Drawings are incredibly important, whether or not you have any artistic talent.) Confidentiality respected.

PRESENT INFORMATION

Name and mailing address:

Phone number (indicate if an unlisted number):

Highest grade level attained in school:

Major subjects or interests in school:

Present occupation:

Present religious affiliation and/or spiritual practices:

Marital/co-partner status (state if divorced):

Give ages of any children (grandchildren too if applies):

Own home or rent?

Status of health:

Hobbies, extra activities, and interests (list special projects):

Present age:

NEAR-DEATH OR NEAR-DEATH-LIKE EXPERIENCE

Age when episode occurred:

Place where episode occurred:

Others present (list names and relationship to you):

Physical circumstances of event:

Subjective experience of event (describe what you can remember):

Afterward, what was your initial reaction?

Did you tell anyone about your subjective experience?

If so, who and how often?

Was any of your experience ever verified?
If so, state what was verified, how long it took to verify, and who verified it:

AFTEREFFECTS

Initially, how did this experience affect you?

If you told others, how did their reaction affect you?

Did manifestations from or because of your experience continue to occur afterward (like sudden or continued "visitations," unusual lights, voices, hauntings, vivid replays of the event, etc.)?

If so, please detail:

If you can, compare your life "before" versus "after" the event—noting any differences:

If you can, compare other people's reaction to you and your relationship to them—using the same before-and-after-format:

SPECIFICS

Did your mind work differently afterward? Explain if yes.

Was there any difference in your faculties? Explain if yes.

Did your intelligence level change? Explain if yes.

Was there any difference in flavor of and preference for food and drink afterward? Explain if yes.

Did the effect of light change afterward? Sunshine? Explain if yes.

Did the effect of sound change afterward? Music? Explain if yes.

Did your energy affect electricity or electronic equipment? Explain if yes.

Was there any difference in your physical body and how it functions, or in your appearance, afterward? Explain if yes.

Did your relationship to animals/nature change afterward? Explain if yes.

Did your relationship to your parents and siblings change? Explain if yes.

Did your relationship to friends and strangers change? Explain if yes.

Did your experience in school and with your teachers/coaches change afterward? Explain if yes.

If you had a counselor or therapist in the years following, was that helpful; did you tell that person about your episode? Please explain.

What was your health like afterward and in the years that followed?

What was your spiritual/religious experience like afterward?

What was the intuitive/psychic and dream world like for you afterward?

How have you dealt with any desire to return to where you once were?

Do you have any regrets about what happened to you?

Do you have a sense of "mission"? If so, explain what you have done or are doing about it:

How do you now handle work, money matters, ownership?

How do you now handle stress, conflicts, negativity?

Did any changes you experienced fade with time? Remain as is? Or, increase over the years? Explain.

Please share your present philosophy of life and the extent to which your episode shaped it:

_____

PERMISSION-TO-USE LETTER

I, _____, hereby give permission to _____ to use what materials I have supplied, as _____ sees fit, in _____ current study of children's near-death and near-death-like experiences, including the publication of same whether in articles, scholarly papers, and/or a book.

I understand that this "permission-to-use" does not restrict me from using my own material in projects of my own making, but simply secures the right for _____ to use my material without fees involved and without recrimination.

Signed:_____

Date:_____

CONCERNING YOUR IDENTITY IN THIS STUDY

May you be referred to by your present name?

If not, give the pseudo-name you want used:

May your present city/state be used?

If not, give any other preference:

It is the custom of _____ to send to _____ research participants a draft copy of _____ initial rendering of any quoted material from their case, so it can be checked over for errors or misinterpretations. Projection for _____ doing this is _____, although no definite date can be set at the present time. Thus, it will be advantageous for you to keep _____ informed should you move, so you can be certain to receive that mailing. Return this form when completed.

Thank you!

ADDITIONAL THOUGHTS ABOUT RESEARCH

I do not use the standard double-blind/control group method most professionals do in my research of near-death states, because I don't trust it during inital screening. This standard screening practice, whether in person or by mail, is dependent upon questions that use terms in advance of the experiencer's response and "lead" in the sense of how certain questions tend to inspire certain answers. And most of the question formats deemed "suitable" have the same antecedent, geared to proving or disproving a single "acceptable" model.

Certainly, when everyone uses the same basic research style and instruments, better and more accurate comparisons can be made. And this is desirable on one level. But, what if the original work was incomplete or perhaps biased in the sense of "preference"—either the researcher's *or* that of the experiencer? consciously *or* subconsciously?

No criticism is intended here, for I know how sincere and diligent both experiencers and researchers are and how difficult it is to maintain objectivity. Nevertheless, we need to admit that:

- No allowance was made during the early years in the field of near-death studies for inquires about unpleasant and/or hellish experiences, or for brief episodes that had little if any imagery.
- Experiencers who had problems accepting or integrating their episode were in essence "ignored."
- The full spread of psychological and physiological aftereffects went unrecognized for more than a decade.
- Children's scenarios were assumed to be the same as adults', their responses similar, until my study indicated otherwise.
- Attempted suicides afterward to get back to the Other Side were completely "missed."
- Correlations between life experiences and what was met in the near-death scenario, the sense that what happened was "needed," were generally bypassed in favor of the notion that near-death states were a distinctly "separate" phenomenon.
- Negative aspects and responses received short shrift compared to the positive ones.
- The three distinctly different types of subjective light were "lost" in a rush to declare near-death states as experiences of brilliant bright, oft times "white" or "golden-white" light.
- The "tunnel" component never was that common; even the "classical" model as established by early research was not and still isn't all that classical.

Both the "preference factor" (seeing in the experience what we want to see) and the "pathological approach" (thinking it something we can dissect, like heart disease) fail utterly to address the complex dynamic known as "the near-death experience."

Today, in almost every discipline, previous studies are being overturned or revamped, not because past authors were inept, but because their research base was not broad enough to adequately cover their field of inquiry. Since I've already mentioned heart disease, let me use it as an example. We now know that the original model for the treatment of heart disease was faulted—its primary source came from work done on men. When women were finally studied separately, vast differences were uncovered in how each sex reacted—which led to the creation of a more efficient and effective model of treatment.

I am not suggesting that near-death states are in any way a pathology, but I am saying that the same premise applies . . . *we need to broaden our research base*. Few people realize that Sigmund Freud, the founder of psychoanalysis, formulated his theories while treating *only twenty-two people*. That humankind is ennobled and spiritual by nature was lost in his investigation of the dark, animalistic urges these twenty-two people exhibited. Exactly like the situation with heart disease, a model of limited parameters was accepted as true for all. Over the years since, more people have been hurt than helped by the distortions in Freud's theory.

Near-death studies have been caught up in the same situation, a tendency to over-rely on a single approach based on singular measurements. Empirical research can be conducted utilizing a number of different approaches, and I count mine as one of them. *Past discoveries in the field of near-death studies are praiseworthy, but, observer/analysts like myself are needed to track myriad details control-group studies cannot address.* If we are ever to understand the near-death phenomenon, we must examine it from 360 degrees. Anything less is unacceptable.

For instance, why do we keep relying on medical investigators in surgical wards for verification of the phenomenon when, neither with adults nor children, is the principle venue "death during surgery"?

This choice was a reasonable one during the early years of research, but modern hospitals are turning more and more to the use of a new drug that causes amnesia in patients. *Are near-death cases on the decline, as a recent but limited study indicates, or are the patients simply unable to remember because of the new drug?* If we are serious about seeking people within the confines of a hospital, why aren't we "hanging out" in emergency wards? The majority of cases, especially with children, come from drownings, suffocation, and accidents (minor surgery, *not* necessarily major surgery)?"

To be fair, the control-group method of research developed about one hundred years ago is a reliable way to study the effect of a single agent acting upon a single illness that in all probability has a single cause. But that method becomes ineffectual when exploring complex issues that have variable causes—like transformations of consciousness (this includes near-death states). A good reference for an illuminating discussion of the pitfalls inherent in standard research styles is *Scientific Literacy and the Myth of the Scientific Method,* Henry H. Bauer (University of Illinois Press, Urbana, IL 1992). Bauer makes the point that scientific accomplishments are often tied to the politics of "prevailing consensus," and that "textbook science" cannot by its very nature convey either the value of the empirical process or the appropriate attitude necessary for such investigation.

Charles Tart, Ph.D., terms such abuse *"scientism."* Tart, internationally known for his experiments that explored altered states of consciousness, and as one of the founders of transpersonal psychology, is the author of two classics in the field of consciousness studies: *Altered States of Consciousness* (reissued by HarperSanFrancisco, San Francisco, CA 1990); and *Transpersonal Psychologies* (also reissued, only this one under Harper, New York City, 1992). According to Tart, *the job of science is to give us information in order that we can make sense of life experiences.* Scientism, on the other hand, states in rigid and dogmatic terms what reality is and should be. He identifies a true skeptic as one who searches for truth, withholding the temptation to establish finality, and "pseudo-skeptics" as those who insist on only one path to truth and only one reality. Tart reminds us that science evolved from philosophy and depends on open inquiry.

Sensationalism teaches the public not to think. To avoid this malaise while exposing yourself to thought-provoking theories on near-death states and related topics, I recommend that you subscribe to *Journal of Near-Death Studies.* All articles are subject to peer review. I would call your attention to Volume 16, No. 2, Winter 1997, as it contains an in-depth report from Kenneth Ring, Ph.D., and Sharon Cooper, M.A., on their research of near-death experiences with the blind. Yes, they did find blind people who could see during their episode, but maybe not as a sighted person sees with physical eyes. Their work suggests that a person's awareness can be omnidirectional and transcendent. In the words of Ring and Cooper: "What we have called transcendental awareness is at least the beginning of the reversal of that process by which, even though the traces of an everyday dualism remain, the individual is enabled, however temporarily, to experience the world from a perspective independent of brain functioning and the operation of the senses." Or, as one of their subjects put it, "Having no eyes, I 'saw' with whole con-sciousness." For more information about the *Journal*, contact: IANDS, P.O. Box 502, East Windsor Hill, CT 06028-0502 or e-mail them at office@iands.org.

I am gratified that China, through the Xinhua news agency, has finally released the results of research conducted by psychiatrists of one hundred sur-vivors of the 1976 Tangshan earthquake, which killed 242,000 people and injured thousands. The survivors, who had been seriously injured, reported about forty different experiences as they came close to death, including a "total recall of past events." Other common reactions were extreme clarity of thought, a sense of calmness, a feeling of having no emotions, a "strange sense about their bodies," and feeling a dreamlike state. No mention was made of aftereffects or of any follow-up investigations with these people.

I am also gratified that the research of Todd Murphy, San Francisco, Cali-fornia, has been recognized, including his investigations of children's near-death episodes in Thailand. I have read several of his case studies and noted the predominance of accusations and admonishments as part of the child's scenario. The notion that experiencers *always* encounter heaven's forgiveness and unconditional love in dying is a misnomer. I suspect, as Murphy does, that cultural superstitions may have a lot to do with this, although not in all cases (refer to the previous discussion of Judith Werner's case, and in chapter 7 the story of Black Elk). Obviously, more research needs to be done in this area. (Murphy's paper on this was published in *Journal of Near-Death Studies*, Vol. 19, No. 3, Spring 2001.)

Before I close, I want to share a most unique case with you—*a collective near-death experience*—where more than one person participated in the same episode. And it is one of the most evidential cases I have encountered. It involves four adults (three men and one woman) on a climb to the summit of Mt. Shivapuri in Kathmandu Valley, February 2, 1996. Julian Rowe, M.D., was one of them. A condensed version of Rowe's account follows:

"My trek in the mountains of the Kathmandu Valley was arranged to go somewhere and see something for four days with a guide, porter, and cook. At the time I thought I would feel like Eddie Murphy in [the movie] *Coming to America*. My royal aspirations were dashed when I was asked if another from the group, Brenda [a nurse], could join me. I had not met her but said yes. The next day we were asked if two American men could join us. Again I said sure. A real party in the works; four people, having never met, going who knows where to see who knows what.

"At dusk, after a difficult climb, we reached the summit. Scott and [his friend] Jeffrey Knapp arrived about ten minutes later and complained of being very tired. Jeff appeared pale and required Brenda's help to remove his backpack. Jeff complained of nausea, and quickly chewed some gummy bears. As we set up our tents and started to get settled, Jeff leaned over the side of the mountain, vomited, and fell backward to the ground. Brenda noted a lack of respirations; and, unable to obtain a pulse, we initiated cardiopulmonary resuscitation (CPR). Scott did mouth-to-mouth and I did the chest compressions. I knew Jeff was sick, but I thought we could slowly get fluids into him to stablilize him. This optimism fled as he suffered another arrest. CPR again initiated, I now received a wave of pure worry, and realized our predicament: three medical personnel on a mountain without any medical supplies. With each compression, I felt a greater weight on my heart. This was all too real.

"The Nepali troops, numbering about ten, refused to call Kathmandu for assistance or a helicopter for two hours. Meanwhile, Jeff again recovered and we moved him into a tent, where we again piled him with sleeping bags and placed warm plates under his back. He suffered several more arrests. All seemed so hopeless. We stopped giving him fluids as he repeatedly vomited more than the fluids we gave him. Scott lay to his left, I to his right, and Brenda gathered supplies and worked to get assistance from the Nepali troops. Around 9:30 A.M., Brenda discovered that even with the U.S. Embassy's assistance, we could not get a rescue helicopter until morning. Shortly thereafter, we decided to send our porters and guide down the mountain to obtain medical supplies.

"Jeff suffered several more arrests, although brief, but I just could not believe he would not survive. His breathing changed, and he slipped into a coma. I briskly rubbed his chest with my knuckle, but no response. His pupils fixed. So we watched, talked, and waited to see if he might be . . . dying. In this silence came the realities and images of the moment, including the smell of vomit and burning coals in the tent, a mass of sleeping bags. The temperature had fallen to around freezing. Scott yelled that 'He could not go now.' Brenda and I chimed in. After approximately thirty minutes, Jeff awoke, and shared his experience.

"Rosy red cheeks with a pale border highlighted Jeff's face. We stared at him with concerned faces, not quite sure what could possibly happen next. After writhing in cramps, and maybe another bout of vomiting, he told us of an amazing near-death experience that included many of our deceased relatives. He told us all several very detailed messages from our deceased relatives and then rested a bit. He also told us that it was time for him to die and he wanted to die. We all could not believe this. He told us that he was told to tell us that we were to take the lesson of doing all that we can do, and that is what we must accept—that the decision of life or death is not really decided by us.

"He suffered another episode or two of CPR, now totaling about ten for the evening. In an attempt to connect with him and help him to hang on, we placed the tape player on his abdomen soothingly playing 'That's What Friends Are For.' We clung to each other in one of the most intense and moving moments of my life. We watched, listened, and cried."

Supplies finally arrived and an IV was set up to get fluids into Jeff's veins. He responded. "The sunrise approached and I had an eerie feeling in my gut. So much occurred on February 2, Ground Hog Day, why should we presume this was over. Jeff remained on top of the mountain without transport and with the trauma of a night of arrests and comas. But he was *supposed* to make it now. I kept these thoughts to myself; and with the warmth of the sunrise, we transported Jeff out of the tent to a resting spot underneath a Hindu shrine, his IV bottle shining in the early morning sun. News of the helicopter transport came a little after 6."

Jeffrey Knapp had a near-death experience under the most threatening of conditions. The tent where he lay became a war zone of three people fighting to save his life. The near-death scenarios he experienced lasted unabated throughout the entire night. *His episodes involved the lives and deceased relatives of everyone present, with specific messages delivered privately to each person when Jeff was conscious enough to do so.* His episode was a collective one in the sense that three people besides himself participated together in the scenario "story form" as it occurred. Of those present, the physician, Julian Rowe, documented the event. The information that was revealed from the Other Side *could not have been known by Jeffrey Knapp in advance, yet it was breathtakingly accurate and consisted of intimate details that each individual regarded as highly personal.*

Although he is an adult experiencer, I have presented Jeffrey Knapp's case as a reminder to all of us how raw and sometimes violent the moments leading to death can be, and how awe-inspiring is the ecstasy of being able to pass through death and return. No skeptic can deny this, or argue away the impact of such an event with the arrogant claim of "it's just a hallucination." Equally deluded are "true believers," for, just because television talk shows and bestselling books have legitimized the subject, does not mean everything an experiencer says is true or that the researcher has done a proper job of investigation.

We seem to have forgotten something in our quest to understand the near-death experience, and that is the power of mystery.

Knapp's tussle with the aftereffects, what his wife and children have been subjected to, is both inspiring and disturbing. Any assessment is premature at this writing. It can be said, however, that the lives of all four people who trekked to that mountaintop in Kathmandu have been radically and forever changed because of the near-death phenomenon. Sensationalizing this or any other near-death case serves no one. Experiencers and their loved ones need time to deal with what comes next—years, in fact. The greater challenge, however, is to society. Near-death states are capable of restructuring the brain and reawakening the heart, even for nonexperiencers who merely hear about the stories. Results are often beyond the reach of research to clarify, or of governments to contain, or of rigid belief systems to control.

Unleashed by near-death states . . . is the majesty of the soul.

The First Decade
THE TRUTH IS BORN
The truth is born
into the world
always seeking expression—

> *when we are taught*
> > *not to communicate;*
> > *not to express;*
> > *not to speak;*
> > *and not to be heard so early in life,*

> *We then learn at a very, very early age,*
> > *to express*
> > *to speak*
> > *to be heard and*
> > *to communicate at a higher, deeper level;*
> *we learn to communicate through the unspoken word*
> *and thought.*

> *At this level spirits seek union.*
> *At this level One learns to listen;*
> > *at this level one learns to listen, feel,*
> *speak, and be at one with nature and its beings.*

—SUSAN FIRTH, FREE UNION, VA; NDE AT TWO IN AN ACCIDENT, AND NDE AT SIX FROM DROWNING

APPENDIX THREE

Web Site of P. M. H. Atwater, L.H.D.

www.cinemind.com/atwater

My Web site exists as a cyber-library of my research with near-death states, the spiritual approach to life, and the positive use of intuitive abilities. Changes are made from time to time, especially regarding my travel schedule, announcements, and news.

When you visit the Web site, look up how to obtain my five self-published books:

I Died Three Times in 1977. A compilation of articles written shortly after my experiences—illustrated with thoughtform drawings.

The Frost Diamond: A true story about my first encounter as a child with hoar frost—a colorbook.

Life Sounds: Poetry and small drawings.

Brain Shift/Spirit Shift: Phase II of a theoretical model using near-death states to understand transformations of consciousness.

The Challenge of September 11: A mini-book, free to all.

Other features include a section for actual near-death cases, reference lists for educational opportunities/holistic therapies/hospitals with a heart, and The Marketplace. The Marketplace of NDE-Related Items of Interest is a treasure trove of offerings from a host of near-death experiencers or those like them. Offerings include such items as: videos, music, art, paintings, all types of inspired products and services, a spiritual seminary, and so forth. It is operated as a public service. Products and services are posted free of charge. The purpose is to help people connect with inspired work, while enabling experiencers to have a way of promoting what they do. The Marketplace exists no where else. Take advantage of it!

Web Site of International Association for Near-Death Studies (IANDS)

www.iands.org

IANDS exists to impart knowledge concerning near-death experiences and their implications, to encourage and support research dealing with the experience and related phenomena, and to aid people in starting local groups to explore the subject. They have numerous publications, among them the scholarly *Journal of Near-Death Studies,* a general-interest newsletter *Vital Signs,* and various brochures and materials. Membership in this nonprofit organization is open to anyone; dues are annual and include various benefits.

Donations to cover operating expenses are always needed and always welcome, especially for the NDE Research Fund. Audiocassette tapes of IANDS conference speakers are available. Ask for their list of national and international chapters (Friends of IANDS), should you be interested in visiting any of them. Individual reports about near-death episodes are solicited for the archives; to make a report you will need to fill out a form, so please ask for one.

Memberships, back issues of their publications, and conference tapes can now be ordered directly from their Web site. Check out their section on actual experiencer episodes; it is growing as more and more people are willing to share their stories. Do start an IANDS group in your area if there isn't one already; invite members from the group Compassionate Friends to come, as those who have lost a child find great comfort when exposed to near-death experiencers and materials. The annual IANDS Conference is held in different cities each year; in 2004 it will be in Chicago.

International Association for Near-Death Studies
P.O. Box 502
East Windsor Hill, CT 06028-0502
phone (860) 644-5216
fax (860) 644-5759
e-mail: office@iands.org

Notes

Do not wait for leaders; do it alone, person to person.
— MOTHER TERESA

Preface

1. P. M. H. Atwater, *Coming Back to Life: The Aftereffects of the Near-Death Experience* (New York: Dodd, Mead & Co., 1988; Ballantine Books, 1989; New York: Citadel Press, 2001).

2. P. M. H. Atwater, L.H.D., *Future Memory: How Those Who "See the Future" Shed New Light on the Workings of the Human Mind* (New York: Birch Lane Press, 1996; Charlottesville, Va.: Hampton Roads Publishing Co., 1999).

One: Evolutions Nod

1. William Strauss and Neil Howe, *Generations: The History of America's Future, 1584 to 2069* (New York: William Morrow, 1991). This is the best reference I have found for identifying the distinctive agendas each generation brings to the fore, and addressing the historical context of the years in which they lived.

2. Sharon Begley "The IQ Puzzle," *Newsweek,* May 6, 1996, 70–72.

3. Melvin Morse, M.D., with Paul Perry, *Closer to the Light: Learning from the Near-Death Experiences of Children* (New York: Villard Books, 1990).

4. "Is There Life After Death?" *U.S. News & World Report,* March 31, 1997, 58–64.

5. Michael Cremo and Richard Thompson, *Forbidden Archaeology: The Hidden History of the Human Race* (Alachua, Fla.: Govardhan Hill, 1993).

6. Richard Milton. *Shattering the Myths of Darwinism* (Rochester, Vt.: Park Street Press, 1998).

7. Michael J. Behe. Ph.D., *Darwin's Black Box: The Biochemical Challenge to Evolution* (New York: Free Press, 1996).

Two: Brain Shift/Spirit Shift

1. P. M. H. Atwater. L.H.D., *Phase II—Brain Shift/Spirit Shift: A Theoretical Model Using Research on Near-Death States to Explore the Transformation of Consciousness.* Available as a sixty-four-page, single-spaced cyberbook research report on my Web site: http://www.cinemmd.com/atwater (various options for payment).

2. This finding of mine, that it takes at least seven years for adults to integrate their near-death experience, has been verified in the clinical, prospective study of cases in Holland, conducted by cardiologist Pim van Lommel and associates. This study was published in *The Lancet* (medical journal), Vol. 358, No. 9298, 12–15-01.

3. *New Scientist* magazine (January 8, 1994) cited the latest findings of Nicholas Humphrey, a senior research fellow at Cambridge University who discovered that emotions are primary. His work concerns "sensory consciousness," a term he coined for the brain's role in feeling. Other researchers have joined in, each adding more information about the importance of emotion and how it influences the mind. A good book on this subject is Antonio R. Damasio's *Descartes' Error: Emotion, Reason, and the Human Brain* (New York: Grosset/Putnam, 1994).

4. Marianne Frostig and Phyllis Maslow, "Neuropsychological Contributions to Education." *Journal of Learning Disabilities* 12, no. 8 (October 1979): 538–552. Also refer to the book *Evolution's End,* by Joseph Chilton Pearce (San Francisco: Harper San Francisco, 1992).

5. Glen Rein is a senior researcher at the Institute of Heart Math, and can be reached through them at 14700 West Park Avenue, Boulder Creek, CA 95006; (408) 338-8700.

6. Refer to Richard E. Cytowic. M.D., *The Man Who Tasted Shapes: A Bizarre Medical Mystery Offers Revolutionary Insights into Emotions, Reasoning, and Consciousness* (New York: Tarcher/Putnam, 1993).

7. Howard Gardner, *Creating Minds* (New York: Basic Books, 1993). Howard Gardner, a psychologist and codirector of the Harvard Project on Human Potential, profiled great minds of the twentieth century in an attempt to characterize genius. He discovered: that discarding accepted ideas of what is possible can make it easier to take new ideas seriously; that connecting the unconnected leads to insight; and that a tolerance for ambiguity is crucial to creativity. He points out that the word "intelligence" means "to select among," indicating the importance of detail recognition. But genius shakes together or clusters information, much as a child would, to arrive at different or larger concepts.

8. Refer to Anna Wise, *High Performance Mind* (New York: Putnam, 1995). The brain normally operates at varying brainwave speeds. Wise created audiocassettes of music and sound frequencies so that anyone who wanted to could have an opportunity to achieve simultaneous "awakened" mind states. These tapes are available from: Kit Walker, Tools for Exploration, 47 Paul Drive, San Rafael, CA 94903; (800) 456-9887.

9. Refer to the article "Brain Waves Move Computer Cursors," *New York Times,* March 7, 1995.

10. Atwater, *Future Memory,* 20.

11. Ibid, 169–170.

12. Todd Murphy, "The Structure and Function of Near-Death Experiences: An Algorithmic Reincarnation Hypothesis." Published in *Journal of Near-Death Studies*, Vol. 20, No. 2, Winter 2001. Murphy's paper "Recreating Near-Death Experiences: A Cognitive Approach," was published in *Journal of Near-Death Studies*, Vol. 17, No. 4, Summer 1999. His groundbreaking research of child experiencers in Thailand, entitled "NDEs in Thailand," appeared in *Journal of Near-Death Studies*, Vol. 19, No.32, Spring 2001.

13. Arnold J. Mandell, "Toward a Psychobiology of Transcendence: God in the Brain," in Richard and Julian Davidson, eds., *The Psychobiology of Consciousness* (New York: Plenum Press, 1980).

14. Michael A. Persinger, Ph.D., *Neuropsychological Bases of God Beliefs* (Westport, Conn.: Praeger, 1987).

15. Wilder Penfield, M.D., *The Mystery of the Mind* (Princeton, N.J.: Princeton University Press, 1977).

16. Raymond A. Moody Jr., M.D., with Paul Perry, *Reunions: Visionary Encounters with Departed Loved Ones* (New York: Villard Books, 1993). Moody coined the term "near-death experience" and launched the entire field with his first book, *Life After Life*.

17. P. M. H. Atwater, L.H.D, *Beyond the Light: What Isn't Being Said about the Near-Death Experience* (New York: Birch Lane Press, 1994). The title was altered in the paperback edition to *Beyond the Light: The Mysteries and Revelations of Near-Death Experiences* (New York: Avon Books, 1995).

18. For more information about the imagery in otherworld journeys, peruse the following: Joseph Campbell, with Bill Moyers, *The Power of Myth* (New York: Doubleday, 1988); Ioan Couliano, *Out of This World: Otherworld Journeys from Gilgamesh to Albert Einstein* (Boston: Shambhala, 1991); Manley P. Hall, *The Secret Teachings of All Ages* (Los Angeles: Philosophical Research Society, 1978); Richard Heinberg, *Memories and Visions of Paradise: Exploring the Universal Myth of a Lost Golden Age* (Los Angeles: Tarcher, 1989); Carl G. Jung, *Man and His Symbols* (New York: Laureleaf, 1997).

19. For an enlightening discourse on this force, refer to Adolf Holl, *The Left Hand of God: A Biography of the Holy Spirit* (New York: Doubleday 1998).

20. James Hillman, *The Soul's Code: Character, Calling and Fate* (New York: Random House, 1996).

21. David Spangler, *The Call* (New York: Riverhead Books, 1996).

22. Larry Dossey, M.D, *Prayer Is Good Medicine* (New York: Harper Collins, 1996). Also, Larry Dossey, M.D., *Healing Words: The Power of Prayer and the Practice of Medicine* (New York: Harper Collins, 1997).

23. Kathleen Norris, *The Cloister Walk* (New York: Riverhead Books, 1996). Also, Kathleen Norris, *Amazing Grace* (New York: Riverhead Books, 1998). The quote I used came from *Amazing Grace*. I find the title of her latest work intriguing, because many researchers attach the notion of "amazing grace" to the near-

death phenomenon, and Norris herself behaves and writes as if she once had such an experience (and she could have when younger).

24. Ken Wilber, *A Brief History of Everything* (Boston: Shambhala, 1996).

25. Kathleen J. Forti's *The Door to the Secret City* is available both as a book and as an audiocassette dramatization. Contact her at 12401 Wilshire Blvd., Suite 306, Los Angeles, CA 90025; e-mail kjforti@aol.com. Although considered fiction, another excellent book about a child's near-death experience is *Wenny Has Wings,* Janet Lee Carey (New York: Simon Schuster/Atheneum Books, 2002).

26. To obtain a copy of Henry Reed's paper "Intimacy and Psi: Explorations in Psychic Closeness," or to be notified of his workshops and speaking schedule, contact: Henry Reed, Ph.D., Creative Spirit Studios, Flying Goat Ranch, 3777 Fox Creek Road, Mouth of Wilson, VA 24363; 1-800-398-1370; Web site http://www.creativespirit.net.

Three: A New View of Near-Death States

1. Raymond A. Moody Jr., M.D., *Life After Life* (Covington, Ga.: Mockingbird Books, 1975).

2. Kenneth Ring, Ph.D., *Life at Death* (New York: Coward, McCann & Geoghegan, 1980).

3. International Association for Near-Death Studies (IANDS), P.O. Box 502, East Windsor Hill, CT 06028-0502; (860) 644-5216; fax (860) 644-5759; Web site: http://www.iands.org; e-mail office@iands.org. Ask for brochure "Active Support Groups." Also, refer to page 257 for more information about the IANDS Web site.

4. Howard Gardner, *Frames of Mind* (New York: Basic Books, 1983). An excellent review of this book appeared in *Utne Reader,* September/October 1990, 82–83. It was written by Thomas Armstrong of *Mothering* magazine. I would especially call your attention to Silverman's book, *Upside Down Brilliance: The Visual-Spacial Learner* (Denver, Colo.: DeLeon Publishing, 2002). Her findings in this study strongly suggest that visual-spatial kids are the forerunners of new generations of conscious children (who, I would add, are born with the distinct characteristics that near-death kids come to have).

5. Linda Kreger Silverman, Ph.D., and her assistant, Betty Maxwell, can be reached through the Institute for the Study of Advanced Development, 1452 Marion Street, Denver, CO 80218; (303) 837-8378. Silverman's work in the field of gifted children is extensive and well documented. I would encourage anyone interested to investigate her offerings.

6. To obtain Silverman's monograph on Dabrowski, ask for a copy of "The Moral Sensitivity of Gifted Children and the Evolution of Society" when you contact her. Also request her rendition of Dabrowski's theory, which discusses his ideas about positive disintegration of psychological structures in favor of compassion, integrity, and altruism. Refer to note 5 for address and phone number.

Five: The Impact of Aftereffects

1. Marlene Spencer, M.Ed., "Dissociation: Normal or Abnormal?" *Journal of Near-Death Studies* 14, no. 3 (Spring 1996): 145–157.

2. To inquire about the hospice work of Nadia McCaffrey, contact her directly at 334 Roosevelt Avenue, Sunnyvale, CA 94086; phones (408) 836-4727 and (408) 733-8672; e-mail nadiaiands@aol.com;
Web site http://www.changingthefaceofdeath.org.

3. These two books are excellent sources to explore: Mary Ann Block, D.O., *No More Ritalin* (New York: Kensington, 1996); Judith Ullman, *Ritalin Free Kids: Safe and Effective Homeopathic Medicine for ADD and Other Behavior and Learning Problems* (Rockland, Calif: Prima, 1996).

4. Diane K. Corcoran, R.N., Ph.D., regularly travels across the nation and through other countries teaching thousands of nurses and health-care providers about their role in supporting patients who have had a near-death experience. As a two-term past president of the International Association for Near-Death Studies, she has been privy to the latest in research and information on experiencer needs. As another adjunct to her work, she has teamed up with Maggie Callanan, R.N., a hospice nurse and coauthor of the book *Final Gifts: Understanding the Special Awareness, Needs, and Communications of the Dying* (with Patricia Kelley; New York: Simon & Schuster, 1992). Together, these two dynamic speakers offer Shades of the Rainbow, a full-day workshop on near-death states and nearing-death awareness, to any group willing to sponsor them. To discuss this further, contact Dr. Corcoran at 2705 Montcastle Court, Durham, NC 27705; cell phone (919) 634-0547; e-mail diane.corcoran@kapa.net.

5. The entire story of Cheryl Pottberg's amazing recovery and Dr. Gerald M. Lemole's equally amazing conversion to holistic health measures is chronicled as a front-page feature article in the Life & Leisure section of the (Wilmington, Delaware) *Sunday News Journal* (July 13, 1997, section J). Contact Dr. Lemole through his office at the Medical Arts Pavilion, Suite 205, 4745 Ogletown Road, Newark, DE 19713-2070; (302) 738-0448. His title is Chief of Cardiovascular Surgery, and his training and credentials are impeccable. Teaming up with two other surgeons, he has established the M.D.'s Medical Healthline at (900) GET-WELL ($1.99 per minute) to provide recorded information on more than fifty diseases and problems, and to give "the truth about natural remedies." Anyone can avail him- or herself of this service. The average call lasts about five minutes.

6. Betty Eadie, *Embraced by the Light* (Placerville, Calif: Gold Leaf Press, 1992).

7. Aafke's self-published book is truly a remarkable feat. It is by far the best rendition of a child's near-death experience that exists at this writing. No English translation has been made so far. It is my hope that a publisher for it will soon be found. Should you wish to speak with Aafke directly, or if you have any ideas about getting her book published, contact: Aafke H. Holm-Oosterhof, Steenderkamp 26, 7921 HE Zuidwolde, The Netherlands; phone 31-528-373103; fax 31-528-370864; e-mail aafke@holm.myweb.nl.

8. *Play with Your Food*, Joost Elffers. New York City; Stewart Tabori & Chang, 1997.

Six: Many Types, One Pattern

1. The purpose as stated on Timothy O'Reilly's forty-minute video *Round Trip* is to "educate, enlighten, and heal." To obtain a copy, order from Wellspring Media, 65 Bleecker Street, New York, NY 10012; (800) 538-5856.

2. Amanda Csanady, then seven, did the drawing for the month of June in the 1987–1988 Mead Johnson Enfamil Calendar, published by Mead Johnson Nutritionals, 2400 West Expressway, Evansville, IN 47721-0001; (812) 429–5000. My thanks to Mead Johnson for allowing me to use Amanda's winning entry.

3. I wrote extensively about correlations of significance between the color yellow and the chemistry of the brain in *Beyond the Light* (pages 180–182 in the paperback version). A further discussion can be found in my research report *Brain Shift/Spirit Shift: A Theoretical Model Using Research on Near-Death States to Explore the Transformation of Consciousness*. The report can be purchased through my Web site at www.cinemind.com/atwater.

4. "Students' Post Near-Death Experience Attitude and Behavior Toward Education and Learning," a Ph.D. dissertation by Joseph Benedict Geraci, is on file at the University of Connecticut, Storrs, Connecticut.

Seven: Cases from History

1. For more information about Lincoln, see: L. Pierce Clark, *Lincoln: A Psycho-Biography* (New York: Charles Scribner's Sons, 1933); Ida M. Tarbell, *The Early Life of A. L.* (New Brunswick, N.J.: A. S. Barnes and Co., 1974); Emanuel Hertz, *The Hidden Lincoln, from the Letters and Papers of Wm. H. Herndon* (New York: Viking Press, 1938); Joseph E. Suppiger, *The Intimate Lincoln* (Lanham, Md.: University Press of America, 1985); Ward H. Lamon, *The Life of A. Lincoln, from His Birth to His Inauguration As President* (Boston: James R. Osgood & Co., 1872); Richard N. Current, *The Lincoln Nobody Knows* (New York: McGraw Hill, 1958).

2. *Einstein: The Life and Times*, Ronald W. Clark (New York: Thomas Y. Croweil Co. [World Publishing], 1971; and *Subtle Is the Lord. . .: The Science and The Life of A. Einstein*, Abraham Pais (Oxford, U.K.: Oxford University Press, 1982).

3. Summarized from the paper "Did Near-Death Experiences Play a Seminal Role in the Formulation of Einstein's Theory of Relativity?" by J. "Joe" Timothy Green, Ph.D., *Journal of Near-Death Studies*, Vol. 20, No. 1, Fall 2001.

4. The case for Edward deVere, the 17th Earl of Oxford, having authored all the works accredited to Shakespeare is so compelling, I detailed it, complete with references, in Appendix Five of my book *Future Memory* (Hampton Roads Publishing, Charlottesville, VA 1999).

5. Refer to John Neihardt, *Black Elk Speaks* (New York: Pocket Books, 1972). Also obtain audiocassette #SU-6 from the 1995 IANDS conference on the near-death phenomenon. This is a tape of a talk by Steve Straight on the connection between Black Elk and his biographer John Neihardt: *both had had childhood near-death experiences and understood each other perfectly.* The tape is still available and can be ordered from: IANDS, P.O. Box 502, East Windsor Hill, CT 06028-0502; (860) 644-5216; Web site www.iands.org; e-mail office@iands.org.

6. Walter and Lao Russell passed on years ago, but their University of Science and Philosophy is still active and growing. Their home-study correspondence course, all their books, plus Glenn Clark's biography of Walter Russell, titled *The Man Who Tapped the Secrets of the Universe,* are available to anyone interested. Contact: University of Science and Philosophy, P.O. Box 520 Waynesboro, VA 22980; (800) 882-5683; VA; phone (540) 887-5030; fax (540) 553-1007; Web site http://www.philosophy.org. Dr. Timothy Binder is the current director and president of the Board.

7. *Infinite Mind: Science of the Human Vibrations of Consciousness* is a 1996 version of Valerie V. Hunt's original book, *Infinite Mind: The Science of Human Vibrations* (Malibu, Calif.: Malibu Publishing Co., 1989). Little changed between the two editions except for the title and a few corrections. Contact: Malibu Publishing Co., P.O. Box 4234, Malibu, CA 90265. Many of Hunt's music and sound audiocassette tapes are also available, as is a video on the human energy field. (Details in the back of her book or through the publisher.) My thanks to Dr. Hunt for the right to quote from her material.

8. Inquire about newsletter subscriptions by contacting Raymond A. Moody Jr., M.D., Ph.D., at Theater of the Mind, P.O. Box 417, Anniston, AL 36202; (205) 831-0199; fax (205) 831-9889. His Web site address is: http://www.lifeafterlife. com/body_index. html.

9. My own work with "empathic experiences" is explained along with instructions in how to engage in creating them, in my book *The Complete Idiot's Guide to Near-Death Experiences* (with David Morgan) (Indianapolis, Ind.: Macmillan/Alpha Books/Pearson, 2000), pages 48–51. Further details are covered in another book of mine—its working title is *Not Here, Present Elsewhere: The Real Truth about Death and Dying* (Virginia Beach, VA: ARE Press, 2004).

Eight: Evidence for a Life Continuum

1. In the paperback edition of *Beyond the Light* (Avon Books, 1997), I discussed the case of Berkley Carter Mills as an example of the Transcendent Experience. The quote that appears here is from page 73 of the paperback and is used with his kind permission.

2. The Pleasant and/or Heavenlike Experience of Alice Morrison-Mays appears on pages 56–60 of the paperback edition of *Beyond the Light* (Avon Books). My thanks to Alice for giving me the right to reuse some other material and for permission to quote from her additional comments. She has since passed away *at the very moment* her physician daughter held in her hands a newborn she had

just delivered. The synchronicity of this, of one soul leaving when another entered, deeply affected Alice's daughter, transforming her grief to joy.

3. Arvin S. Gibson, "Near-Death Experience Patterns from Research in the Salt Lake City Region," *Journal of Near-Death Studies* 13, no. 2 (Winter 1994). The specific quote used appears on page 125. Gibson wrote a series of three books, each a collection of accounts from the near-death survivors he interviewed. These are: *Glimpses of Eternity* (1992), *Echoes from Eternity* (1993), and *Journeys Beyond Life* (1994), all published by Horizon Publishers in Bountiful, Utah.

4. Robert L. Van de Castle, Ph.D., *Our Dreaming Mind: A Sweeping Exploration of the Role That Dreams Have Played in Politics, Art, Religion, and Psychology from Ancient Civilizations to the Present Day* (New York: Ballantine Books, 1994).

5. Rand Jameson Shields is currently writing a book of his reincarnation memories entitled *There Is No Death*. Publication date as yet unknown. He can be reached via e-mail at rjameson@vgernet.net.

6. "Elvis and His Angelic Connection" by Maia C. M. Shamayyim, appears on page 22 of *Angel Times Magazine*, Vol. 1, Issue 4 (no date declared). No longer in print, the magazine was originally published by Angelic Realms Unlimited, Inc., 4360 Chamblee-Dunwoody Road, Suite 400, Atlanta, GA 30341.

7. Caryl Dennis, with Parker Whitman, *The Millennium Children: Tales of the Shift*. Dennis self-published this book in 1997. The book is available through: Rainbows Unlimited, 1415 Main St., #295 Dunedin, FL 34698; e-mail caryl@gte.net; Web site http://www.rainbowsunlimited.com. Prepare yourself, for the book is printed on lavender-colored paper. The section about vanishing twins is on pages 138–166.

8. Raymond W. Brandt, Ph.D., publishes both *Twins World* magazine and *Twinless Twins* newsletter. To obtain these publications plus information about annual conferences, contact: Twinless Twins Support International, 11220 St. Joe Road, Fort Wayne, IN 46835; (219) 627-5414.

9. The research bulletin "Multiple Personality—Mirrors of a New Model of Mind?" vol. 1, no. 3/4, is a double issue and is available from: Institute of Noetic Sciences, 101 San Antonio Road, Petaluma, CA 94952-9524; 1-800-383-1394 and in California (707) 775-3500; Web site http://www.noetic.org.

10. *Newsweek* magazine, special edition, "From Birth to Three" (Spring/Summer 1997). The quote is from Geoffrey Cowley's article, "The Language Explosion," on page 17.

11. Thomas Verny, M.D., with John Kelly, *The Secret Life of the Unborn Child* (New York: Dell, 1981).

12. David Chamberlain, Ph.D., *Babies Remember Birth* (Los Angeles: Jeremy Tarcher, 1988).

13. David B. Cheek, M.D., "Are Telepathy, Clairvoyance, and 'Hearing' Possible in Utero? Suggestive Evidence As Revealed During Hypnotic Age-Regression," *Journal of Pre- & Peri-Natal Psychology* 7, issue 2 (Winter 1992): 125–137.

14. Ian Stevenson, M.D., *Twenty Cases Suggestive of Reincarnation* (New York: American Society for Psychical Research, 1966), and *Where Reincarnation and Biology Intersect* (Glenview, Ill.: Praeger, 1997).

15. Tom Shroder, *Old Souls: The Scientific Evidence for Past Lives* (New York, N.Y.: Simon & Schuster, 1999).

16. Carol Bowman, *Children's Past Lives: How Past Life Memories Affect Your Child* (New York: Bantam, 1997).

17. Two leaders in the field of NDA (nearing-death awareness) are Maggie Callanan and Patricia Kelley. Their book is *Final Gifts: Understanding the Special Awareness, Needs, and Communication of the Dying* (New York: Simon & Schuster, 1992).

18. Two pioneers in ADC (after-death communication) are Bill Guggenheim and Judy Guggenheim, authors of *Hello from Heaven: A New Field of Research Confirms That Life and Love Are Eternal* (New York: Bantam Books, 1996). Contact them directly if you wish to report an ADC or participate in their research: The ADC Project, P.O. Box 916070, Longwood, FL 32791; (407) 862-1260.

19. Works by those spearheading research into PBEs (prebirth experiences) are: Sarah Hinze, *Coming from the Light: Spiritual Accounts of Life Before Birth* (New York: Pocket Books, 1994). Hinze is actively seeking more accounts of the PBE. Contact her through: Royal Child Studies, P.O. Box 31086, Mesa, AZ 85275-1086; (602) 898-3009. Craig Lundahl and Harold Widdison, *The Eternal Journey: How Near-Death Experiences Illuminate Our Earthly Lives* (New York: Warner Books, 1997). Elisabeth Hallett, *Soul Trek: Meeting Our Children on the Way to Birth* (Hamilton, Mont.: Light Hearts Publishing, 1995). Elizabeth M. Carman and Neil J. Carman, Ph.D., *Cosmic Cradle: Souls Waiting in the Wings for Birth* (Fairfield, IA: Sunstar Publishing Ltd., 1999).

Nine: Alien Existences

1. An intriguing collection of stories about the missing fetus syndrome is found in Jenny Randles, *Star Children: The True Story of Alien Offspring among Us* (New York: Sterling Publishing Co., 1995). *Caution:* Randles's list of characteristics that she says distinguish "star children" is *exactly the same as the list that identifies average, typical child experiencers of near-death states.* There is reason to question this "coincidence" and wonder what differences would emerge if research between the phenomena were compared in a more thorough and careful manner. The fact that a child fits Randles's list *does not mean he or she is "alien."*

2. Ben Okri, *The Famished Road* (New York: Anchor Books, 1993). My thanks to Doubleday for their generous permission in allowing me to quote from Okri's work. My thanks also to Donald Riggs of Thorigne Sur Due, France, for recommending Okri to me. Okri writes from a child's perspective of modern Nigeria that is most extraordinary, and creates striking word pictures.

3. Flavio M. Cabobianco, *Vengo del Sol (I Come from the Sun)* (Buenos Aires, Argentina: Organizacion Zago S.R.L., 1991). French and German translations are available; an English version does not exist at this writing. I want to thank Flavio

and Marcos Cabobianco for their many kindnesses, and Alejandra Warden for translating our conversation and Flavio's book. Thanks also go to Florin Lowndes for bringing along a German copy of Flavio's book when he stayed in our home. What I saw as he translated each page convinced me that I had to locate the Cabobianco family, and I did so with the help of Stephany Evans.

4. Peter Graneau, "Is Dead Matter Aware of Its Environment?" *Frontier Perspectives 7,* no. 1 (Fall/Winter 1998): 50–52. The Institute for Frontier Sciences has since moved to: 6114 LaSalle Avenue, PMB 605, Oakland, CA 94611; (510) 531-5767; e-mail brubik@compuserve.com; Web site http://www.healthy-net/frontierscience.

5. Kenneth Ring, Ph.D., *The Omega Project: Near-Death Experiences, UFO Encounters, and Mind at Large* (New York: William Morrow, 1992).

6. Greta Woodrew, LL.D., and her husband, Dick Smolowe, LL.D., were publishers of the newsletter *Woodrew Update* until the fall of 1997, when they retired the periodical after seventeen years of "holding forth." Copies of volume 17, number 3 are still available, as are other past issues, Woodrew's books *On a Slide of Light* and *Memories of Tomorrow,* and her storybook for children, titled *Hear the Colors! See the Music!* Contact: Woodrew and Smolowe, 122 Bayberry Place, Advance, NC 27006; (336) 940-2339; e-mail STARFDN@PRODIGY.NET

7. Ruth Montgomery, *Strangers among Us* (New York: Coward, McCann, Geoghegan, 1979).

8. Proponents of the walk-in theory, or "soul switching," have formed an organization that sponsors regular conferences. Contact: WE International, P.O. Box 120633, St. Paul, MN 55112; e-mail WalkinsLiz@aol.com

Ten: A New Race Aborning

1. Stauss and Howe, *Generations.* Refer to note 1, chapter 1.

2. Refer to note 5 in chapter 3 for contact information about Dr. Silverman. I want to thank her for allowing me to quote from the material she sent me, and from our phone calls.

3. This is an old Sumerian legend sculpted in relief on actual dated artifacts, thought to be symbolic by most archaeologists, but taken as factual by researcher Zecharia Sitchen in many of his books. Refer to Zecharia Sitchen, *Genesis Revisited: Is Modern Science Catching Up with Ancient Knowledge?* (Santa Fe, N.M.: Bear & Co., 1990).

4. For more than forty years Edgar Cayce would close his eyes, enter an altered state of consciousness, and speak to the very heart and spirit of humankind on subjects such as health, dreams, prophecy, meditation, and reincarnation. Dubbed the "sleeping prophet," he has since passed on, but his work continues through the Association for Research and Enlightenment (ARE), 67th and Atlanta Ave., Virginia Beach, VA 23451; general information is available at (800) 333-4499; the bookstore phone number is (888) ARE-0050. Anyone can visit their extensive library. Membership is yearly; they offer a wide range of services and products and have active study groups of the Cayce material worldwide.

5. One interpretation of this is found in Kirk Nelson, *The Second Coming* (Virginia Beach, Va.: Wright Publishing Co., 1986).

6. An excellent reference for the legend of the White Buffalo is Robert B. Pickering, *Seeing the White Buffalo* (Denver, Colo.: Denver Museum of Natural History Press, 1997).

7. Gordon-Michael Scallion, *Notes from the Cosmos: A Futurist's Insights into the World of Dream Prophecy and Intuition—Includes Global Predictions for 1998–2012.* Originally published by his company in 1997, it should be available in any bookstore. If not, contact: Matrix Institute, Inc., P.O. Box 367, West Chesterfield, N.H. 03466-0367; (603) 256-6520; fax (603) 256-6614; e-mail service@IntuitiveFlash.com; Web site: http://www.IntuitiveFlash.com. Scallion publishes the monthly *Intuitive Flash* newsletter and a large map of what his visions have shown him the world will be like after "the changes." All quotes are used with his kind permission.

8. Swami Amritasvarupananda, *Mata Amritanandamayi: A Biography* (San Ramon, Calif.: Mata Amritanandamayi Center, 1988). This book should be available through any bookstore. Or, order from: Mata Amritanandamayi Center, P.O. Box 613, San Ramon, CA 94583-0613; (510) 537-9417; fax (510) 889-8585; Web site www.ammachi.org. Quotes are excerpted from pages 14–16 and 193. I want to thank Swami Paramatmananda for giving me permission to use the quotes, and Helen Williams of Vancouver, British Columbia, for telling me about Mata Amritanandamayi.

9. John White has written fifteen books, which have been translated into nine languages; among them is the classic *The Meeting of Science and Spirit* (New York: Paragon House, 1990).

10. Stauss and Howe, *Generations*, p. 341. Also consider their latest book, *Millennials Rising: The Next Great Generation* (New York: Vintage Books, 2000).

11. E. Alan Meece, *Horoscope for the New Millennium* (St. Paul, Minn.: Llewellyn, 1997). Meece excerpted parts of his book for the article "The Generations: An Overview," which was carried in the May/June 1997 issue of *Welcome to Planet Earth* magazine. Contact the publisher: The Great Bear, P.O. Box 12007, Eugene, OR 97440; (541) 683-1760. Although this magazine has been discontinued, back issues should still be available at the address given.

12. The Adawee Teachings are produced as part of the Honor Series of Entertainment/Educational Tools. For more information, contact: Linda Redford, 1034 Ninth Street, Apt. 9, Santa Monica, CA 90403; (310) 392-1200; Web site www.honorkids.com.

Eleven: The Promise

1. *The Cultural Creatives: How Fifty Million People Are Changing the World,* Paul H. Ray and Sherry Ruth Anderson. (New York: Harmony Imprint Crown Publishing Group, 2000).

2. Charlene Spretnak, *The Resurgence of the Real: Body, Nature, and Place in a Hypermodern World* (Reading, Mass.: Addison-Wesley, 1997).

3. Third-way principles are discussed in chapter 20 of *Future Memory* (New York: Birch Lane Press, 1996; Charlottesville, Va.: Hampton Roads Publishing Co., 1999). Also, see chapter 3 in John Nelson, ed.. *Solstice Shift: Magical Blend's Synergistic Guide to the Coming Age* (Charlottesville, Va.: Hampton Roads Publishing Co., 1997). I penned both chapters.

4. Walter Starcke, *It's All God* (Boerne, Tex.: Guadalupe Press, 1998). Should you have any difficulty obtaining this book, or want to avail yourself of Starcke's past works, contact: Guadalupe Press, P.O. Box 877, Boerne, TX 78006; 1-800-460-2005 or (830) 537-4837; e-mail wstarcke@walterstarcke.com. I want to thank Walter Starcke for his kind permission in allowing me to quote him.

5. The most documented of weather-pattern study and human-behavior links is James DeMeo, *Saharasia: The 4000 B.C.E. Origins of Child Abuse, Sex-Repression, Warfare and Social Violence in the Deserts of the Old World* (Greensprings, Ore.: Orgone Biophysical Research Lab, 1998). If you are unable to locate this book, contact: Orgone Biophysical Research Lab, Inc., Greensprings Center, P.O. Box 1148, Ashland, OR 97520; (541) 552-0118; e-mail demeo@mind.net.

6. Refer to Jeremy Rifkin, *The Biotech Century* (New York: Tarcher/Putnam, 1998).

7. New Visions for Child Care, Inc., focuses on preschool and after-school learning opportunities, as well as functioning as an umbrella for New Global Visions for Children's Television. Muriel Freifeld's mission is to tailor learning programs to meet children's individual needs. "It's the kids who tell me what they need," she explained, "not someone's theory." To avail yourself of her expertise or to inquire about her innovative programs, write to her at 10737 Deborah Drive, Potomac, MD 20854.

8. Refer specifically to the work of Rupert Sheldrake in his books, *A New Science of Life: The Hypothesis of Formative Causation* (Los Angeles: Tarcher, 1981), and *The Presence of the Past: Morphic Resonance and the Habits of Nature* (New York: Times Books, 1989).

9. Ken Wilber, *The Spectrum of Consciousness* (Wheaton, Ill.: Theosophy Publishing House, 1993). This is the twentieth-anniversary edition.

10. *Mark Matousek,* "Up Close and Transpersonal with Ken Wilber," *Utne Reader,* July/August 1998, 50–55, 106–107.

11. Ken Wilber, *The Marriage of Sense and Soul: Integrating Science and Religion* (New York: Random House, 1998).

12. Ursula King, *Spirit of Fire: The Life and Vision of Teilhard de Chardin* (Maryknoll, N.Y.: Orbis Books, 1996).

Appendix One: Tips for the Child in All of Us

1. Newsclip submitted by L. A. Justice of *The National Examiner*, 20 May, 1997 issue. *A Window to Heaven: When Children See Life in Death,* Diane M. Komp, M.D. (Grand Rapids, Mich.: Zondervan Books, 1992).

2. An excellent reference to psychiatry's "disease labels" and how they can be misused, is Paula J. Caplan's *They Say You're Crazy: How the World's Most Powerful Psychiatrists Decide Who's Normal* (Reading, Mass.: Addison-Wesley, 1995).

3. On the subject of false memories, refer to *Unchained Memories: True Stories of Traumatic Memories, Lost and Found,* Lenore Terr, M.D. (New York: Basic Books, 1994). And, *The Myth of Repressed Memory: False Memories and the Accusations of Sexual Abuse,* Elizabeth Loftus and Katherine Ketcham (New York: St. Martin's Press, 1994).

4. Refer to *Ritalin-Free Kids: Safe and Effective Homeopathic Medicine for ADD and Other Behavior and Learning Problems,* Judith Ullman (Rockland, Calif.: Prima, 1996). Refer also to Mary Ann Block, D.O, *No More Ritalin* (New York: Kensington, 1996).

5. The real problem with television is the element of "startle" necessary to hold a person's attention, and more specifically the effect that has on children. Investigate the work of Keith Buzzell, M.D. His research is contained in *The Children of Cyclops: The Influence of Television Viewing on the Developing Human Brain.* Available from Association of Waldorf Schools of North America, 3911 Bannister Road, Fair Oaks, CA 95628.

6. Howard G. Hunter, "Did You Hear the One about Plato? Students Need Stories of the Past to Experience the Present," *Newsweek,* 14 November, 1994, 20.

7. Time-Life Books published *What Life Was Like: The First World History of Everyday Lives* (a series) to fill this need. Also get *Zarafa* by Michael Allin, about an unbelievable event in history that teaches all of us many lessons about life (New York: Walker Publishing, 1998). Memoirs and autobiographies are good sources as well. A gentle but enjoyable one I recommend is Edgar Allen Imhoff's *Always of Home: A Southern Illinois Childhood* (Carbondale: Southern Illinois University Press, 1993).

Appendix Two: Research Methodology

1. John Philo Dixon, Ph.D., *The Spatial Child* (Springfield, Ill.: Charles C. Thomas Publisher, 1983), 9.

⑥

I am brilliant. I am golden. I am a starchild of God.
I illumine my world with the light of the highest heaven.

—THE REVEREND COCO STEWART

Index

abortion, 137, 138
  encounters with unborn, 142
  missing twin from, 144, 150
abuse, 64–67, 69, 85, 110, 137–38,
  147, 163–64, 236
acceptance, 70
accident, 109–11, 120, 124, 126
Adawee Teachings, 175–76, 206–7
adults
  of alien (walk-in), 153–54, 157
  alien abduction, 153–54, 157,
    163–64
  brain shift/spirit shift as growth
    event for, 13–14, 182
  child's aftereffects v., 81, 84–91,
    98–99, 112, 120
  counseling of, 194–97, 201–3
  experiencers helping child, 206
  integration of NDE by, 96, 98–99,
    194–97
  near-death experiences of, 6, 20,
    40–41, 47–48, 81, 146–47,
    153–54, 161–62, 175, 250–53
  as suicide deterrent, 70
  visualization techniques for, 194–96
"Adventure Camp," 224
Adventurers Beyond the Body
  (Buhlman), 212
after-death communications (ADC),
  151
aftereffects, 81–103. *See also* brain
  shift; counseling; light; spirit shift
  advice for, 101–3
  alcohol and, 70, 86, 97, 218
  of alien walk-ins, 165
  blood pressure and, 83, 94
  cascade effect/imprinting of limbic
    system on, 18
  characteristics of, 82–84, 91–92
  in children v. adults, 81, 84–91,
    98–99, 112, 120
  communication ability influenced in,
    81–82, 83

dealing with, 193
desire to return to "home," 67–70,
  84, 86, 89–90, 91, 94, 96, 103,
  113, 138
of electrical sensitivity, 83, 85, 103,
  119
family/friend alienation, 70–72, 82,
  83, 85–86, 87, 89, 91, 95, 101–2
health and, 83, 92–95
increase in, over time, 84
insanity-like, xv, 146
integrating phases of, 95–98
integration, counseling and, 190–91,
  192–99
intelligence and, 29, 51–61, 75
judgment and, 78, 83–84, 89–90
of light sensitivity, 75, 83, 85, 94,
  103, 124, 125, 160
long-term, 81–82
marriage and, 83, 84, 118, 119, 181
money, mission, home and, 84,
  89–90, 91, 94, 96, 113, 118, 119,
  120, 121, 124, 185, 241–42
with no recall of NDE, 104
"off course" feeling of, 29
pharmaceuticals decreased tolerance
  with, 94
(brain shift and) physiological, 15,
  57, 82
psychic abilities, 33–37, 52, 74–75,
  78–80, 83, 89, 91, 119, 125, 194,
  213
(brain shift and) psychological, 16,
  81–84
questionnaire on, 7–8, 236, 245
repression of, 82–93, 95–96, 120–22
social service and, 6, 30, 55, 62, 94,
  121, 124, 181, 185
of sound sensitivity, 75, 83, 94, 125
suicide and, 70, 86–89, 97, 247
without memory of NDE, 111–22
without physically dying, 104–5
afterlife, 187, 188–89

About the Author

P. M. H. Atwater is one of the original researchers of the near-death phenomenon, having begun her work in 1978. Today, her contribution to the field of near-death studies is considered on a par with that of Raymond Moody and Kenneth Ring. Her first two books, *Coming Back to Life* and *Beyond the Light* (in-depth studies of what happens to adult experiencers), are considered the bibles of the near-death experience. With the publication of *Future Memory,* she expanded her work into areas of brain development that call for a reconsideration of what is presently known about transformations of consciousness.

Rune casting with the elder yin or Goddess Runes became therapy for her after she survived three death events that produced three different near-death experiences in 1977. Her investigation of these primordial runic glyphs led to her books *The Magical Language of Runes* (out of print) and *Goddess Runes* (now available through A. Merklinger Publishing), offered as thanks for what she has gained and also to pass on the skill of rune casting.

Children of the New Millennium, an in-depth study of child experiencers of near-death states (the original version of this book), has been greatly expanded into *The New Children and Near-Death Experiences.* Her book, *The Complete Idiot's Guide to Near-Death Experiences* (with David Morgan), is an encyclopedia of the entire phenomenon, both the experience—its aftereffects and implications, positive/negative—and the genre of consciousness transformations/otherworldly journeys.

We Live Forever: The Real Truth about Death, combines her research, her personal experiences and those of others, into an uncommon guide of spirit realms and soul power. She is currently working on a book about our newest generations—bearers of light in a world of upheaveal. Check on her Web site www.cinemind.com/atwater for announcements.

Also available on P. M. H. Atwater's Web site are her publications *I Died Three Times in 1977, The Frost Diamond, Life Sounds, The Challenge of September 11,* and *Brain Shift/Spirit Shift: A Theoretical Model Using Research on Near-Death States to Explore the Transformation of Consciousness,* three new research papers, and "A Book of Columns."

Happily married, Atwater is the mother of three, grandmother of four (in bodies) and one now in spirit. She has dedicated the remaining years of her life to writing and speaking about the soul, spirit realms, the power of prayer, and helping to dispel the fear associated with death and dying.

BOOKS OF RELATED INTEREST

The Edison Gene
ADHD and the Gift of the Hunter Child
by Thom Hartmann

The Child of Your Dreams
Approaching Conception and Pregnancy with
Inner Peace and Reverence for Life
by Laura Archera Huxley and Piero Ferrucci

Children at Play
Using Waldorf Principles to Foster Childhood Development
by Heidi Britz-Crecelius

Parenting Begins Before Conception
A Guide to Preparing Body, Mind, and Spirit For
You and Your Future Child
by Carista Luminare-Rosen, Ph.D.

From Magical Child to Magical Teen
A Guide to Adolescent Development
by Joseph Chilton Pearce

Shapeshifting
Shamanic Techniques for Global and Personal Transformation
by John Perkins

Psychonavigation
Techniques for Travel Beyond Time
by John Perkins

Return of the Children of Light
Incan and Mayan Prophecies for a New World
by Judith Bluestone Polich

Inner Traditions • Bear & Company
P.O. Box 388
Rochester, VT 05767
1-800-246-8648
www.InnerTraditions.com

Or contact your local bookseller